Ideological Battlegrounds –
Constructions of Us and Them
Before and After 9/11
Volume 1

Ideological Battlegrounds – Constructions of Us and Them Before and After 9/11 Volume 1: Perspectives in Literatures and Cultures

Edited by

Joanna Witkowska and Uwe Zagratzki

CAMBRIDGE
SCHOLARS
PUBLISHING

Ideological Battlegrounds – Constructions of Us and Them Before and After 9/11
Volume 1: Perspectives in Literatures and Cultures,
Edited by Joanna Witkowska and Uwe Zagratzki
Technical Assistant Colin Phillips

This book first published 2014

Cambridge Scholars Publishing

12 Back Chapman Street, Newcastle upon Tyne, NE6 2XX, UK

British Library Cataloguing in Publication Data
A catalogue record for this book is available from the British Library

ISBN (10): 1-4438-5891-9, ISBN (13): 978-1-4438-5891-5

TABLE OF CONTENTS

INTRODUCTION

The end of the Cold War in 1989 spelt out the hope of a more peaceful world and visions about global unification, chiefly economically motivated, prospered. Nearly twenty-five years after these earth-shaking events, in particular Europeans appear to enjoy the political and – not as a rule – the economic fruits of the post-communist era. In contrast, the underside of the new order reveals global warming caused by unleashed capitalist forces, international bank terrorism and ideological and religious war-fare on a large scale.

The East-West conflict of the past has been replaced by a North-South divide or rather an ideological battle between the free-market, democratic Europe-North America on the one side and the antagonistic concepts of religious and political Islam on the other. But while the relations between the antagonists used to be determined by economic exploitation and political oppression of one by the other since colonial times without the possibility of reversal, the rise of Islamic extremism signals that the Euro-American political hegemony and its economic (Capitalist) and ideological (human rights and Western democracy) allies have come to be not only opposed by the power of the Koran, but also by guerrilla warfare and suicide militancy.

This became most drastically visible on 11 September 2001, when al-Qaeda "declared war" on what they judged to be a decadent, secular Western, that is US, liberalism epitomised by the WTC Towers and the Pentagon.

The events on 11 September 2001 – since then orthographically represented as "9/11" and hence graphically recognisable for its symbolic value in the present political discourses and future history case books – with hindsight bear resemblance to historic events of similar explosive potential in the cultural arenas.[1] The Crusades and the Inquisition, the violent proselytization of millions of indigenous peoples in the South and North Americas, the Holocaust, the inexorable prosecution of the Christian

---

[1] The explosivity of the event has been poignantly captured by Alexander Kluge, a German film director and author: "On 11 September 2001 he [Osama Bin Laden, U.Z.] is the projectile, which derails our century." [my translation, U.Z.] Welt online 9.5.2011. Alexander Kluge interviewed by Andreas Rosenfelder.

population in some Muslim countries, also daily racism and rabble-rousing xenophobia in modern nation states of the Old and New Europe, the outrageous persecution of homosexual citizens in some ex-communist countries in Eastern Europe or the inherent degradation of women by the doctrines of the Catholic Church – wherever we go we find the construct, the representation of the strange, unadaptable, non-conforming, curious, bizarre, threatening, evil and finally hostile Other at the heart of power politics.

Unlike the long periods of time the other conflicts took from their ideological origins to becoming instruments of oppression, the events on 11 September 2001 seemed to explode within one day. Each and every one of us recalls this particular day in their own way, our personal memories are different, though most of us – depending on our cultural affiliations – share the bitter impressions and the sense of despair entailed by the atrocious images brought into our living rooms via TV and the Internet. Instant comments by US governmental and media commentators pointed to the unimaginable brutality of the attacks, intertwined with hate speeches from the highest political ranks – not only directed to al-Qaeda, but to any Muslim Other inside and outside the States. When the hysteria – created for political purposes by the Bush Administration and fired by conspiracy theories on the other end of the political spectrum – died down, more moderate voices came to be heard which reflected on the roots of the events reaching deep down into the history of the cultural relations between the Occident and the Orient, or the North and the South and their respective constructions of the Other. Bearing the long evolution of all kinds of links between East and West in mind, from a historical perspective hurt feelings, embitterment about real or alleged suppression and the fear of extinction in Eastern cultures and religions in the face of a pervasive Western capitalism climaxed in the attacks. Several discourses, secular and religious, tied in with the attacks, all pointing to Western, especially US, economic and colonial hegemony via the World Bank, International Monetary Fund or G8 trade policy in these times of Globalisation. Yet, the reactions to real or imagined Western injustices went out of all proportion, as bottled-up hatred and revenge were articulated by extremist Islamist groups struggling themselves for political and ideological leadership in the Muslim world. In short, the attacks were made possible by a melange of technological expertise, Western economic power, an unshakeable dogma which rests in the extreme Islamist belief of a godly mission, and the utter unscrupulousness of the executors. The attacks were not triggered by a fundamental evil-mindedness often read into the Koran by Western ideologues, but by the elitist interest of a radical faction within the Islamic world. Thus the perpetrators, seen through unbiased eyes, could not justify their terrorist acts on behalf of the majority of Muslims.

Having reasoned that the attacks on the one hand brought to a climax the disastrous nature of the relations between Western and Islamic cultures – which in the Islamic world at large was felt to be unjust, offending and aggressive, but, on the other hand, because of its outrageous violence left radical Islamists without any justification among millions of common believers – is only half of the story. As the assassinations transmuted into the code "9/11" they gained symbolic relevance which is underscored by the material objects of the attacks – the World Trade Towers – which not only from a radical Islamist perspective stood for capitalism at its most despicable. Detached from their historical connections the events soon began to live a life of their own in a metaphorical realm. No longer the climax of deteriorating relations between cultures, "9/11" in the aftermath of the events came to represent the disruption of communication between the "Eastern Them" and the "Western Us" and, hence, the secret code, the cipher, to start a new round of hatred across cultural and political boundaries. Condensing history into such a code played into the hands of extremists on both sides – here the Bush administration, there al-Qaeda and the Taliban – and helped sharpen the "evil profile" of the respective cultural Other at the expense of cutting off any empathy and intercultural competence between cultures. The return of the hawks – in both camps – served the same aims of consolidating power politics in the interest of elites.

Our personal memories are supplemented by our collective memories, which are shaped, if not dictated, by our respective cultural norms. Edward Said in his ground-breaking study has pointed to Western re-constructions of the Orient. The same applies in reverse.

Discourses about the Other have too long been infused with aggressions and violence. The aim of this book is twofold: to trace "9/11", the cipher and the code, in the fields of various academic disciplines – occasionally "9/11" can thus precede the historic event – and to contribute to the return of the intellectuals´ original function: reading between the lines!

The authors assembled in this volume specialise in different fields from cultural studies and literature. **Cultural studies** are represented by :

Thomas Bauer, whose theoretical reflections investigate Western constructions of Islam. He illuminates four major strategies of inventing the image and, in parts, the self-image of modern Islam. Bauer argues that this discourse, including the "medievalisation" of Islam, gained new

vigorous currency through the 9/11 events. **Ryan Dorr** takes a cultural
perspective to look for authenticity determinants in the post 9/11 film
depiction (*World Trade Center*, 2006) that would account for the positive
reception of the otherwise politicized content. He demonstrates the
techniques which neutralize the ideological message of the film images
and draws our attention to the influence of this endeavour on the critical
analysis of the movie. **Jarema Drozdowicz** casts light upon the
appropriation of scientific discourses by the military "machinery in times
of war and conflict" exemplified by the program *Civil Operations and
Revolutionary Development Support (CORDS)* in the 1960s and the
Human Terrains System (HTS) of 2005. He delineates the impact these
programs had on the image of the Muslim Other as either a terrorist and/or
a martyr with the purpose of establishing a hegemonic rule over defining
and maintaining intercultural dialogues. **Krzysztof Inglot**'s article proves
the totality of the 9/11 events, which entered also the realm of the video
game industry. The interactive nature of this medium makes one ponder on
the potential influence of the sensitive contents on the gamers' identity.
Self-censorship of the industry when it comes to the issue of terrorism
seems to be a barometer of the public attitudes and prove that 9/11 has not
been fully integrated yet. In this respect, the author argues, the terrorists
won. **Michał Różycki** reveals the mechanisms of dealing with a reality too
horrible to be accepted. By going back into history he analyses cultural
patterns that led to the acceptance, by some portion of the US society, of
the conspiracy theories which came back with a vengeance after 9/11.
Danial Šip takes up the issue of justifying and legalising torture as it was
discussed in the fourth season of the US TV-series *24*. He examines the
active role of popular media cultures in not only representing torture but
also in making strong statements about the pros and cons of exerting
torture as it is expressed by the dramatisation of the plots. **Elżbieta
Wilczyńska** traces representations and misrepresentations of Muslims in
2006-2011 Hollywood productions. She shows how the movie industry
participates in and influences the contemporary discourses about Muslims.
In this way, apart from the picture of the Other, the films, by implication,
become also a source of knowledge about the power relations between
countries – but also inside the USA. The article points to the mechanisms
of the formation of stereotypes and makes us rethink the validity of our
perceptions. Proceeding on the assumption that cultures for the sake of
self-identification borrow from other cultures, **Ákos Windhager** contrasts
the classical symphonies and concerts which commemorated wars and
which were written by European composers like van Beethoven,
Tchaikovsky or Bartók with modern American classics written in

remembrance of 9/11. As `meaning´ is subject to transmigration, the establishing of an authentically American funeral music inspired by earlier models has been halted by the fleetingness of notions like "national musical identity".

Literary studies are represented by:

Sabine Ernst who ploughs a largely neglected field. Her article takes stock of the impact 9/11 has had on contemporary ethnic Dutch novels. She lays bare the twofold approach of the novels under consideration, since on the one hand they thematise a growing mutual mistrust between the Dutch mainstream society and the Moroccan-Dutch communities and on the other utilise `writing-back-strategies´ for the propagation of mutual respect in ethnically diversified modern urban communities. **Brygida Gasztold** identifies Michael Chabron´s novel *The Yiddish Policeman´s Union* (2007) as a 9/11-novel as she claims it internalises the sensibilities and feelings of the post-9/11 period, which are linked with assumptions of global religious wars. At the novel´s heart, however, we find a fictional treatment of a Jewish diaspora in Alaska in the post-World War II years. Ethnic identities and religious fanaticism hold a prominent place in the prose and thus link up with major concerns in the post-9/11 discourses, like the rupture of history or "the struggle for political and ideological supremacy." **Karolina Golimowska** characterises *The Reluctant Fundamentalist* (2007) by Mohsin Hamid and *Home Boy* (2009) by H.M. Naqvi as articulate prose texts which capture the changed perceptions of the United States after 9/11 among the Muslims living there. Being forced to take sides in a now unyielding Islamophobic environment, the two protagonists grow disillusioned in the course of the novels, which culminates in their drastic personal decisions. Consequently, the idea of American exceptionalism is called into question. In consequence, 9/11 is regarded to be the catalyst rather than the origin of cultural stereotypes. The world of fantasy by its very nature evades a definitive reflection of real world events. Bearing this in mind, **Dorota Guttfeld** tries, cautiously, to trace the impact of 9/11 events on Terry Pratchett's Discworld novels. She points to the visible changes in the relations between the Anglophone cultures and the Other in the series. The message behind the plot in some novels may be read as a comment on the post 9/11 solutions and the roles ascribed to the West. **Barbara Poważa-Kurko** deals with *You have to be careful in the Land of the Free* (2004) by the contemporary Scottish novelist James Kelman. On the surface it is shown to provide the personal observations of an ordinary Scottish immigrant to the US, on a broader scale the novel mirrors the decline of what originally were considered American values, in particular the spirit of freedom, while desperately safeguarding them against violation. In the context of 9/11 the US in Kelman's fiction appears as the very rigid authoritarian system US ideologues have come to discover exactly in the Other. Whereas other articles in this section stress the post-9/11 traumas, **Uwe Zagratzki** reaches back in time for a thorough examination of the political and economic mechanisms of Imperialism based on stereotypical Othering. Exemplified by George Orwell's *Burmese Days* (1934) it is shown how stereotypes of the colonial Other in terms of race and gender under the rule of Imperialism turn against the colonising subaltern. Hence not only the constructedness of stereotypes is revealed but also – within the range of possibilities – their `sudden death´ under conditions of unrelenting power.

Joanna Witkowska and Uwe Zagratzki

THE ISLAMIZATION OF ISLAM

THOMAS BAUER

Der Spiegel ("The Mirror") is the most widely read and most respectable German weekly political magazine. It should come as no surprise that Islam has appeared on its front cover several times. One of these covers dedicated to Islam reads: "Blutiger Islam" ("Bloodthirsty Islam"). It would be an obvious guess that this was the cover after 9/11. But it was not. The bad guy was not Bin Laden, but Ayatollah Khomeini, and it is not an issue from 2011, but from 1987.[1] However, in several respects the image of Islam depicted in this issue does not differ significantly from the coverage post-9/11. Already Islamic fundamentalism was presented as irrational, fanatic, violent, irreconcilable with democracy and a threat to the entire world.

In the years that followed, the coverage of Islam in *Der Spiegel* went along the same lines, but Islam did not make it onto the cover again until 2001, a year in which – unsurprisingly – several cover stories were dedicated to Islam. One of them reads "Wer war Muhammad? Das Geheimnis des Islam" ("Who was Muhammad? The Secret of Islam"), and it is here that we find the whole distorted and prejudiced image of Islam which has dominated in the West since 9/11. Bin Laden also makes an appearance in this issue of *Der Spiegel*: "Die Terror-GmbH. Religiöse Fanatiker verfluchen den 'satanischen' Westen und bedrohen auch Deutschland" ("Terror Inc. Religious fanatics curse the 'Satanic' West and also threaten Germany"). All this would come as no surprise if the issue were a post-9/11 issue, but again, it is not. Despite Bin Laden's appearance in this number of *Der Spiegel* (which is not normally known for its prophetic skills), it is again a pre-9/11 issue, dating from June of that year.[2]

---

[1] *Der Spiegel* 1987, no. 33 (online: http://www.spiegel.de/spiegel/print/index-1987-33.html).

[2] *Der Spiegel* 2001, no. 23, title and 172-173 (online: http://www.spiegel.de/spiegel/print/index-2001-23.html and http://wissen.spiegel.de/wissen/image/show.html?did=19337203&aref=image025/E0122/SCSP200102301720173.pdf&thumb=false).

This short press-survey shows that 9/11 did not create the present image of Islam, but rather fostered and enforced it. The construction of Islam as the arch-enemy of the West must have begun earlier, to be more exact: somewhere in the 1970s. Of particular interest is the *Spiegel* issue from July 1973. The occasion for its cover story was the fact that the number of Turks in Germany had reached one million. The cover showed a Turkish family with five children, and the headline read: "Gettos in Deutschland. Eine Million Türken" ("Ghettos in Germany. One Million Turks").[3] The different articles that were dedicated to this subject are plainly xenophobic. The main article bears the headline "Die Türken kommen! Rette sich wer kann!" ("The Turks are coming! Escape if you can!").[4] The whole issue presents a nightmare of German towns full of slums and ghettos worse than the Bronx, populated by illiterates who cannot understand German and controlled by criminal gangs. It can only be recommended to reread this issue of the Spiegel today, forty years later, in order to see how successful integration in Germany really is. In the context of the present article, however, another fact is more interesting. Despite all the horrible scenarios that are presented in this issue of *Der Spiegel*, Islam is not mentioned with a single word. It still took some time until xenophobia was replaced by Islamophobia.

The year 1973 was also the year of the oil crisis. The "oil sheikh" became a topic in the November issue.[5] Here, in fact, Islam was mentioned as a unifying force for the Near Eastern countries, but the breakthrough for the scaring image of Islam was still a few years ahead. It was, in fact, the Iranian revolution and the constitution of the Islamic Republic of Iran in 1979, which drastically changed the public image of Islam in the West. We will have a look at a title page of *Der Spiegel* from that year later. For the moment, it suffices to state that the beginning of the construction of Islam as an enemy reaches back to the late seventies of the 20th century, and not to 9/11. Further, it was a political event, the Iranian Revolution, and not a religious event which nevertheless made the *religion* of Islam appear as a *political* threat. Thanks to this strategy, Islam could be successfully built up as a new enemy able to replace communism, when during the late 80s the threat of the "Eastern Bloc" waned. US military expenditure did not

---

[3] *Der Spiegel* 1973, no.31 (online: http://www.spiegel.de/spiegel/print/index-1973-31.html).

[4] Ibid., 24 (online:
http://wissen.spiegel.de/wissen/image/show.html?did=41955159&aref=image035/E0539/PPM-SP197303100240034.pdf&thumb=false).

[5] *Der Spiegel* 1973, no. 46 (online: http://www.spiegel.de/spiegel/print/index-1973-46.html).

decrease significantly after the end of the "Cold War" (contrary to what happened after World War II). It is certainly not too risky to ascribe an important role in this development to the fear of Islam.

The strategies for creating an Image of Islam as a threat did not have to be newly invented; they were already present in the Western scholarly approach to Islam[6] and had only to be adapted to their new purpose. Ironically, at the same time when in scholarship these old, essentialist approaches were abandoned, they were taken up by the media and by political propaganda.

The main strategy is what could be called the "alienization" of Islam. The June 2001 issue of *Der Spiegel* formulates this quite frankly: "Keine Weltreligion ist uns so fremd" ("No other world religion is as alien to us as Islam").[7] Given the fact that Islam is a monotheistic religion quite close to Christianity (and even closer to Judaism), whereas Hinduism and Buddhism are grounded on very different principles, this statement may cause astonishment. Islam as a religion can hardly be more foreign to a Christian than Jainism and Shintoism. But this is exactly what happened, consciously or not: Islam as a religion was presented as strange and as alien as a religion could possibly be. This "alienization" of Islam, however, would not have been possible if Islam had been conceived of only as a religion. Instead, "Islam" was and is conceived of not only as a religion, but also as a culture and even as a political movement.

A strange coincidence came to foster this conception. As a matter of fact, nearly all cultures bear as their name either a geographic term, the name of a people, or a historic period. So we speak about the culture of Japan, India and Europe, of the Aztecs and the Maya, of the culture of the Bronze Age or the ancient Middle East. Islam is more or less the only case in which a culture is named by its prevalent religion.[8] Labelling the cultures of North Africa, the Middle East and parts of South- and Southeast Asia as "Islamic" suggests, however, that the religion of Islam plays a more important role in them than religion does in cultures named otherwise. Historically, this is definitely not the case. The culture of the people of Baghdad in the 10th century, of Cairo in the 14th, of Malacca in

---

[6] The standard text on this issue is still Edward W. Said, *Orientalism* (London 1978).

[7] *Der Spiegel* 2001, no. 23, 158 (online: http://wissen.spiegel.de/wissen/image/show.html?did=19337202&aref=image025/ E0122/SCSP200102301580178.pdf&thumb=false).

[8] See Almut Höfert, "Europa und der Nahe Osten: Der transkulturelle Vergleich in der Vormoderne und die Meistererzählungen über den Islam", *Historische Zeitschrift* 287 (2008): 561-597; 577.

the 16th or of Beirut in the 19th century was not dominated by religion to a larger degree than was the culture of their contemporaries in India or Europe. The general impression, however, is different. Again and again we read that Islamic culture is "permeated" by religion, that every aspect of life is "regulated" by religion, and so on.

The pure terminological coincidence is not enough to explain such an image of the culture of Islam. Another factor must be involved, and this is what I call, using an expression borrowed from Aziz al-Azmeh, the *Islamization of Islam*[9] and to which I will dedicate the rest of my paper. My main thesis is that through the mechanism of the *Islamization of Islam* the very different cultures of the different parts of the Islamic world (if there is such a thing) are unified into a single culture, which is seen as restlessly dominated by a single religion, a religion which, in addition, is fanatical and atavistic and deeply rooted in the Middle Ages. "No other world religion is as foreign to us as Islam": This sentence from *Der Spiegel* only makes sense if the word "Islam" does not only denote the religion, but also the culture as a whole. It is this very process of the *Islamization of Islam* which allows to display Islam as a stranger and consequently as a menace and a threat.

In the following, I will discuss the four major strategies of the *Islamization of Islam*, which, besides, are not only relevant for shaping the image of Islam in the West, but also contribute to a degree to the self-image of Islam in Muslim countries at the present time. Let me start with the question of importance:

(1) Non-religious discourses in Islamic societies are disregarded or considered unimportant.

Was (and is) Islamic culture in fact as radically dominated by religion, as permeated by the sacred, as is generally assumed? Of course, it was not. Many aspects of life were dominated by completely or predominantly secular discourses. A page from an Arabic manuscript written and illustrated in 1273 (today in the Ambrosiana library, Milan) directs us to several of them.

First, the author, a certain Ibn Buṭlān, was Christian, which points to the fact that nearly all Islamic societies were always and are to this present day multi-religious societies. But the fact that the author was a pious Christian, who died in the year 1066 in a monastery, is irrelevant for the text, which is not intended for a Christian, but for a general, predominantly

---

[9] Aziz Al-Azmeh, *Die Islamisierung des Islam. Imaginäre Welten einer politischen Theologie* (Frankfurt a.M./New York, 1996). (The original English edition is entitled *Islams and Modernities*, London/New York, 1993).

"Banquet Scene", from *The Medical Dinner Party*. 1273

Muslim readership. The book, entitled *The Medical Dinner Party*, is "a witty skit on quacks, their ignorance and arrogance, with remarks on the ethics of the medical profession."[10] It is full of irony and satire, something many people deny ever existed in Islamic societies in the aftermath of the affair of the Danish cartoons. Along with this light-hearted book, the author, a professional physician, wrote a number of more serious books in the field of medicine. Medicine is one of those fields in Islamic societies, which were completely secular, even as concerned their ethical aspects. Physicians were expected to take an oath before being admitted to work. But it was not an oath on the Quran (or the Bible). Instead, they had to swear the Hippocratic Oath. Obviously, it was a heathen Greek from which Islamic medicine took its ethical basis, but so why then do we call it "Islamic" medicine?[11]

Perhaps the most important secular discourse in Islamic societies was poetry. Arabic poetry started as completely secular literature before the advent of Islam. 500 years later, it was still a nearly exclusively secular discourse, and, apart from some mystical texts and poems in praise of the prophet, it remained as such until the very present. Poetry was one of the leading discourses in society, omnipresent in all Islamic lands. Every learned person, religious scholars included, was expected to estimate and to compose poetry. Even Ayatollah Khomeini published a book of worldly ghazal-poems. Of course, poetry is also present in Ibn Buṭlān's book. Even in the page that is reproduced here we find a poem (lines 3 to 6), and it doesn't make things less complicated when we learn that it is a homo-erotic love poem. In Western Oriental studies, however, poetry plays a completely marginal role, and in all the popular books on Islam under which the shelves of our bookshops are bending, poetry is hardly ever mentioned.

Let us have another look at the illuminated manuscript from the year 1273. The pure fact alone that there *is* an illustration might seem surprising to readers of the aforementioned books on Islam, since they have learned that Islam prohibits the portrayal of human beings, if not drawing in general. A visit to any museum of Islamic art can prove to us the contrary, and again, it seems problematic that "Islamic art" should be called "Islamic", since most of the works of art in the museum are purely secular, if not even contradictory to Islam, such as the copper wine bowls.

---

[10] J. Schacht, "Ibn Buṭlān", in *Encyclopaedia of Islam*. Second Edition. 12 vols. (Leiden, 1954-2004), 3:740-742; 740a.
[11] See Thomas Bauer, *Die Kultur der Ambiguität. Eine andere Geschichte des Islams* (Berlin, 2011), 194-198.

Wine-drinking is also going on in the scene depicted in the illustration. Of course, wine-drinking is a clear violation of the rules of Islam, but no other world literatures have composed anything close to the numerous wine poems we find in Arabic and Persian, much to the discomfort of many pious Arabs and Iranians, and completely ignored by the many self-appointed "experts" on Islam.

But there's not only wine-drinking going on, there is also music. Music was prohibited by the Taliban and is still prohibited in Saudi-Arabia and in several provinces in Pakistan. In Iran, pop music is banned and women are forbidden from singing for an audience of men. Is it true to say that Islam prohibits music? Certainly not, since many Islamic scholars wrote treatises in favour of music, and there is a rich and extremely sophisticated and diversified tradition of Classic music in the lands of Islam. Again, Sufis apart, music is a secular phenomenon. It is nevertheless called, according to the mixing-up-culture-and-religion-terminology, "Islamic music", but no student of "Islamic studies" in the whole Western world is ever given an introduction in this fascinating field to so-called "Islamic" music.

Even this one single, innocent book page shows us that the image of "Islamic" culture in the West and among Islamic fundamentalists (who to a large extent share this image) is quite distorted by the fact that non-religious discourses in Islamic societies are disregarded or considered unimportant. They are largely disregarded in Western Islamic studies, and considered unimportant or even deviant by Islamic fundamentalists.

The first point was about secular discourses in Islamic societies, which are neglected or marginalized today. A similar reaction can be found in cases in which discourses are shaped by both religious and non-religious elements or in fields in which both religious and non-religious discourses exist. Here the rule is:

(2) Discourses that contain both religious and non-religious elements are reduced to their religious component. In fields in which both religious and secular discourses exist, secular discourses are given less weight.

A good example for the first part of strategy 2 is Islamic Law. *Fiqh,* Islamic law or rather Islamic jurisprudence, is not the same as the Shari'a. Instead, Shari'a, the sum of God's judgements of human acts, is the *basis* for Islamic law – the methodology of which is not fundamentally different from other legal systems. Islamic law uses exegetical methods, rational procedures and makes use of non-religious sources such as customary law and public welfare.[12] All these elements and procedures are generally

---

[12] See Thomas Bauer, "Normative Ambiguitätstoleranz im Islam," in Nils Jansen and Peter Oestmann (eds.), *Gewohnheit, Gebot, Gesetz. Normativität in Geschichte*

neglected in the media. This is why the public was rather scared when the Libyan rebels announced that they would make shari'a the basis for future legislation.

This brings us to the second point to be discussed in this context, the relation between the state and Islam. It is one of the most common prejudices about Islam that there is no separation between state and religion, and this is why Islam is not reconcilable with democracy. In fact, the slogan "Islam is *dīn wa-dawla*", "Religion and State", was created in the 19th century by Muslims who developed an Islamic ideology as a counterpart to the Western ideologies with which the Muslim world was confronted at the time.[13] This was the birth of political Islam, which is considered today by many people in the West (and, of course, Muslim fundamentalists) characteristic of Islam as a whole. But history teaches a different lesson. Political thought in pre-modern Islam was not limited to the religious discourse. Instead, a secular, philosophical approach existed side by side with the religious one. Poetry again drew a rather secular picture of the state and the ruler.

Let us take as an example the poet and secretary of the chancellery of Damascus Ibn Nubātah al-Miṣri (1287-1366).[14] He was one of the most famous and celebrated poets and prose authors of his time. All of his prose texts are purely secular, and so is the bulk of his poetry. The main exceptions are a number of poems in praise of the Prophet. Among the addressees of his poems were the sultans al-Malik al-Mu'ayyad and his son al-Malik al-Afḍal, descendants of the Ayyubids, the dynasty that was founded by Saladin. Though the dynasty had come to an end, the new rulers, the Mamluks, employed them as governors of the Syrian town Ḥamāh between 1310 and 1341. In his many poems on al-Mu'ayyad and al-Afḍal, Ibn Nubātah praised their determination and prowess, their wit and generosity, but does not mention their religious legitimation with even a single word. When in 1332 al-Afḍal succeeded his father, Ibn Nubātah dedicated to him a book of advice, which – two hundred years before the posthumous publication of Machiavelli's *Il principe* – displays a complete

---

und Gegenwart: Eine Einführung (Tübingen, 2011), 155-180; Mathias Rohe, *Das Islamische Recht. Geschichte und Gegenwart* (München, 2009).

[13] See Almut Höfert, Europa und der Nahe Osten, 578; Reinhard Schulze, "Islam und Herrschaft. Zur politischen Instrumentalisierung einer Religion," in Michael Lüders (ed.), *Der Islam im Aufbruch? Perspektiven der arabischen Welt* (München, 1992), 94-129.

[14] On him see Thomas Bauer, "Jamāl al-Dīn Ibn Nubātah" in Joseph E. Lowry, Devin J. Stewart (eds.), *Essays in Arabic Literary Biography* (Wiesbaden, 2009), 184-202.

secular approach to politics. In this book, religion is presented as an object of politics, which is governed by its own rules. Never is the prince advised to stick to Islamic law or care for the salvation of himself and his subjects. Even more interesting is Ibn Nubātah's view of history. Contrary to what is generally held as the world view in the so-called "Middle Ages", Ibn Nubātah did not consider history as the result of divine predestination, but as man-made. History, according to him, is driven forward by the passions of men. Consequently, the competent ruler has to master his own passions and to bring other people's passions into his service in order to be successful.[15] Ibn Nubātah was not alone with this anthropocentric world view. It must have been common ground for the intellectuals of his time, as the ideas about history of his younger (and today much more famous) contemporary Ibn Khaldūn show.[16]

"Strategy 2" also shapes our perception of violence in the Islamic context. First, violence committed by Muslims attracts much more attention in the media than violence committed by members of other religions. The massacre of thousands of Hindu Tamils committed by the Sri Lankan army or the persecution of the Muslim Rohingya in Burma were not in the media focus and did not affect Western perception of Buddhism as a particularly peaceful religion. Second, not all violence practiced by Muslims is Islamic. The first suicide attacks in Palestine were not conducted by Islamists, but by the communist PFLP. Third, even if violence committed by Muslims is justified with religious arguments, religion is never its immediate cause and its only (or even main) reason. Hamas, for example, is of course the Palestinian branch of the Muslim Brotherhood. This does not mean, however, that the acts of violence of Hamas are motivated primarily by religion, even if religion provides for a language to glorify extreme and self-destructive acts of violence such as suicide bombings. But Hamas is first and foremost an organization with a Palestinian nationalist agenda. To deny its political agenda and to reduce Hamas to its religious background furnishes a most welcome pretext for not negotiating with this organization, since, as is generally assumed, it is possible to argue about political positions but not with religious fanatics.

The same holds true even for the events of 9/11. Bin Laden's speech in the aftermath of 9/11 was a propaganda speech, in which he presented the terror attacks against a mainly religious background. Speeches by Ayman aẓ-Ẓawāhirī and Abū Ghaith on the same occasion, however, focused much more on the political background, especially what they considered

---

[15] See Thomas Bauer, *Die Kultur der Ambiguität*, 324-339.
[16] See Aziz al-Azmeh, *Ibn Khaldun: An Essay in Reinterpretation* (London, 1982).

"US imperialism" and the catastrophic consequences of the US embargo on Iraq. Much of what they had said could have also been said by Fidel Castro. It is no surprise that Bin Laden's speech was given great attention in the media, whereas the other speeches were hardly mentioned. Whereas Bin Laden's speech was translated into German very quickly, the two other speeches were not.[17] I strongly suggest that, in general, the political background of 9/11 is still largely unknown to the Western public. I will only deal shortly with strategy 3:

(3) If several religious discourses exist, the most radical and uncompromising discourse is considered "orthodox", the others are regarded as deviant.

Whenever the Western media deal with subjects like "women and Islam" or "homosexuality and Islam"[18] or whatever floats the boat in the contemporary discourse on Islam, the Taliban and Saudi Arabia are quoted as main authorities. The Wahhabis in Saudi Arabia are considered by the Western media as a particularly "orthodox" form of Islam. "Orthodox" means "confessing the true belief", and this is what most Muslims in the world would deny as far as the Wahhabis are considered. As a matter of fact, since the first appearance of the Wahhabis as a political force in the early 19th century, scholars from all parts of the Islamic world and from all Islamic schools and movements, both traditional and liberal, Sunni and Shi'i, have issued statements according to which Wahhabism is a deviant form of Islam, if not even not Islamic at all. It is, therefore, not correct to call Saudi Arabia's Wahhabism an especially "orthodox" form of Islam. It is rather the opposite.[19]

(4) The "medievalization" of Islam

Finally, I would like to mention a fourth and final strategy of "alienating" Islam. It is quite an old one and does not properly fall under the headline of the "Islamization" of Islam. Instead, I call it the "medievalization" of Islam. It has long become customary to call classical Islamic culture "medieval". We are speaking of "the Islamic Middle Ages", and in this way we impose on Islamic history a periodization, which was originally devised for European history (and has often enough been criticized by historians of Europe). But does the tripartite division

---

[17] See Hans-Gerhard Kippenberg, Tilman Seidensticker (eds.), *Terror im Dienste Gottes: die "Geistliche Anleitung" der Attentäter des 11. September 2001* (Frankfurt a.M., 2004).
[18] See Khaled El-Rouayheb, *Before Homosexuality in the Arabic-Islamic World, 1500-1800* (Chicago, 2005); Joseph A. Massad, *Desiring Arabs* (Chicago, 2007).
[19] See Hamid Algar, *Wahhabism: A Critical Essay* (New York, 2002).

"antiquity – middle ages – modernity" fit the case of Islamic history? After all, we would rather not speak about "medieval Japan" or the "Aztec Middle Ages". My suspicion is that it does not make more sense to speak of the Islamic Middle Ages than of the Chinese Middle Ages. For in order to bring about Islamic Middle Ages, we have to extinguish a whole empire and invent another one, which never existed.

I am speaking, of course, about the Roman Empire, which had to be declared dead, and the Byzantine Empire, which had to be invented. Most of us probably learned at school that the Roman Empire ceased to exist in the year 476, but in that year the Roman Empire just lost some of its Western provinces. Its Eastern half survived for more than a millennium. When Sultan Mehmet conquered Constantinople in 1453, he conquered the capital of the Roman Empire and added the title Qayṣar-e Rūm "Emperor of Rome" to his other titles. What is more, neither Sultan Mehmet nor any of the subsequent Sultans changed the name of the capital from Constantinople to Istanbul, as you might also have learned at school. As a matter of fact, the official name of the city, as represented on coins, remained Constantinople until the end of sultanate in 1922.

What remained of the Roman Empire after the fall of the Western provinces was called nothing other than "Rome" by its inhabitants, and the Arab armies besieged no other enemy in Anatolia than Rūm, i.e. "Rome".

And what holds true for politics also holds true for culture. As recent studies by British historians like Peter Heather[20] and others have recently confirmed, there was indeed a remarkable decline in the economy, material culture and education in the Western parts of the Roman Empire during the 4th, 5th and 6th centuries. But in the East, the economy flourished, material culture continued on a high level, and the cultural heritage did not fall into oblivion. The Arab conquest did not change this situation. To mention just a few examples: People continued to pay with coins in gold, silver and bronze, whereas Europe became a barter society. People did continue to visit bath houses, whereas Roman bath culture came to an end in the West. Large buildings of stone and brick continued to be constructed in the East, whereas in the West many settlements were abandoned and cities decayed. Whereas the West ceased to be an urban culture, in the East new urban centres (like Wasit, Fustat – later Cairo – and Baghdad) were founded. Whereas the scientific knowledge of antiquity went into oblivion in the West, it was transmitted, translated and enlarged in the Roman and Islamic East.

---

[20] Peter Heather, *The Fall of the Roman Empire. A New History* (London, 2005), see also Bryan Ward-Perkins, *The Fall of Rome and the End of Civilization* (Oxford, 2005).

To sum up: Whereas the transformation of the Roman Empire was so drastic that it is justified to consider it as a break between antiquity and a new epoch, the "Middle Ages", there was no similar break in the East, where both politically and culturally, antiquity simply continued. It is, therefore, quite reasonable to see the so-called "Byzantine" and the Islamic empire as the natural heirs to the empires of the antique world.

In the West, however, the elites were rarely willing to admit the continuity of antiquity in the East. In the Middle Ages, the Latin Church and the "Emperor of the Holy Roman Empire" in Europe had every motivation to style themselves as the true and only heirs to the ancient Roman Empire. The Roman Emperor of the East was called "the Emperor of the Greeks" in order to blur any continuity between the Empire of Constantinople and the Roman Empire. By calling the Roman Empire Greek, the West could claim the real heritage of the Romans. By the 18th century, this terminology became problematic again. At that time, Europe had discovered not only its Roman, but especially its Greek heritage. In order to claim the heritage of both the Romans and the Greeks, the term "Greek" for the latter Roman Empire was no longer suitable. "Greek" had to be reserved for the "classical", pre-Christian Greeks. Therefore a new term had to be invented in order to designate the "Greeks" of latter times. This term was successfully coined in 18th century France. It was the term "Byzantine", which soon became popular as a derogatory term for the latter Roman Empire. As a matter of fact, an empire that had called itself "Byzantine" had never existed. But it had to be invented in order to make the West appear the one and only legitimate heir to the Greeks and Romans.

It is no wonder that Islam fared even worse than the Greeks. Hardly ever was Islamic culture seen as a continuation of the cultures of antiquity. It was and is generally admitted that Islamic scholars played a certain role in transmitting Greek knowledge and thereby bringing some light into the otherwise dark Middle Ages. But they were always seen as part of these Middle Ages, though maybe a slightly lighter version of it, but still firmly in the Middle Ages, from which they never escaped. "Byzantium" was invented to "medievalize" the latter Roman Empire. Islam, having its origin as a religion in the 7th century, was medieval *per se* regardless of the continuities with classical Greek and Persian cultures (again, Religion is equated with Culture). And, even more importantly, by medievalizing Byzantium and Islam, they were excluded from modern European history, if not from the history of modernity altogether.

Modern Europe largely defines itself as the culture that has overcome the Middle Ages. The Middle Ages is the antithesis of the Modern West, and the point of utmost strangeness. And this is the point with which Islam is quite often identified. The stoning of adulterers is considered "medieval", though no case is known from Islamic lands during the time which we call the Middle Ages. Protests against the Danish caricatures were ascribed to a "Muslim medieval mentality"[21], and it is easy to find further examples in which modern Islam is accused of being "stuck in the Middle Ages". This "medievalization" of Islam has immediate political consequence. So, e.g., Wolfgang Merkel, a political scientist and advisor to influential politicians argued against Turkey's candidature of membership in the European Community with exactly this pseudo-historic argument:

> The central problem as regards the compatibility of Islam and democracy is the fact that Islam has never experienced a real enlightenment. (…) There was no renaissance, during which already Machiavelli powerfully replaced the concept of divine order by the principle of human self-government. (…) In Islam, the theocentric worldview has never been superseded by an anthropocentric one, which, however, is a precondition for democracy.[22]

As we have seen before, with Ibn Nubātah and others, the Arabs had their Machiavelli even two hundred years earlier. If there was no renaissance in Islam, this is simply due to the fact that there were no Middle Ages. If antiquity did not die, it could not be born again. Nevertheless, the similarity between several periods in Islamic history to the European renaissance is so striking that several scholars made use of the term "renaissance" also in respect of Islamic history.[23]

Still many European intellectuals favour a model which is called by Jürgen Gerhards "historical substantialism". According to Gerhards, "Historical substantialists believe that Europe's cultural exceptionality is based in its intellectual roots, which stretch from Judeo-Greco-Roman antiquity via the Renaissance and Enlightenment to the modern scientific consciousness."[24]

---

[21] *The Massachusetts Daily Collegian*, February 09, 2006 (http://dailycollegian.com/2006/02/09/muslim-medieval-mentality/ [10.08.2012]).
[22] Wolfgang Merkel "Islam und Demokratie," *Eurasisches Magazin* (2003), no. 10 (online: http://www.eurasischesmagazin.de/artikel/?artikelID=101603 [12.08.2012], translation T.B.
[23] Adam Mez, *Die Renaissance des Islams* (Heidelberg, 1922); Joel L. Kraemer, *Humanism in the Renaissance of Islam. The Cultural Revival during the Buyid Age* (Leiden, 2nd ed., 1992).
[24] Jürgen Gerhards, "Europäische Werte – Passt die Türkei kulturell zur EU?," *Aus Politik und Zeitgeschichte* (13. September 2004): 14-20, 14 (translation T.B.).

If, according to historical substantialists, European history is constituted by antiquity, Renaissance, Enlightenment and Modernity, where are the Middle Ages? "The Middle Ages, it's the others!"[25] The "medievalization" of Islam is one of the most successful strategies of "othering" Islam and Muslims.

In the conception of Islam as a medieval phenomenon, all four strategies of constructing Islam as a stranger are combined. Islam is, as is allegedly typical for the Middle Ages, all religion and nothing but religion; there is no place in it for secular discourse, and, of course, no place for enlightenment and democracy. This picture is neither correct historically nor for our time, but it is powerful, as another *Spiegel* cover shows. Again, the topic is the Iranian revolution. The cover shows a "medieval" Islamic warrior on horseback with a scimitar in his hand. Behind him on the horse is a woman deeply veiled in her chador. The headline is "Back to the Middle Ages".[26]

The prejudices of 1979 are still at work, reinforced as they were by 9/11. At present it is important to understand the strategies of the "Islamization" and "medievalization" of Islam in order to properly react to the present developments in the Middle East and North Africa, where Islamic people seem to be having more success in developing a modern Islamic society than previous generations ever had.

---

[25] Valentin Groebner, *Das Mittelalter hört nicht auf. Über historisches Erzählen* (München, 2008), 148: "Das Mittelalter, das sind die Anderen".
[26] *Der Spiegel* 1979, no. 7 (online http://www.spiegel.de/spiegel/print/index-1979-7.html).

Bibliography

Algar, Hamid. *Wahhabism: A Critical Essay.* Oneonta, NewYork: Islamic Publications International, 2002.

Al-Azmeh, Aziz. *Die Islamisierung des Islam. Imaginäre Welten einer politischen Theologie.* Frankfurt a.m./New York: Campus, 1996.

—. *Ibn Khaldun: An Essay in Reinterpretation.* London: Frank Cass, 1982.

—. *Islams and Modernities.* London/New York: Verso, 1993.

Bauer, Thomas. *Die Kultur der Ambiguität. Eine andere Geschichte des Islams.*Berlin: Verlag der Weltreligionen im Insel Verlag, 2011.

—. "Jamāl al-Dīn Ibn Nubātah." In *Essays in Arabic Literary Biography*, edited by Joseph E. Lowry, Devin J. Stewart, 184-202. Wiesbaden: Harrassowitz, 2009.

—. "Normative Ambiguitätstoleranz im Islam." In *Gewohnheit, Gebot, Gesetz. Normativität in Geschichte und Gegenwart: Eine Einführung*, edited by Nils Jansen and Peter Oestmann, 155-180. Tübingen: Mohr Siebeck, 2011.

El-Rouayheb, Khaled. *Before Homosexuality in the Arabic-Islamic World, 1500-1800.* Chicago: UoC Press, 2005.

Gerhards, Jürgen. "Europäische Werte – Passt die Türkei kulturell zur EU?" *Aus Politik und Zeitgeschichte* (September 13, 2004): 14-20.

Groebner, Valentin. *Das Mittelalter hört nicht auf. Über historisches Erzählen.* München: Beck, 2008.

Heather, Peter. *The Fall of the Roman Empire. A New History.* London: Macmillan, 2005.

Höfert, Almut. "Europa und der Nahe Osten: Der transkulturelle Vergleich in der Vormoderne und die Meistererzählungen über den Islam." *Historische Zeitschrift* 287 (2008): 561-597.

Kippenberg, Hans-Gerhard and Seidensticker, Tilman (eds.). *Terror im Dienste Gottes: die "Geistliche Anleitung" der Attentäter des 11. September 2001.* Frankfurt a.M.: Campus, 2004.

Kraemer, Joel. *Humanism in the Renaissance of Islam. The Cultural Revival during the Buyid Age.* Leiden: Brill, 1992.

Massad, Joseph. *Desiring Arabs.* Chicago: UoC Press, 2007.

Mez, Adam. *Die Renaissance des Islams.* Heidelberg: Georg Olms, 1922.

Rohe, Mathias: *Das Islamische Recht. Geschichte und Gegenwart.* München: C.H. Beck Verlag, 2009.

Said, Edward W.. *Orientalism.* London: Routledge, 1978.

Schacht, Joseph. "Ibn Buṭlān." In *Encyclopaedia of Islam*, edited by Bernard Lewis et al., volume III, 740-742. Leiden: Brill, 1971.

Schulze, Reinhard. "Islam und Herrschaft. Zur politischen Instrumentalisierung einer Religion." In *Der Islam im Aufbruch? Perspektiven der arabischen Welt*, edited by Michael Lüders, 94-129. München: Piper, 1992.

Ward-Perkins, Bryan. *The Fall of Rome and the End of Civilization.* Oxford: Oxford University Press, 2005.

Online resources

Der Spiegel 1973, no. 31 (online: http://www.spiegel.de/spiegel/print/index-1973-31.html).

—. 1973, no. 31 (online: http://wissen.spiegel.de/wissen/image/show.html?did=41955159&aref =image035/E0539/PPM-SP197303100240034.pdf&thumb=false).

—. 1973, no. 46 (online: http://www.spiegel.de/spiegel/print/index-1973-46.html).

—. 1979, no. 7 (online http://www.spiegel.de/spiegel/print/index-1979-7.html).

—. 1987, no. 33 (online: http://www.spiegel.de/spiegel/print/index-1987-33.html).

—. 2001, no. 23 (online: http://www.spiegel.de/spiegel/print/index-2001-23.html).

—. 2001, no. 23 (online:http://wissen.spiegel.de/wissen/image/show.html?did=19337203&aref=image025/E0122/SCSP200102301720173.pdf&thumb=false).

—. 2001, no. 23 (online: http://wissen.spiegel.de/wissen/image/show.html?did=19337202&aref =image025/E0122/SCSP200102301580178.pdf&thumb=false).

Eurasisches Magazin 2003, no. 10 [Merkel, Wolfgang. "Islam und Demokratie."] (online: http://www.eurasischesmagazin.de/artikel/?artikelID=101603).

The Massachusetts Daily Collegian, February 09, 2006 (online: http://dailycollegian.com/2006/02/09/muslim-medieval-mentality/

Illustration

Illustration from Ibn Butlan, *The Medical Dinner Party.* 1273. (in Biblioteca Ambrosiana Milano, sign. A125, fol.29v.)

Ideology, Authenticity, and Reception in *World Trade Center*

Ryan Dorr

Introduction

As one of the first mass-entertainment depictions of the terrorist attacks on September 11th, 2001, the film *World Trade Center* (dir. Oliver Stone, 2006) was, upon its release, confronted with a unique set of concerns and questions on the part of its prospective audience: how authentic would the film be? Would its depiction of the events of 9/11 (in general) and of the rescue of Port Authority officers Will Jimeno and John McLoughlin from under the collapsed towers (in particular) be accurate and, perhaps most importantly, appropriately respectful and reverent? Moreover, what political stance, if any, would the film take *vis-à-vis* not only on the events of 9/11 themselves, but the nearly five years of subsequent U.S. foreign policy as well? Would the film pander to or align itself with the political left or right, or would it attempt to distance itself from any kind of political ideology?

Of course, this last concern is somewhat of a trick question if one wants to read the film from a cultural studies perspective, an approach which (broadly speaking) presupposes that any cultural artefact must necessarily contain some kind of ideological content. The question then becomes not whether the film is political, but rather in what way the film (or the implicit act of making the film itself) is political. Unsurprisingly, *World Trade Center* (as will be detailed later) is firmly rooted in a conservative political perspective, offering the presumably American viewer a rousing affirmation of the United States in general, and of the basic goodness of Americans in particular.

Such a reading of *World Trade Center*, however, becomes immediately problematic in terms of the film's hypothetical audience, as discussed earlier. Given the highly sensitive nature of the topic of 9/11, it would be highly unlikely that an audience would accept any depiction of 9/11 which could be perceived as being politically coloured in any way. Nevertheless,

World Trade Center was a more-than-modest success in terms of both the domestic and international box office[1]; moreover, the film was never the subject of widespread critical condemnation, as reflected by the film's generally positive ratings on the review aggregation websites *metacritic. com* and *rottentomatoes.com*[2]. How, then, can we account for this apparent discrepancy between the film's definite ideological stance and the generally warm reception accorded the film by both critics and movie-going audiences?

One key to solving this seeming paradox might lie in the aforementioned notion of authenticity. Following Barthes, we can view authenticity not as the degree to which events as depicted in a novel, film, or the like correspond to real-life events, but rather the *impression* (created by both textual and extratextual means[3]) that this is indeed the case. In other words, the authenticity of a text has little to do with whether a text actually recreates historical events in an accurate manner, but rather with whether a text convinces its recipient that it is an accurate recreation of historical events, along with whether accompanying extratextual materials provide a context within which the text itself can be thus received.

Even a cursory viewing of *World Trade Center* (and/or a brief perusal of interviews, magazine articles, etc. dealing with the film) demonstrates that both the filmmakers and many of those dealing with the film on the extratextual level were indeed highly concerned with constructing a sense of authenticity, with creating the impression within the viewer that this cinematic version of 9/11 closely resembles the actual events upon which the film is based. One effect of this construction of authenticity is that it renders the film *World Trade Center* itself somehow "appropriate"; by positing the film as authentic, the filmmakers deftly avoid accusations of exploiting 9/11 for financial gain at the expense of the victims of the attack and their families. Another effect of *World Trade Center*'s construction of authenticity, I would argue, is that it obscures, negates, or "naturalizes" the film's ideological content. After all, according to the logic of the filmmakers, as well as that of so many journalists and critics

---

[1] According to Wikipedia, the film earned 162 million dollars internationally, on a budget of 65 million dollars.
http://en.wikipedia.org/wiki/World_Trade_Center_%28film%29
[2] Cf. http://www.metacritic.com/movie/world-trade-center;
http://www.rottentomatoes.com/m/world_trade_center/
[3] One can also consider how authenticity can be generated on the intratextual level as well (i.e. in the interaction between a given text and other existing texts, such as those belonging to the same genre or those dealing with the same subject matter); this discussion, however, will be omitted from the present paper.

who have written on the film, if the film is "authentic", it must necessarily be ideologically neutral, and thus immune to charges of political bias and the like (thus, again, rendering the film more appropriate for a mass audience).

It is the rejection of this logic which shall form the basis of the present paper. Here, I intend to demonstrate that *World Trade Center* has a very definite, easily discernible ideological stance, one expressed by the use of cinematic technique as well as in terms of the narrative itself, and that this ideological stance is downplayed or obscured completely by *World Trade Center*'s construction of authenticity, both by textual and extratextual means. After discussing how the film *World Trade Center*, along with extratextual materials on the film, construct the effect of authenticity, and how this construction of authenticity renders the film's ideological content invisible or seemingly inconsequential, I will consider how these notions of authenticity and ideology figured into the critical reception of the film upon its 2006 release.

Textual means of constructing authenticity in *World Trade Center*

World Trade Center's construction of authenticity using textual means begins even before the narrative proper has begun, as the viewer is informed via on-screen text that "these events are based on the accounts of the surviving participants." Clearly the film, from the very onset, is concerned with establishing a context in which its narrative is likely to be accepted by the potential viewer as authentic via recourse to participant accounts of the events of 9/11 – a strategy frequently employed in extratextual materials on the film as well. Beyond this rather obvious observation, however, the filmmakers' choice of the word "events" to describe the narrative of the film is rather remarkable, as the term "event" would normally refer to something which has happened in real life, not a plot point of a narrative work, whether based on real-life events or not. The closing text of the film, which insists that the narrative is "based on the true life events of John & Donna McLoughlin and William & Allison Jimeno," further complicates matters, as here the term "event" is used in the conventional sense (as described above), to refer to the real-life events upon which the narrative is based, and not to the narrative itself.

At any rate, the onscreen text which opens and closes *World Trade Center* is clearly concerned with framing the filmic narrative itself as authentic – a preoccupation which extends to the movement and placement of the camera throughout the film. Point-of-view shots are frequently used, usually from within a vehicle showing the exterior setting as it passes by. Many shots in the film are unstable in terms of both movement and reframing, such as the shot in which McLoughlin, played by Nicolas Cage, exits his vehicle at the scene of the attacks. In this shot, the tracking does not occur on a steady, linear axis, while the camera refuses to frame the subject of the shot – McLoughlin himself – in a conventional manner, leaving some or even most of McLoughlin's face and body out of the frame throughout the shot. Even in static shots, unconventional framing is frequently used, often in the form of an extreme close-up, thus establishing an uncomfortably reduced distance between the viewer and the "events" on-screen. Furthermore, the film – especially in scenes involving the attack itself – often refrains from employing long shots, thus denying the viewer any comfort that might be derived from the spatial overview which long shots typically provide, as well as contributing to the impression that the viewer is not privy to more information than are the characters in the film themselves[4]. All of these techniques – POV (point-of-view) shots, unstable framing and tracking, extreme close-ups, lack of long shots – have by now become typical cinematic signifiers of authenticity due to their rejection of classical Hollywood filmmaking practice, and thus contribute to the film's construction of authenticity on the textual level.

Various elements of *World Trade Center*'s *mise-en-scène* also contribute to its construction of authenticity. First, the locations used in the film were recreated as accurately as possible, a point which highlights the overlap and interplay between textual and extratextual means of constructing authenticity – after all, how would the average viewer, presumably unfamiliar with New York City, know how faithfully Stone's film recreates locations where the real-life events of September 11th took place unless he/she had been primed by newspaper and magazine articles, reviews, etc. pointing this out? Second, televisions showing archival news footage broadcast on September 11, 2001, are a constant presence in the film, whether as part of the background or as the focal point of a scene (as in the viewer's introduction to the character of Dave Karnes, for example)[5].

---

[4] Perhaps oddly (or perhaps not), *World Trade Center* closely parallels Steven Spielberg's remake of *War of the Worlds* (2005) in its abandoning of long shots during key sequences (in *War of the Worlds*, the first alien attack is shown largely with ground-level tracking shots, with the alien aggressors themselves appearing only in the background in many shots); interestingly, many critics discussed the possible presence of a political subtext involving 9/11 and subsequent U.S. foreign policy in the latter film upon its release.

[5] In this respect, *World Trade Center* (again, quite oddly) strongly recalls the

Finally, although *World Trade Center*, as pointed out in many reviews and articles, does not recreate the image of the aeroplanes crashing into the towers (though this is clearly referenced by the shot showing the silhouette of an aeroplane slowly passing over the surface of another skyscraper), the film does recreate many other images which now belong to the iconography of 9/11 – the towers themselves before the attacks, the people jumping from the towers, the massive clouds of dust and debris produced by the collapse of the towers, and so on. The prevalence of familiar 9/11 imagery in the film's *mise-en-scène*, coupled with the textual and extratextual assurance that non-familiar elements of the film's *mise-en-scène* have been recreated by the filmmakers as faithfully as possible, thus plays a key role in the film's construction of authenticity as well.

Finally, *World Trade Center* also employs editing in its construction of authenticity, though in a more indirect and subtle (but no less effective) manner. Editing is used at least twice in the film to establish a connection between, or to blur the lines separating, the film itself and the real-life situations which the film recreates. This first happens at the beginning of the film, when shots of New York City at dawn are intercut with footage of the actors playing Will Jimeno and John McLoughlin as these characters wake up and go to work. The effect here is not one of juxtaposition; rather, this sequence is shot in such a way as to situate the actors in a situation non-specific enough to plausibly stand-in for New York City on the morning of September 11th before the attacks (a man walks his dog in silhouette, for example). Thus, the actors (and, by extension, the narrative they play central roles in) are associated with New York City on the morning of September 11th – or at least a reasonable facsimile thereof.

This happens in even more striking fashion in the sequence directly after Jimeno and McLoughlin are trapped under the collapsed towers. Here, the camera, in an extended, computer-assisted long take, zooms out from beneath the rubble to an overhead shot of the wreckage of the towers. From this recreation (obviously part of the narrative re-telling), the film cuts to ostensibly authentic footage showing various reactions to the attacks, thus briefly re-situating the film in a non-fictional, non-narrative context. After this brief excursion, the film returns us to the narrative proper by introducing the character of Allison Jimeno (played by Maggie Gyllenhaal) as she watches the same news broadcasts being watched by the people in the previously-shown news footage. By editing the sequence in this manner, the filmmakers once again blur the line between their

---

seminal horror film *Night of the Living Dead* (dir. George Romero, 1968); in this film, the survivors of a zombie outbreak watch television news reports on several occasions in order to gain more knowledge about their predicament.

narrative re-telling of the events of 9/11 and the actual events themselves (or at least their representations in news media, traditionally expected to more closely approximate reality than other forms of media) by introducing another main character in a way that cleverly situates this character (and, again, the narrative to which that character belongs) in the context of real-life events rather than only in the context of the film's narrative recreation of those events.

Thus, *World Trade Center* employs editing, as well as the manipulation of camera movement, camera placement, and *mise-en-scène*, in order to construct a sense of authenticity. This process is accompanied by the concurrent construction of authenticity on the part of extratextual materials dealing with the film. It is to this extratextual construction of authenticity which we will now turn.

Extratextual means of constructing authenticity in *World Trade Center*

As the film itself directly references the involvement of surviving participants in the making of *World Trade Center* as a means of constructing authenticity, it is not surprising that extratextual material on the film does precisely the same thing. According to a *New York Times* article from July of 2006 leading up to the film's U.S. release in August of that year, Will Jimeno and John McLoughlin (the men upon whose experiences the film is based) both "say the script and the production took very few liberties except for the sake of time compression"[6]. In a National Public Radio interview, Jimeno offers the following anecdote:

> The people, the gaffers, the sound mixers, the electricians, would come up to me and say, are they doing this right. And I would say, well, yeah, they are, why? They said because if they're not, I don't want to be part of this project.[7]

Beyond the involvement of Jimeno and McLoughlin, not to mention the apparent concern of the entire crew, extratextual material on *World Trade Center* emphasizes the filmmakers' attempts to contact and involve

---

[6] David M. Halbfinger. "Oliver Stone's 'World Trade Center' Seeks Truth in the Rubble." *New York Times*, July 2nd, 2006. Accessed August 30th, 2012. http://www.nytimes.com/2006/07/02/movies/02halb.html

[7] Anne Hawke. "Real Cops Say 'World Trade Center' Gets It Right." *National Public Radio*, August 10th, 2006. Accessed August 30th, 2012. http://www.npr.org/templates/story/story.php?storyId=5635107

both family members of 9/11 victims (in a 2005 Associated Press article published as shooting on the film had just begun, one family member is quoted as expressing his appreciation for the "outreach and sensitivity of the filmmakers" as well as his desire to ensure "that the day's events [...] are represented accurately"[8]) as well as other survivors of 9/11 who were not directly involved in Jimeno and McLoughlin's story. As the *New York Times* piece puts it, "the studio is running all of its [promotional] materials by a group of survivors to avoid offending sensibilities"[9]. Clearly, this constant reference to the participation of those who were involved in (or whose lives were affected by) 9/11 in some way contributes to the perceived authenticity of *World Trade Center*, providing a context on the extratextual level within which the text's construction of authenticity is likely to be positively received by audience members.

Another way in which extratextual material on *World Trade Center* portrays the film as authentic concerns the film's director, Oliver Stone, and his directorial persona. While Oliver Stone is typically portrayed in the media as a larger-than-life personality known for making films with the potential to outrage on both the intellectual and stylistic level, with his 1994 film *Natural Born Killers* perhaps serving as the best reference point for both of these perceived tendencies, extratextual material on *World Trade Center* repeatedly portrays Stone as a changed director who has foregone his usual stylistic tics and conspiracy theories in the making of this particular film, ostensibly in the service of telling the "true" story of 9/11 (or at least that of Jimeno and McLoughlin's experience) as accurately as possible. The Associated Press article, for example, mentions those who "were concerned about how Stone – whose more controversial films include *JFK*, which offered conspiracy theories about the Kennedy assassination – might interpret the attacks in the film," but then hastens to allow Stone the opportunity to assure the reader that his 9/11 film will not traffic in this sort of political speculation:

> But in July, Stone called the untitled project "a work of collective passion, a serious meditation on what happened, and carries within a compassion that heals."
>   "It's an exploration of heroism in our country – but it's international at

---

[8] Associated Press. "Oliver Stone shoots Sept. 11 movie in New York." *USA Today*, November 2nd, 2005. Accessed August 30th, 2012.
http://www.usatoday.com/life/movies/news/2005-11-02-stone-filming-new-york_x.htm
[9] Halbfinger. "Oliver Stone's 'World Trade Center' Seeks Truth in the Rubble."

the same time in its humanity," he said.[10]

Even more explicit in its characterization of *World Trade Center* as an atypical work in Stone's oeuvre (and thus more "authentic"), both in terms of style and content, is the *New York Times* article, which truly goes out of its way to portray Stone as a changed director, and perhaps even a changed man, since his earlier days as a director, perhaps as a result of the gravity of the project:

> There are many people of course who have been driven a little crazy for other reasons by some of Mr. Stone's more controversial films, *JFK*, *Natural Born Killers* and *Nixon* chief among them. But in several interviews, sounding variously weary, wounded and either self-deprecating or defensive, Mr. Stone spoke as if his days of deliberate provocation were behind him.
> "I stopped," he says simply. "I stopped."[11]

Later, the article states explicitly that in Stone's opinion, the making of *World Trade Center* "would require a different approach from, say, *JFK*," emphasizes the involvement of screenwriter Andrea Berloff (perhaps in a bid to cast doubt upon the degree of Stone's authorship of the film), and touches upon co-star Michael Peña's concerns about an Oliver Stone-directed movie on 9/11 ("'I'm like, let me read it first – just because you're aware of the kind of movies that he does'"), before ending on a note of self-effacement on the part of Stone ("'I hope the movie does well,' he adds, 'even if they say in spite of Oliver Stone'"[12]). This portrayal of Stone contributes to *World Trade Center*'s construction of authenticity by implying and in some cases explicitly stating that, since the film's director has reined in his usual political slant and dialled down his stylistic excesses, the film itself must be more authentic as a result.

Factors having to do with the making of the film itself are also frequently cited in extratextual material on *World Trade Center* in order to cement the film's authenticity. The Associated Press article points out that "Cage, Pena [sic] and the other actors playing officers are using authentic equipment"[13] (whatever this might entail), while the *New York Times* article begins with a lengthy description of a computer-assisted recreation of the collapse of the World Trade Center presumably used by the filmmakers to ensure the accuracy of their sets and locations. The article

---

[10] Associated Press. "Oliver Stone shoots Sept. 11 movie in New York."
[11] Halbfinger. "Oliver Stone's 'World Trade Center' Seeks Truth in the Rubble."
[12] Ibid.
[13] Associated Press. "Oliver Stone shoots Sept. 11 movie in New York."

goes on to describe how Peña and Cage employed method acting techniques in their preparations for the shooting of the film and their portrayals of Jimeno and McLoughlin, respectively:

> Mr. Cage says he focused on getting Mr. McLoughlin's New York accent right, and spent time in a sense-deprivation tank in Venice, Calif., to get a hint of the fear and claustrophobia one might experience after hours immobile and in pain in the dark. Mr. Peña all but moved in with Mr. Jimeno.[14]

Thus, we can say that the extratextual material on *World Trade Center* is as invested in establishing the film's authenticity as is the film itself.

Another thread running throughout the extratextual material on the film (and here I shall return to the authenticity/ideology logic discussed in the introduction of this paper) is the notion that, since the film recreates the events of 9/11 in an authentic manner, the film itself must therefore be ideologically neutral, and must necessarily not take any sort of political stance. For instance, in a *Sight and Sound* interview, Oliver Stone first insists on the authenticity of the film ("It was crucial that [the film] be responsible and accurate to the story") before lambasting his (apparently mostly European) critics who took him to task for the film's ideological content:

> You should have seen Germany and Spain. It's insane. It's all politics. But the critics lose sight of the heart. The movie's about heart. It's about people helping each other.[15]

Later, in the same interview:

> I don't believe the intellectuals of Europe are really in touch with people. They are so politicised by 9/11. It's not their fault. It's anti-Bush, pro-Bush, anti-Iraq. They've lost sight of something. [...] They politicise everything. Every movie has to be seen through political glasses. They're insane. I'm not a political film-maker Goddamnit![16]

The *New York Times* article, for its part, makes the perceived connection between authenticity and lack of ideological content a great deal more

---

[14] Halbfinger. "Oliver Stone's 'World Trade Center' Seeks Truth in the Rubble."
[15] Ali Jaafar. "I'm not a political filmmaker goddamit!" *Sight and Sound*, September 2006. Accessed August 30th, 2012.
http://old.bfi.org.uk/sightandsound/feature/49325
[16] Jaafar. "I'm not a political filmmaker goddamit!"

explicit ("'This is not a political film,' [Stone] insists. [...] He said he just wants to depict the plain facts of what happened on Sept. 11"[17]), while the Associated Press article is even more blunt in conveying the producers' assertion that "because Berloff's script focuses entirely on McLoughlin and Jimeno's experience on Sept. 11, the film will not interpret the politics or meaning of Sept. 11" while simultaneously claiming that "Stone has taken great care to portray the event as it happened"[18].

It is clear, then, that a kind of consensus or unspoken agreement exists between the film *World Trade Center* as a text, the filmmakers, and much of the extratextual material on the film to the effect that, since the film has achieved a certain level of authenticity, it follows logically that the film must be ideologically neutral and lacking any kind of political message. The next section of this paper will attempt to prove the opposite – that *World Trade Center* does in fact take a clear ideological and political stance, in spite of these attempts to construct authenticity.

Ideology in *World Trade Center*

One clear ideological stance taken by *World Trade Center* throughout its running time is, unsurprisingly, that Americans are essentially good people and that the United States (as a place, as a political and economic entity, etc.) is also essentially good. One of the first shots of the film, showing McLoughlin watching his sleeping children before he leaves for work, already characterizes Americans (and, by extension, the United States itself) as innocent, incapable of doing harm to others. Scenes of Jimeno striking up a random conversation on a bus and the Port Authority officers horsing around in the locker room, both of which take place before the attacks, further characterize Americans as genial, friendly, and inclusive. Even before the severity of the attacks is understood, Jimeno is reassured by a fellow officer that there are "a lot of good people here." From this point on, the essential goodness of Americans is repeatedly emphasized, culminating in the outpouring of support for McLoughlin upon his rescue and the film's closing voice-over narration, which overlays a recreation of a barbecue commemorating Jimeno and McLoughlin's rescue: "[9/11] brought out a goodness we forgot could exist [...] people taking care of each other for no other reason than it was the right thing to do." Thus, *World Trade Center* can be seen as a baldly expressed paean to American exceptionalism – which also becomes problematic when we

---

[17] Halbfinger. "Oliver Stone's 'World Trade Center' Seeks Truth in the Rubble."
[18] Associated Press. "Oliver Stone shoots Sept. 11 movie in New York."

take into account that the film, barring the montage of ostensibly archival reaction footage after the attacks, *only* depicts Americans, therefore inviting viewers to characterize the Other (which, in the vague terms of the film itself, might comprise the attackers themselves, the governments and/or populations of Middle Eastern countries, or even all non-Americans, depending on the viewer) in opposition to the Americans in the film, i.e. as essentially bad.

Relatedly, the film also uses various means to highlight the relative economic prosperity of the United States. This is first underlined by the shots of impressively daunting skyscrapers which pepper the opening sequence, as well as a shot in the same sequence which lingers on the famed "Charging Bull" statue near Wall Street, a pronounced symbol of a robust American economy (the radio broadcast on the soundtrack here refers none-too-subtly to rising stock prices). On Jimeno's car ride to work, the car radio blasts the song "Only in America" by Brooks and Dunn, with its references to the "sun coming up over New York City" and the "promise of the promised land" allowing the film's general pro-American ideology and emphasis on the strong American economy to be expressed in terms of the soundtrack; the Jimeno character's positive reaction to the song can thus be seen as a tacit endorsement of these sentiments. Moreover, the music here is clearly diegetic, as emphasized by the shot of Jimeno turning up the volume of the car radio and the corresponding increase in volume on the film soundtrack, which might serve to both naturalize the song's sentiments by situating them in a thus far painstakingly accurate recreation of New York City and to encourage the viewer to share in these sentiments (along with Jimeno, who for viewers at all familiar with any extratextual material on the film might well already be a figure of identification, even at this early point in the film).

From this perspective, the terrorists attacks on September 11, 2001, as portrayed in the film, could be read as attacks on the economic system of the United States, the long-term effects of which are ultimately rejected by the end of the film, with its emphasis on renewal, reconstruction, and rejuvenation – in addition to the aforementioned barbecue scene, with a recovered Jimeno and McLoughlin perhaps standing in for a recovered United States, the final sequence focuses on the rescue efforts and the clearing of debris, and features "God Bless America" signs prominently in *its mise-en-scène*. Thus, it is difficult not to read the film as an endorsement of the United States' status as a global economic and political superpower (and, implicitly, of the questionable foreign policy decisions made by various U.S. governments throughout the 20th and 21st centuries to establish and maintain this status).

Related to, and perhaps offered as a justification for, *World Trade Center*'s enthusiasm for the United States' global economic and political status is the film's portrayal of the U.S. as a multicultural, socially tolerant land. Among the shots included in the film's aforementioned opening montage of city life are shots of Asian tourists and of a black woman (who might well be a man in drag); the fact that these shots, editorially speaking, are not made to stand out from other shots of the city or from shots of white New Yorkers creates the effect of inclusivity and harmony. Throughout the film, the multiracial and multi-ethnic composition of various groups – the Port Authority officers, the people responding to the attacks, the rescuers – is emphasized, while one of the final scenes of the film includes a pointed reference to "bratwurst", and therefore to the multi-ethnic composition of New York in particular and the United States in general. This diversity is highlighted by the closing text of the film, which points out that "citizens from 87 countries" were murdered in the 9/11 attacks. As this multicultural aspect of the United States is solely presented in a positive light, with an emphasis on harmony and coexistence (and the conspicuous absence of any resultant problems or tensions), this aspect of the film also contributes to *World Trade Center*'s pro-United States ideological stance.

Accompanying this message is the film's unambiguous embrace of religion, a subtext which is expressed not only in terms of plot (as many of the film's major plot points – Karnes' discovery of Jimeno and McLoughlin, Jimeno's ability to endure his harrowing predicament – are directly facilitated by religion), but also by the use of cinematic technique. Take the scene showing Karnes in the church, for example, in which he asks God for guidance before deciding to assist the rescue efforts at Ground Zero. In terms of plot, religion is shown as a major – if not the sole – impetus for Karnes' subsequent heroism; in terms of technique, this scene is striking in that the camera movement here becomes more stable, the frequency of the cutting more regular, and the framing more conventional than in the previous sections of the film – involving the attack, Jimeno and McLoughlin's predicament, and the efforts of their families to obtain information and to maintain some semblance of normality. Thus, this scene conveys Karnes' peace of mind and clarity of purpose to the viewer in cinematic terms, while making it clear, plot-wise, that Karnes was only able to achieve this state with the help of religion.

Significantly, this scene is also framed symmetrically. This use of symmetrical framing, which also makes this scene stand out from the chaos and confusion depicted earlier, becomes a motif used throughout the film as a kind of visual shorthand for the influence of religion and, ultimately, the implied presence of God or another "higher power". Symmetrical framing is used when Jimeno has a hallucination of Jesus after being trapped under the rubble of the towers for hours. Here, the implication that the appearance of Jesus (or a delirium-inspired version thereof) provides Jimeno with the presence of mind necessary to survive his ordeal is obvious, a connection which is made explicit in the subsequent dialogue, when Jimeno tells McLoughlin that his vision of Jesus means that they will live.[19] Later, the rescue of McLoughlin is also symmetrically framed; the re-use of this motif, along with the circumstances of the rescue (McLoughlin is excavated to the surface from under the ground, strongly bringing to mind the biblical idea of resurrection) and the choice of inspirational music, lend this scene a definite religious tone. The shot of Jimeno and McLoughlin recovering together in the hospital after the rescue is also symmetrically framed; the use of symmetrical framing here, which has by now practically come to explicitly represent religion and its influence, along with the placement of the camera (the characters are filmed from above in a long overhead shot), convey not only the presence and influence of religion, but also the unmistakable impression that McLoughlin and Jimeno are being watched over by God, thus encouraging the interpretation that it is in fact God who makes their recovery (and the happy ending of the film) possible. Through a combination of plot points and cinematic technique, then, *World Trade Center* clearly espouses a pro-religious ideology.

Most strikingly, *World Trade Center* seems to implicitly argue that 9/11 calls for retaliation and must be avenged; whether intentionally or not, this message is communicated in such a way as to strongly imply that the United States' military involvement in Iraq was a justified response to 9/11, thus placing the film squarely in the pro-war ideological camp. The general characterization of the United States and of Americans as essentially good and innocent throughout the film (as discussed earlier in this section) provides the basis for this implication, as does the emphatic reference to the attackers as "bastards" repeated twice in the film, which furthermore establishes a clear "us vs. them" dichotomy, as the attackers are never mentioned otherwise throughout the film, and encourages the viewer to see the attackers as purely evil and the United States as purely good, with no shades of grey.

It is through the character of Dave Karnes, however, that this pro-war

---

[19] Amazingly, this bit of dialogue (according to Jimeno himself in his National Public Radio interview) was an invention of the filmmakers.

ideology is most clearly expressed. We are introduced to Karnes as he informs his colleagues that "this country's at war" before leaving to join the rescue effort; while walking away from the wreckage of the collapsed towers after the rescue, Karnes (now clad in his former Marines uniform and sporting a typical military crew cut) proclaims that "they'll need good men to avenge this." The closing text of the film informs the viewer of Karnes' post-9/11 fate: "Dave Karnes re-enlisted in the Marines and served two tours of duty in Iraq." Though Stone insists that the text was added after test audiences thought the Karnes character was entirely fictional,[20] the fact that this information is presented uncritically, in conjunction with the pro-war thrust found in many other aspects of the filmic narrative, produces an obvious effect: America's military involvement in Iraq can be seen as an appropriate response to the attacks on 9/11.

The notion that *World Trade Center* could be seen as politically or ideologically neutral, then, seems to be a rather far-fetched one, as the film quite clearly espouses a pro-America, pro-religion, and (most problematically) pro-war ideology, while encouraging viewers to engage in the typical binary thinking that posits a purely good United States and a purely evil set of shadowy entities opposed to the United States. Once again, I would argue that these ideological positions are obscured by recourse to the notion of authenticity, on the part of both the film itself and the extratextual materials on the film, which provide a context within which it can be read as an authentic depiction of historical events.

Critical reception and concluding thoughts

In closing, I would like to return to the idea of "reception" touched upon in the introduction of this paper. If, as I have argued, the film *World Trade Center* constructs authenticity in order to obscure or draw attention from its ideological content, and if much of the extratextual material on the film is engaged in the same project, how might this interplay between authenticity and ideology influence, and/or find expression in, the critical reception of the film (i.e. in reviews by film critics)? While a thorough examination of this question is beyond the scope of this paper, it is fortunately not completely beyond the scope of this conclusion – and, indeed, a cursory look at newspaper and magazine reviews of *World Trade Center* lends at least some credence to the idea that the construction of authenticity and (thus) the disavowal of any ideological or political stance indeed played at least some role in the critical reception of the film.

---

[20] Jaafar. "I'm not a political filmmaker goddamit!"

Firstly, many reviews of *World Trade Center* either downplay or explicitly deny the presence of any sort of ideological or political stance in the film itself. The *USA Today* review of the film is perhaps most explicit in this regard, describing *World Trade Center* as "a powerful film told without any discernible political agenda"[21]. Richard Schickel's review of the film in *Time* also argues that Oliver Stone's "sometimes loopy political opinions – not to mention paranoia – [are] nowhere in evidence," while later calling attempts by the "political right" to co-opt the movie "nonsense"[22]. David Denby, in his *New Yorker* review, concurs in arguing that "some of the [political right's] euphoria […] is not only inane, it's enough to turn you off moviegoing altogether"[23].

In order to account for its supposedly apolitical stance, reviewers frequently cite the notion that *World Trade Center* is an "atypical" Oliver Stone film – an idea which, as we have seen earlier, is expressed repeatedly in the extratextual material on the film as well. In addition to Schickel's aforementioned comments, Ty Burr's review of the film for the *Boston Globe* offers the rather backhanded compliment that "the best thing I can say about [*World Trade Center*] is that it doesn't feel like an Oliver Stone movie. There are no conspiracies here"[24]. Likewise, the *USA Today* review argues that while "some might have expected a more controversial angle from the director of films such as *JFK* and *Natural Born Killers*," the film itself is in fact a "more conventional rendering"[25] of the events of 9/11. A.O. Scott's review of the film in the *New York Times* also touches upon the idea that Oliver Stone has in *World Trade Center* somehow transcended his own directorial persona, this time citing the possible influence of screenwriter Andrea Berloff in this regard (again recalling similar claims made in the extratextual material on the film):

> [After the 9/11 attacks] there would be complications, nuances, gray areas, as the event and its aftermath were inevitably pulled into the murky, angry

---

[21] Claudia Puig. "Intimate 'Trade Center' tells larger tale." *USA Today*, August 8th, 2006. Accessed August 30th, 2012.
http://www.usatoday.com/life/movies/reviews/2006-08-08-wtc-review_x.htm
[22] Richard Schickel. "Fine Movie on a Bad Day." *Time Magazine*, July 31st, 2006. Accessed August 30th, 2012.
http://www.time.com/time/magazine/article/0,9171,1220510,00.html
[23] David Denby. "On Duty." *The New Yorker*, August 21st, 2006. Accessed August 30th, 2012. http://www.newyorker.com/archive/2006/08/21/060821crci_cinema
[24] Ty Burr. "Emotional rescue." *Boston Globe*, August 9th, 2006. Accessed August 30th, 2012. http://articles.boston.com/2006-08-09/ae/29246914_1_andrea-berloff-movie-star-world-trade-center
[25] Puig. "Intimate 'Trade Center' tells larger tale."

swirl of American politics. But that is territory Mr. Stone, somewhat uncharacteristically, avoids.

> *World Trade Center* is only the second film [...] that he has directed entirely from someone else's script, and Andrea Berloff's screenplay [...] imposes a salutary discipline on some of the director's wilder impulses.[26]

Toward the end of the review, Scott further argues that "Mr. Stone and Ms. Berloff [...] keep their distance from post- – or, for that matter, pre- – 9/11 politics,"[27] thus cementing the idea that *World Trade Center* is an apolitical work, echoing the sentiments of both the filmic text itself and much of the extratextual material on the film.

Moreover, many of the reviews of *World Trade Center* also indicate acceptance of the notion that the film is "authentic", thus making it plausible that the textual and extratextual construction of authenticity with regard to the film had at least some influence on reviewers' interpretation and characterization of the film as apolitical. Scott's review refers to "the sober carefulness of this project" as well as "the film's astonishingly faithful re-creation"[28] of 9/11, while Denby tells his readers that "[Stone] doesn't exaggerate or hype anything"[29]. (Oddly enough, two sentences later, Denby praises "a fine shot, in slow motion, that passes across the astonished faces of the policemen in the bus,"[30] which begs the question as to what this particular reviewer would actually term "exaggeration", if not the manipulation of the frame rate to create a slow-motion effect.) The *USA Today* review praises the "almost matter-of-fact style" of the film as well as Stone's attempts to "avoid sensationalism,"[31] while Schickel's *Time* review emphasizes that "[Jimeno and McLoughlin's] survival story is true"[32].

Thus, it would seem as though a general acceptance of the film's "authenticity" figures prominently in the critical reception of *World Trade Center*, which, when coupled with the general disavowal of the film's ideological content on the part of critics, certainly supports the central

---

[26] A.O. Scott. "Pinned Under the Weight of Skyscrapers and History in 'World Trade Center'." *New York Times*, August 9th, 2006. Accessed August 30th, 2012. http://movies.nytimes.com/2006/08/09/movies/09worl.html?pagewanted=all

[27] Scott. "Pinned Under the Weight of Skyscrapers and History in 'World Trade Center'."

[28] Scott. "Pinned Under the Weight of Skyscrapers and History in 'World Trade Center'."

[29] Denby. "On Duty."

[30] Denby. "On Duty."

[31] Puig. "Intimate 'Trade Center' tells larger tale."

[32] Schickel. "Fine Movie on a Bad Day."

proposition of this paper – that the textual and extratextual construction of authenticity with regard to *World Trade Center*, whether intentionally or not, obscures the presence of ideology in the film.

Bibliography

Primary sources

World Trade Center, DVD. Directed by Oliver Stone. 2006: Paramount Home Entertainment, 2007.

Secondary sources

Associated Press. "Oliver Stone shoots Sept. 11 movie in New York." *USA Today*, November 2nd, 2005. Accessed August 30th, 2012. http://www.usatoday.com/life/movies/news/2005-11-02-stone-filming-new-york_x.htm

Burr, Ty. "Emotional rescue." *Boston Globe*, August 9th, 2006. Accessed August 30th, 2012. http://articles.boston.com/2006-08-09/ae/29246914_1_andrea-berloff-movie-star-world-trade-center

Denby, David. "On Duty." *The New Yorker*, August 21st, 2006. Accessed August 30th, 2012. http://www.newyorker.com/archive/2006/08/21/060821crci_cinema

Halbfinger, David M. "Oliver Stone's 'World Trade Center' Seeks Truth in the Rubble." *New York Times*, July 2nd, 2006. Accessed August 30th, 2012. http://www.nytimes.com/2006/07/02/movies/02halb.html

Hawke, Anne. "Real Cops Say 'World Trade Center' Gets It Right." *National Public Radio*, August 10th, 2006. Accessed August 30th, 2012. http://www.npr.org/templates/story/story.php?storyId=5635107

Jaafar, Ali. "I'm not a political filmmaker goddamit!" *Sight and Sound*, September 2006. Accessed August 30th, 2012. http://old.bfi.org.uk/sightandsound/feature/49325

Puig, Claudia. "Intimate 'Trade Center' tells larger tale." *USA Today*, August 8th, 2006. Accessed August 30th, 2012. http://www.usatoday.com/life/movies/reviews/2006-08-08-wtc-review_x.htm

Schickel, Richard. "Fine Movie on a Bad Day." *Time Magazine*, July 31st, 2006. Accessed August 30th, 2012. http://www.time.com/time/magazine/article/0,9171,1220510,00.html

INFIDELS AND MARTYRS: POPULAR AND SCIENTIFIC DISCOURSES ON PICTURING MUSLIMS AFTER 9/11 IN THE CONTEXT OF THE US MILITARY PRESENCE IN IRAQ AND AFGHANISTAN

JAREMA DROZDOWICZ

When speaking about the phenomenon of the cultural implications of the so called "War on Terror" we have to include in the ongoing debate a vast amount of existing positions on this issue. Each of them is expressed on a different level of public discourse. The multi-vocal character of the post-9/11 discourse seems to be the consequence of a strong differentiation of political views, depending on whether the fight against what is called a global network of Muslim terrorism is considered as just or not. The growing level of that differentiation influences also the contemporary debates and contributes to a polarization of positions in the political, as well the academic field. The academic approach to the post 9/11 world order does not differ much from the mechanism constructing the political and public discourse in the USA, especially when it comes to grasping the matter of the cultural shifts following the events in New York. This very relation between the academia and politics, mostly visible in the way American scholars express their views on the problem, might be considered an obstacle in an objective academic view, but on the other hand it also might be taken into account as an immanent part of the whole problem. Therefore it seems appropriate to consider this phenomenon as an object of study in the perspective of cultural studies, including media discourse, popular culture and the academic practice.

The attack on the Taliban regime in Afghanistan was an important turning point in conceptualizing the 9/11 aftermath. The US military presence in Afghanistan did contribute to the emergence of a specific geo-political context, which affected not just the military strategies, but also American universities. American scholars had to take up a position in the world, which from now on was taking the state of exception as granted. The American public was expecting them to deliver practical solutions to urgent problems. Therefore the views of science and the academic practice changed significantly. Extreme pragmatism took the place of a free dialogue between various worldviews. Science and the humanities were in a state of war just as the Western society was.

But it was not the first time American scholars were made a part of a political machinery in times of war and conflict. The context of the 1960's may serve here as an example of this relation between academic and military structures, providing us with some of the most striking instances of incorporating scientific ideals into a system of values, which has little in common with science. The Vietnam War became the most significant and nationwide trauma for the American society in those days. The picture of the internally torn apart American society that might have been observed in the 1960s was also reflected in the academic debates and social actions inspired by scholars. At the time when the Afro-American rights movement propagated non-violent forms of civil disobedience in so called "sit-ins", John Lennon and Yoko Ono gave an example of the alleged effectiveness of their "bed-ins", and on universities campuses academics began to implement so called "teach-ins". The counterculture movement shaped the academic discourse just as it had shaped many other fields in American public life in that decade.

The CORDS program (*Civil Operations and Revolutionary Development Support*) was supposed to create in this context an effective initiative, joining the field of civil social research in Indochina and their military applications with the actions of the US Army in Vietnam. The battle for the hearts and minds of the Vietnamese was in this view a much more important battleground than direct military actions on the frontline. Achieving not exactly sympathy, but long term loyalty from the South Vietnamese for the fight against the urban guerilla (along with sympathizers of the Viet Cong in the US) was the strategic mission of this operation. The CORDS program, whose inventor was Robert Komer, an advisor in Lyndon B. Johnson's administration office, included some smaller counter-insurgency programs led by the US Army, the CIA and USAID (*United States Agency for International Development*). Through directing to the ideological frontline large amounts of financial support, CORDS could also further various research initiatives in the United States, as long as they were pointed out as useful allies in fighting with the Eastern Bloc. CORDS supported ethnographic research among the local population of Vietnam and Laos (mostly among the Hmong/Montagnards groups), which were also trained by American advisors in counterinsurgency and fought against the communists. It is also worth mentioning that a side project of CORDS, the classified Phoenix program, whose main goal was to eliminate people suspected of collaboration with the Viet Cong and alleged sympathizers of the North, was part of the whole enterprise. Although most of the assassinations were carried out by US special forces and CIA operatives, Phoenix later became a model solution for many paramilitary groups in Central America during the so called "dirty wars" in the 1970s and 1980s.

In a world of political and economic destabilization science is according to many supposed to fulfil a specific mission. It has to counteract the overwhelming crisis of society and politics as well as to provide practical solutions for current issues. This kind of pragmatic approach towards science, which simultaneously is a political postulate, is typical for many American scholars from the right and the left side of the intellectual barricade. Pragmatism understood as a philosophy of science seems to be in every of these cases the key problem of the theoretical and methodological approach, which in reference to the social sciences finds many controversial examples.

When at the end of 2005 and the beginning of 2006 the chiefs of staff of the US Army initiated a program called euphemistically the Human Terrain System (HTS), the American academic environment of social scientists had been put in a very inconvenient position. Thus we might observe an attempt of a direct transfer of postulates of modern sociology and cultural anthropology related to their applications, which until then had seemed to be effective only on paper, to a socio-cultural situation in the global hot-spots i.e. in Iraq and Afghanistan. Both places were linked together by the situation of a socio-political conflict. This very conflict in consequence occurred to be a cultural phenomenon, the more so as it was associated with current debates on the nature of modern methods of sociology and anthropology. HTS was supposed to be in the eyes of its authors an effective combat tool in the field of the Global War on Terror. American anthropologist Montgomery McFate, one of the main architects of HTS, points to the main tasks of this program : 1) on- the- ground ethnographic research (through interviews and participant observation) in the Middle East and Central Asia, 2) redeployment and advanced cultural training and computer-based training on society and culture, 3) socio-cultural studies of areas of interest (such as North Korean culture and society, Iranian military culture and so on), 4) training and deployment of cultural advisers for planning and operations on request and lectures at military institutions, 5) experimental socio-cultural programs, such as the preparation of the environment – a constantly updated database tool for use by operational commanders and planners[1]. As we can see these goals clearly emphasize that HTS should become not just a set of anthropological directions, which might be useful for the realization of military tasks, but an integral part of the military infrastructure in the fight against terror.

What actually is HTS? Is it just an attempt at an "anthropologization" of the space of military actions, or a form of militarization of anthropology itself; or, as Hugh Gusterson, one of the HTS critics states – a militarization of knowledge? To obtain at least a partially satisfying answer to these questions we have to go back to the scientific, historical and political context surrounding the HTS. This very context was drawn largely by processes of social and political changes in the United States after World War II. The climate of Cold War paranoia affected in this matter also the circle of the prominent representatives of the social sciences. These academic circles would be soon confronted with various political pressures. The frontline of combat with communism was taken into academic campuses, where the intellectual battle for the minds of young Americans was to be fought. The emergence in the late 1950's and early 1960's of the first centrifugal tendencies linked with countercultures and social emancipation movements (like for example the Afro-American movement) contributed quite fast to the situation where the overwhelming crisis of values reported by many followers of counter-cultural ideals also became a part of the political discourse and practice. The appearance of radical social movements like the *Black Panthers* or the *Symbionise Liberation Army* only fomented the cognitive and conceptual instability of the social sciences, from which the public and government officials often demanded a provision of not just moral directions but also information about how to deal with revolutionary movements back home. The American society was seen to be the field of various social experiments, sometimes of even the most peculiar ones (just to recall here the infamous experiments with LSD undertaken by the CIA). Thus social difference became a political and cultural category at the same time. The terrain which was ordered in this manner was also a human terrain, in the sense of a geographical (or even cartographic) description of the world of the human desires for a change of the social status quo. Urban guerillas like the *Black Panthers*, did not differ much in this light from the leftist guerillas in Central America, or the Viet Cong. It is not a surprise that these organizations also had been put under surveillance from the

---

[1] J. Gonzales, *American Counterinsurgency. Human Science and the Human Terrain* (Chicago, 2009), 48.

authorities, similar to the Viet Cong who were targeted as an object of the military actions in Indochina. In this sense American cities evolved into a militarized terrain, like the title of Robert Moss's book *The War for the Cities* might suggest.

With regard to the Vietnam War, it was considered a point of reference in theory as much as in practice for many intellectual debates at the time. Nevertheless, the conflict in Vietnam is also, as far as establishing the direct origins of HTS are concerned, an important part of the debate over the position of this program in a political and scientific context. One of the supporters and inventors of this method of civil protest was Marshall Sahlins, nowadays one of the most popular American anthropologists and a critic of HTS. The years of American military involvement in Indochina provide us with one of the most significant examples of the incorporation of methods and theories of the social sciences into military actions.

US Army officials claim that HTS has been viewed as a CORDS of the 21st Century. Anthropological and other methods of the social sciences are not only to strengthen the cooperation with the local population, but should also enhance the understanding of the motivations of insurgents and groups hostile towards the official governments in Baghdad or Kabul. As US Army officials point out:

> Cultural awareness will not necessarily always enable us to predict what the enemy and noncombatants will do, but it will help us better understand what motivates them, what is important to the host nation in which we serve, and how we can either elicit the support of the population or at least diminish their support and aid to the enemy[2].

HTS brings together specialists from many social disciplines, who are ready to provide analyses of the Human Terrain – a terrain saturated with the category of difference, one of the basic terms in the anthropological dictionary. This difference is set against our Western thought patterns and marks off different structures within a given geographic space. Although this difference has first of all a cultural character (like for example the structure of the Pashtu tribes in Afghanistan), it also has an economic, social, religious, and last but not least political character. At the same time, the anthropological description of difference is an attempt to put it into order and to define its epistemological frames. It is a conceptual intention

---

[2] Major General Benjamin C. Freakley, Commanding General, CJTF-76, Afghanistan, 2006,
http://www.army.mil/professionalwriting/volumes/volume4/december_2006/12_06_2.html.

put against what is empirically available. Thus it is a construction of a specific image of cultural reality, which might differ (as Edward Said tried to show) from the factual state. As Neil L. Whitehead states in his book *War in the Tribal Zone*, such expansive actions like the HTS generate only a specific imagination of a cultural space; a tribal zone which has to be put into well known terms, sometimes through the application of methodologies far from the anthropological workshop. The actions undertaken within the HTS show this very clearly. Five person Human Terrain Teams serve as advisors on a tactical level who provide analyses that might help to shape the strategy in Iraq and Afghanistan. In the words of Steve Kipp, the author of the first HTS concept, a typical Human Terrain Team (HTT) would consist of:
- HTT leader (a major or lieutenant colonel who is also a staff college graduate)
- Cultural analyst (civilian with an MA or PhD in cultural anthropology or sociology)
- Regional studies analyst (civilian with an MA or PhD in area studies with language fluency)
- HT research manager (with military background in tactical intelligence)
- HT analyst (also with military background in tactical intelligence)

Together with the change in US general command that took place in 2010 and the nomination of General David Petraeus "cultural awareness" is pointed to as the key to success, not just in the current, but also in future conflicts. Just as WW I was a war of the chemists, WW II a war of the physicians, and the Cold War a war of politicians, the conflicts of the future would be wars of the social scientists. Hence HTS is not just an experimental research program, but an integral part of the military structure and the HTTs are deployed to particular units together with a set of tasks to fulfil.

These tasks often result from the current needs of the military and the local population. Despite the fact that HTTs coordinate quite often actions to support the modernization of local communities (like drilling wells, building schools and many other such actions) these actions can be hardly called aid work. HTT members are more involved in programs aiming at minimizing the helplessness against acts of insurgency in Iraq and Afghanistan. The use of biometric methods in order to make a proper census might recall obvious associations with the Nazi pseudo-science in Germany in the 1930s and 1940s or a modernized post-colonial system of direct/indirect rule. If these historical associations come to our minds, they are unfounded as we have to take into account the purely postulated goals of HTS and the broader practical dimension in which HTS functions. The frames of that context are not drawn by an anthropological or scientific discourse but by political factors. The incorporation of HTS into new counter-strategies for battling terrorism proves not a militarization of anthropology, but more an "anthropologization" of military structures. This new strategy predicts an incorporation of a dictionary of terms of the social sciences into a structure of a completely different nature. These terms are treated as one of many instruments of military actions. The expectation that the US command will suddenly "think" in anthropological terms is an evidence of scientific naivety, or a more or less conscious submission to opportunistic tendencies visible in many scientific environments. A factual inclusion of the discourse of the social sciences into the language of military structures is an evidence in this matter of a marriage between certain academic traditions and sheer military pragmatism.

Paradoxically, we find the very same terminology in official publications by luminaries of the HTS like McFate, and the former director of the program Steve Fondacaro. The validity of speaking of a militarization of anthropology in the context of HTS is also put into question by the fact that in recent years within the structures of this program we may find fewer and fewer educated anthropologists or sociologists and more often that the position of an HTT member requires nothing more than having a degree in any scientific discipline that fits into the obscure field of "social scientist". Sometimes any doctorate degree would do to join a HTT. At heart this phenomenon reveals a crisis of anthropology, which in its current shape seems to be deprived of a practical standing in a dramatically changing world.

Critics and members of HTS, whose main field of discussion is the Internet and the blogs published by them in the cyberspace, prove also a great level of political activism. An extreme polarization of views in this case shows that the debate over the character of HTS and its influence on the social sciences is marked by the burden of ideological positioning, mostly in the context of American political debates. The main internet forum of the critics is a website called "zeroanthropology.net" (formerly "openanthropology.org") and organized by Maximilian C. Forte and John Stanton. While Forte, an associate professor of anthropology at Concordia University in Montreal, represents a standpoint which might be defined as one of scientific polemic, Stanton represents the media and is an investigative reporter. His comments reveal a highly critical attitude towards the conservative administration and the US Government. Both authors of zeronathropology point out that the criticism of HTS is not just levelled at the deformed ideals of the applied science, but more generally at the system that produces and promotes them as a role model for modern research programs.

The often debated topic of modernization included in the HTS documents refers not only to the alleged modern character of the program itself, but also to the modernization of the societies in which the program finds its application. The modernization of Iraq or Afghanistan is simultaneously regarded as a development of democratic institutions. At this point a number of questions emerge – does the use of the social sciences in the process of the democratization of these societies lead to constructing the relations of power and dominance? Does the commitment of social scientists in the struggle for a better tomorrow conceal American dominance through the use of slogans of progress and the fight against tyranny? These questions automatically direct the discussion over HTS to the post-colonial debates. British or French rule in Africa or Asia also included these slogans of a speeded-up modernization and here also the emergence of anthropology as an autonomous discipline was a part of this positivistic enterprise. However, as I have mentioned before, the use of that rhetoric, no matter how tempting it might be as a style of writing, has to be considered within the specific rhetoric used by the military and government agencies in the US. HTS, CORDS and other similar programs (like Camelot and MINERVA), which boast of themselves as scientific are a phenomenon belonging to the current processes of geopolitical transgressions in Iraq and Afghanistan and have to be considered as such. This does not deny the fact that the history of anthropological thought provides us with some significant examples of similar discussions about the ethical basis of scientific research in the context of military actions and about the militarization of science in the service of ideology.

The memorable open letter issued by the father of American anthropology, Franz Boas, and published in the magazine *The Nation* on October 16th, 1919, raised controversies similar to the criticism of HTS nowadays. The article included an accusation of espionage against unnamed British archaeologists during WW I in the Middle East. Boas, until his death closely bound up with the German research tradition and philosophy of science, argued that this kind of involvement estranged scientific research from the possibility of an objective view on the examined problem. Research would then fall prey to a structure, whose goal is not by any means objective scientific findings, but the realization of tasks set by politicians and military officials. The scientist as a spy, as the title of the article suggests, at this very moment stops being a man of science and turns into a soldier on the frontline of an ideological combat. Boas' imperative of an independent and objective view on conducting research had contributed to his marginalization in the academic environment. His removal from the office in the American Anthropological Association seemed to be dictated by his criticism of American interventionism, but also by his own uncertain status as an American citizen.

The second example relates to Gregory Bateson, a reputable British anthropologist, semiotician and linguist. David H. Price in his book *Anthropological Intelligence* recalls the relation between Bateson and the OSS (*Office of Strategic Services*), the predecessor of the CIA. The collaboration of the British scholar with the OSS during WW II raised concerns of an ethical nature also in Bateson. As he states:

> Both these objections have a certain validity. In helping a military government to govern a population without bloodshed one is aiding a dictatorship to avoid trouble with the masses, but – and this is the applied anthropologist's point of view – one is also helping to avoid the sorts of decisions that not only will lead to more trouble and expense for the administrators, but that will also lead to greater harshness of treatment of the people by their temporary governors[3].

The cooperation of reputable anthropologists with military institutions in the past also concerned Alfred Metroux, Clyde Kluckhohn, or Conrad Arensberg and few other prominent authors. On the one hand Bateson's collaboration with the OSS was a strong expression of his patriotic feelings, of patriotic duties, and his political will to counteract the malicious Nazi system spreading across Europe. On the other it was also an expression of a significant stratification of public expectations towards the social sciences and their moral standards. The epistemological focus of anthropology lies on the assumption that morality is culturally relative in terms of research. The theoretical awkwardness visible in Bateson's words is also typical of the situation HTS members are put into. A theoretical and notional insecurity of anthropology dominates the discussions about the current state and future of this discipline and is also an important factor in the discussion about HTS. The open criticism by the American Anthropological Association and some American anthropologists like the Network of Concerned Anthropologists (including David H. Price and

---

[3] D. H. Price, *Anthropological Intelligence. The Deployment and Neglect of American Anthropology in the Second World War* (Durham and London, 2008), 36.

Roberto J. Gonzales, a professor of anthropology at the San Jose State University) does not reflect the nature of the problem. The problem concerns in the first place a crisis of the anthropological tools of cognition in a culturally diverse world, its adequate ethnographic description and the use of fieldwork data for purposes completely different from the intentional ones. This last issue is the key problem in understanding the nature of HTS.

The question by whom and how the HTS data might be used is the main topic of Barry Silverman's article *Human Terrain Data – What Should We Do With It?* Or: What are the data included in the particular analyses provided by the HTS? As Silverman says:

> (...) human terrain information is open source derived, unclassified, referenced (geospatially, relationally, and temporally) information. It includes the situational roles, goals, relationships, and rules of behavior of an operationally relevant group or individual"[4].

In this view the HTS data are supposed to be an off-the-shelf product, a ready-made set of tools and directions to be applied in the Global War on Terror. Although Silverman is not an apologist of HTS, he articulates, more or less consciously, the imperative of pragmatism. Thus the data provided by the social sciences can assist a schematically shaped cognitive and structural analysis of human social and cultural agencies. As to HTS, the schematic approach can also be understood literally, as creating a computer software making possible a description with quasi cartographic methods and an adequate picture of human motivations and worldviews. The potential advantage here is the possibility of predicting what region of the country may become politically unstable in the close future, the answer to the question which group or clan may be persuaded into cooperation or must be bribed, or, what is here more important, how to modify current strategies on the basis of computer analyses. A computer software called MAP-HT (*Mapping the Human Terrain*) meets all the requirements in the eyes of the experts. Critical voices from the ranks of its users, that is frontline commanders, who admit that the system is useless towards asymmetric warfare, are hushed up in the general admiration over the new combat tool. The ethnographer, if he can still be called one, became a cartographer mapping the Human Terrain.

Anthropological understanding of the cultural implications involved here is not just set in the tradition of ethnographic description and cultural

---

[4] B Silverman, *Human Terrain Data – What Should We Do With It?* (Pennsylvania, 2007), 34.

cartography. We may also look upon the whole phenomenon from the perspective of a broader discussion about cultural contacts and the history of misinterpretations between the West and what anthropologists used to call "the cultural Other", represented in this case by Muslims. Recalling Edward Said's theory of Orientalism, it is a conflict of images – a long lasting history of the imperial gaze of the colonial rulers on their subjects. Nevertheless, the contemporary image of the Afghan or Iraqi population and the cultural landscape emerging from the data gathered by HTT members is transferred to a very technologically understood map of the area of interest, such as today's Afghanistan in a manner similar to ethnographers describing "primitive" societies in the 19th century. As a consequence, the picture of Muslims visible in the public discourse in the West, and based on those descriptions, is often simplified to fit into a monochrome vision of a black/white, good/evil, West/Orient dichotomy. This dialectical discourse is also set in an environment of a moral nature. It's not just a fight against a global network of terrorism, but also an ideological clash of civilizations, as Samuel Huntington named it. In the view of the American scholar, the map of the world's civilizations is in constant turmoil, and the main reasons for this situation of permanent conflict are the discrepancies between the various cultural worldviews represented by particular cultural megastructures, i.e. civilizations. In the context of 9/11 Huntington's theses find common ground among many ideologies describing the ethnocentric domination of the West (and its decline as well), especially when it comes to their application in countries like Iraq or Afghanistan. We have to acknowledge the fact that the war and conflict tormenting these parts of the world for the last years are a significant factor for creating the picture of the political and cultural stagnation of these Muslim societies. Islam is often associated by many Westerners at a popular (or even pop-cultural) level with ideologies of violent confrontation and religious fundamentalism. The idea of Jihad is perceived through the lenses of Islamic extremism, like for example Wahhabism. Although my intention here was not to discuss all the facets of the discourse on Islam and the Western perception of it, in the context of HTS and the presence of the military structures and the social scientists in countries like Afghanistan, the reluctance towards accepting Muslim immigrants into the USA or Western Europe might be regarded as part of the larger question of accepting generally what is different in cultural terms from our own world. This discussion is present at all levels – starting from popular culture, and ending with political and scientific debates. However, what seems to be interesting about it, is the fact, that programs like HTS contribute largely to a legitimization of a specific distorted image of Muslims in the West, due to a specific tradition of social research like the one provided by the history of anthropological fieldwork undertaken in a situation of war.

The above mentioned distortion of the image of Muslims is clearly transferred more often to the American public discourse on homeland security. Recently documents have been revealed by the American press, showing the ways US law enforcement agencies were conducting surveillance operations on Muslim communities in large American cities like New York. The actions undertaken by these agencies were exposed as dubious and regarded by the public as outrageous and unconstitutional. The civil rights violated with these actions were at the same time withheld due to the suspicion of terrorism. What is significant in this case, is the almost immediate association of terror acts and plots with certain ethnic groups. This led to pointing out Muslim communities in the US as a potential background for terrorists and other suspicious activities. What is remarkable is that the acceptance for the actions of the federal agencies and the simplified image of Muslims as terrorists which justified them had fitted well into the existing social frames of otherness being perceived as a threat. Associating Muslims with danger, insecurity, antisocial behaviour or simply religious extremism is clearly a part of the public discourse in the West since 9/11. It is also most interesting to trace how the current visualizations of Muslims in the western media are anchored at the heart of institutions of all sorts or of every day practice. On the other hand these forms of marginalization, or sometimes even clear discrimination of Muslims in the public sphere, today seem to be rooted in the more common cultural patterns of pushing the "other" outside the limits of our world and are not just related to the contemporary context of post 9/11. The significant part of that phenomenon is, however, the construction of a picture shared by many westerners towards Islam and Muslims themselves.

The most important features of this picture are reproduced on various levels, including academic and professional institutions dealing with the cultural realm on an every day basis. The scientific approach claimed by initiatives like the mentioned HTS program might be regarded as an attempt of the rationalization of the existing stereotypes and *apriori* knowledge. The examples of the instrumentalization of anthropological knowledge presented here show a visible tendency of polarization in the western conceptualization of Islam and Muslims. The actual picture of Muslims today is certainly affected by this simplification and spreads also into the popular discourse and popular culture. The latter sphere is today saturated with caricatures, like for example in the well known comedy show by Jeff Dunham – in which the main character named Ahmed the Dead Terrorist incorporates the vision of a Muslim fundamentalism. Furthermore, we might recall the contemporary aesthetics of military "fashion" and the popularity of the so called "morale patches", i.e. graphic representations of slogans especially popular among soldiers and all sorts of gun enthusiasts. One of the most popular of those patches is the "Pork Eating Crusader" distributed by a US-based company named Milspecmonkey. The symbolic significance of this patch fits the stereotypical image of Muslims and shows a clear contempt not just for Islamic fundamentalism itself, but for all Muslims. Historical reference to the crusades is on the other hand associated by many Muslims with western hegemony and military interventionism – a context significant in the relations between Muslims and Westerners also today.

The discourses presented in this article depict a culturally constructed set of contrast images. What is significant is the fact that the black and white worldview is shared by both sides of the barricade. On the one hand we deal with a picture of Islam and Muslim societies proliferated by western institutions (like the HTS) and accepted by large parts of western societies, where terrorism is being put into a mix of politics, cultural "backwardness" and religion. This kind of merging of these realms is according to many a constant element present in the Muslim world. HTS and other programs undertaken by the US military officials today attempt to deliver a roadmap of these areas of agency. They achieve this goal through an extremely pragmatic and objectified manner of acting on the ground in Iraq or Afghanistan. On the other hand the Western world accepts the historical stigma of "crusaders" or "infidels" and uses it as a further tool of maintaining hegemonic rule over Islamic "martyrs" fighting and dying for a long lost cause and inevitable the course of history. The critical trajectories of these political and cultural optics of seeing each other do have an impact on the way intercultural dialogue is being held nowadays, but also has to be taken only as a part of (however highly visible) and not as the whole of the picture.

Bibliography

Gonzales, Roberto J. .*American Counterinsurgency. Human Science and the Human Terrain*. Chicago, 2009.

Gonzales, Roberto J. (ed.). *Anthropologists in the Public Sphere. Speaking out on War, Peace, and American Power*. Austin, 2004.

Gusterson, Hugh. "The Cultural Turn in the War on Terror." In John D. Kelly, Beatrice Jauregui, Sean T. Mitchell, Jeremy Walton (eds.). *Anthropology and Global Counterinsurgency*, 279-295. Chicago & London, 2010.

Huntington, Samuel P. *The Clash of Civilizations and the Remaking of World Order*. New York, 2003.

Human Terrain Team Handbook. Fort Leavenworth, 2008.

Lucas Jr., George R. *Anthropologists in Arms. The Ethics of Military Anthropology*. Plymouth, 2009.

Price, David H. *Anthropological Intelligence. The Deployment and Neglect of American Anthropology in the Second World War*. Durham and London, 2008.

Silverman, Barry. *Human Terrain Data – What Should We Do With It?* Pennsylvania, 2007. *American Anthropological Association's Executive Board Statement on the Human Terrain System Project*. 2007.

Stoddard, Abby, Harmer, Adele, DiDomenico, Victoria. *The Use of Private Security Providers and Services in Humanitarian Operations*. London, 2008.

Wax, Dustin M. "The Use of Anthropology in the Insurgent Age." In John D. Kelly, Beatrice Jauregui, Sean T. Mitchell, Jeremy Walton (eds.). *Anthropology and Global Counterinsurgency*, 153-167. Chicago & London, 2010.

"DIFFICULT TOPICS SUCH AS POLITICS, DISCRIMINATION, ATTACKS AND SO ON": 9/11 IN DUTCH LITERATURE

SABINE ERNST

The attack on the twin towers appears to constitute a turning point in the politics and society of many countries around the world, in the relations between countries and among the people themselves. 9/11 is echoed in several novels of world literature, and its effects on society and individuals are made more or less explicitly topical. In many recent Dutch novels the characters are also confronted with the impact of 9/11 such as growing anti-Islamic tendencies. Particularly interesting among these novels are those which are written by multicultural writers such as Abdelkader Benali, Naima El Bezaz, Khalid Boudou, Said El Haji and Hans Sahar.

I want to consider the following questions: What impact does 9/11 and the social changes have on the characters of the novels? Can we notice if and how something like fear, hate or anger comes into the lives of the characters and their surrounding society? Is there anything like a growing mutual mistrust between the characters or in society? How do these novels take up a position on essentialism and how are they creating an image about self vs. the other? Can the novels be seen as a contribution to current debates where the image of radical Muslims is often predominant?

"Dutch writers avoid the topic 9/11."
Rob Schouten's article in the newspaper *Trouw*

According to an article in the newspaper *Trouw,* literary critic Rob Schouten claims that most Dutch writers have avoided the topic of 9/11 and that still no normative 9/11 novel has been published. Moreover, he claims that the writers also have kept silent about the multicultural debate in recent years. In his opinion, multicultural writers have also avoided these topics. As one of the only exceptions, where 9/11 is partly addressed, he mentions the novel *Tirza* (2007) written by Arnon Grunberg, where the main character sees a reincarnation of Mohammed Atta in the Moroccan-Dutch boyfriend of his daughter Tirza, and so kills the young couple.[1] The novel shows the disease of the white middle class, their more or less latent racism.[2]

Then Schouten refers to novels that expose Dutch fundamentalism, as in *Knielen op een bed violen* [Kneeling on a bed of violets] (2005) by Jan Siebelink, where a closer look is taken at orthodox Protestantism. A second example he gives is the novel *Koetsier herfst* [Coachman autumn] (2008) written by Charlotte Muetsaers, where the animal rights activist Do admires Osama bin Laden. Schouten explains that both novels criticize the indiscriminate Western response to Islamic terrorism.[3]

Thus the question arises: which ingredients are necessary for a 9/11 novel? Do typical 9/11 topics have to have a prominent place in the novel? Is it possible that in the 21st century authors express their commitment in another, more subtle way than in the 20th century? In my opinion, topics such as 9/11 and the multicultural debate are certainly present in contemporary novels.

Case-study: multicultural writers on 9/11

In my case study on 9/11 in Dutch literature, I focused on the following novels by multicultural writers:

Naima El Bezaz: *De verstotene.* (2006) [The outcast]
Said El Haji: *Goddelijke duivel.* (2006) [Divine devil]
Hans Sahar: *De gebroeders Boetkaboet.* (2008) [The brothers Boetkaboet]
Robert Vuijsje: *Alleen maar nette mensen.* (2008) [Only decent people].

I use a broad definition of the term multicultural writer. That means that I not only consider the ethnic roots of the writer as a criterion, but also

---

[1] Cf. Rob Schouten, "Nederlandse schrijvers mijden maatschappelijk engagement." *Trouw* (September 4, 2011).
http://www.trouw.nl/tr/nl/4468/Schrijf/article/detail/2890821/2011/09/04/Nederlan dse-schrijvers-mijden-maatschappelijk-engagement.dhtml (accessed September 8, 2011).
[2] Cf. Schouten and Liesbeth Schulpé, "Vader en een zonnekoningin." *Recensieweb. Nieuwe Literatuur. Nieuwe Gidsen* (October 31, 2007)
http://www.recensieweb.nl/recensie/2283/Vader+van+een+zonnekoningin.html (accessed September 8, 2011).
[3] Cf. Schouten, 2011.

the typical topics in their work.

First I would like to give a short summary of the above-mentioned novels. Amelie, the main character of *De verstotene* [English: The outcast] (2006), written by Naima El Bezaz, is abandoned by her boyfriend Mart during their vacation in New York. Back in Amsterdam, she falls into a deep depression. The reader gradually discovers that she has disguised her Moroccan background after being expelled by her strict Muslim family. She changed her name and hair colour, and after some other cosmetic changes she lived as a native Dutch woman. When the truth about her roots leaks out, she is also no longer accepted by the people in her native-Dutch community.

In *Goddelijke duivel* [English: Divine devil] (2006), by Said El Haji, a Dutch writer of Moroccan-Berber descent flees on a summer day in 2005 from Zatot de Barbaar – a mythical figure – and travels to a prestigious Writers Institute in Ohio. He stays there for a few months and meets lots of colleagues from countries all over the world. Through him, the reader becomes acquainted with many different ideas, opinions and religions.

The brothers Redouan and Fadil, the main characters of *De gebroeders Boetkaboet* [English: The brothers Boetkaboet] (2008) by Hans Sahar, grow up in the quarter Schilderswijk in Den Haag (The Hague). Their father Driss is disappointed about Fadil who has spent six months in prison and praises Redouan, because he is apparently more successful. While Fadil is looking for a job and wants to change his life, Redouan has joined a group of Muslim terrorists. Under the influence of false friends, Fadil also falls back onto the wrong track.

In Robert Vuijsje's novel *Alleen maar nette mensen* [English: Only decent people] (2008), the main character David Samuels, a Jewish boy of 21 years, lives in Amsterdam in the upper class quarter Zuid-West. After graduating from high school, he does not know how to continue with his life. Additionally, he struggles with an identity crisis. Because of his black hair and dark skin he is often mistaken for a Moroccan. While he has doubts about his relationship with his Jewish girlfriend Noemi, he has different liaisons with black girls from the lower class quarter Bijlmer, in which his preference is for a colour that is as dark as possible.

The impact of 9/11 on the characters

Security checks at airports: always in the focus

Many characters experience a clear difference between travelling by plane before or after 9/11. Now there are thorough security checks of the passengers and their luggage. Often characters with migrant roots are searched a bit more carefully, controlled more thoroughly and extensively questioned about the reason for their trip. If passengers are checked randomly, they are almost always picked from a crowd of travellers.

When the main character Amelie, a Dutch woman with hidden Moroccan roots, and her ex-boyfriend Mart, in the novel *De Verstotene* [The outcast] (2006) return from their trip to New York, she is singled out by the customs officer, while Mart is just allowed to walk on and leave the airport.

> 'Excuse me, Madam, may I have a look at your suitcase?' A bearded customs officer pointed to a corner where on a long metal table the suitcase of an unconventional-looking man was being subjected to a thorough inspection. I could imagine that the long-haired sinister-looking man is the loser, but me? I looked flawless in my black pants, black jacket and white blouse. My auburn-coloured hair was washed and sweet-smelling, and so I was stunned.
>
> 'But why?'
>
> 'Routine inspection, Madam,' the customs officer said. He tossed my suitcase on the table and asked me in an unfriendly way to open it.
>
> 'But why me? Why not him – that man there!' I pointed at Mart who embraced the colourless Anne with her spiky salt-and-pepper hair tenderly.
>
> The customs officer looked through my clothes, his rough hands went through bras and panties. I cringed and said nothing.
> I was paralyzed. My neatly folded T-shirts and dresses were randomly rummaged through. Without any emotion he searched my most intimate possessions. I felt assaulted.
>
> 'I will complain,' I hissed at him while I was trying to close my suitcase with some difficulty.
>
> 'Great, Madam. Good night.' [...]
>
> I was really struggling to close my suitcase. My hair dryer and iron stuck out too much. With some effort I pushed everything down until with relief I heard a click. (El Bezaz 2006, 35-36)[4]

At first sight it seems that she was chosen by chance. But later in the novel it becomes more and more clear that Amelie, actually called Mina, has tried hard to hide her Moroccan roots. First the reader notices the discomfort and how a security-check might feel from her woman's perspective. Later it becomes clear that the issue of ethnicity could have played a role.

In the novel *Alleen maar nette mensen* [Only decent people] the main

---

[4] The quote is, like the other quotations from the novels in this article, translated by S.E., because the novels are not otherwise translated as yet.

character David Samuels, who is often taken for a Moroccan because of his black hair, experiences the security checks at airports as discrimination based on his alleged ethnic origin.

> Schiphol is a bad place to look like a Moroccan. When I tried to walk outside with my suitcase, the customs men in blue uniform asked for my passport.
>
> A customs man with a light brown moustache and brown hair with lots of dandruff asked: 'Samuels, is that a Dutch name?'
>
> 'Yes.'
>
> 'Where does Mister originally come from?'
>
> 'From Amsterdam.'
>
> 'But where does Mister really come from? Which country you call home?'
>
> 'I don't know,' I said. 'The Netherlands?'
>
> The customs man asked me to take along my luggage and to put it on a table.
>
> They always do the same. They take all the clothes out of the suitcase and put them on the table. Then, they investigate the empty suitcase, as if there were very dangerous things in it, grab all the clothes and put them back into the suitcase. Then they thank me for my cooperation. (Vuijsje 2008, 266)

David experiences the interrogation as insulting and discriminating. The customs officer continues pushing David into the role of the foreigner, the exotic other. The result is that he, although born and raised in Amsterdam, does not know if he can still feel at home in the Netherlands.

There is a second message between the lines. The customs officer is presented as slightly retarded, because he does not know that Samuel can be an ordinary Dutch name. The Hebrew origin of the name, the Jewish background of David, and the war experiences of his grandparents, who died in Sobibor and Auschwitz, can indicate a latent anti-Semitism, and suggests that Dutch Jews in the past have not always been regarded as truly Dutch. More about this later.

Another possible response to the security checks is astonishment, as the main character in the novel *Feldman en ik* (2006) [Feldman and I] by Abdelkader Benali experiences:

> I had finished reading the book earlier than expected on this flight, which altogether lasted three hours, including checking in with all its exaggerated security measures which has become a part of modern life – so I had to take off my shoes because they assumed that you can take along everything that was explosive, while the book in my hands wasn't worth inspecting. (Benali 2006, 217)

There is not just a wink to the fact that the checks always remain incomplete, because you can hide a bomb in a book. But it does not seem worth submitting a book for closer examination. Literature has no value for the customs officer. Moreover, it indicates that the writer of the book is perhaps fighting with his pen.

In *Goddelijke duivel* [Divine Devil] by Said El Haji, the security check of air travellers becomes comical. The first-person narrator flies from Schiphol Airport to Cedar Rapids and is accompanied by a drunken colleague whom he has just met. While changing planes at Detroit Airport, he helps Ofra come through the security check:

> 'Get your passport out, Ofra, we're here.' [...]
> For reasons of privacy, only one person may stand at the customs counter. People in the queue have to remain standing behind a yellow line, it is strictly controlled. But Ofra understands nothing of the supposed Cabinet of curiosities where she's ended up, and the customs officer refuses to get out of her glass cage for just one second, so I have to assist the drunken skunk. I escort her index finger into the soft sponge with ink, while I support her body from behind to check her stagger, to the hilarious satisfaction of the other people waiting. A few praise me for my heroic helpfulness. Then, I put her finger in the appropriate box, neatly within the line, then I turn her head a quarter turn sideways to the iris scan. The modern world must feel very insecure, if it has to rely on biometric nonsense, apparently no one knows yet who is who.
> It's not easy at all for Ofra to keep her eyes open, she absolutely doesn't see the point of it. But ultimately she succeeds. (El Haji 2006, 25)

It is about a very thorough check to which every traveller has been submitted since 9/11, because security now has absolute priority. But sometimes not:

> You could almost forget that the American can also be wrong, make mistakes or simply ignore something seen. Because of the whole hilarious show with the pharaonic lady it was forgotten to take a fingerprint and iris scan of me. So I simply walk into America, honestly true. (El Haji 2006, 26)

As icing on the cake, the first-person narrator is of Moroccan Muslim descent. All checks and safety measures could be – with or without intent –circumvented.

Growing anti-Islamic tendencies and Islamophobia

The characters are faced with growing anti-Islamic tendencies, which sometimes lead to Islamophobia.

In the novel *De verstotene* (2006) [The outcast] the main character Amelie goes to Samuel and tells him that she is pregnant by him. What started out as a one-night stand now becomes very serious for her, because she is falling in love with him. He reacts with indifference and cold rejection.

'If you're having a baby, it's by somebody else. Go to an abortion clinic and get rid of it. What do you think? That I would raise a child with a Moroccan, a Muslim? Never!'

'What do you mean?' My heart was pounding.

'Esther told me all about you. Your father is on a mosque board, things like that.' […] I could only look at him. The words stuck in my throat.

'Amelie or Mina, or whatever you're called, I can't do anything with it. I am Jewish and I am for the Jewish cause. A large part of my family lives in Israel. I just have nothing to do with Arabs and your Islam... no. If I had known who you are, I wouldn't have touched you with so much as a finger.' He looked at me with disgust. (El Bezaz 2006, 202)

Samuel imports the conflict between Israel and Palestine and projects these and his anti-Islamic sentiments onto Amelie. By using the words 'you' (plural) and 'Arabs', he creates an opposition of *us* versus *them* and places Amelie into the group of the outsider.

Amelie sees that 9 / 11 has caused a change of social climate:

The world had changed. Especially after September 11, 2001. When with two hits the economic heart was touched, and the world changed forever. (El Bezaz 2006, 184)

After the attack on Theo van Gogh, she is afraid that the perpetrator is of Moroccan origin (cf. El Bezaz 2006, 150). Amelie goes to the place where the murder took place and sees how people of Moroccan descent are being abused.

Someone said that all Muslims should be gassed. I was afraid of the unfounded emotions. [...] There was a Moroccan mother with her twins. She put a rose in the sea of flowers and walked away with bowed head. She did not react when a group of rowdies scolded her as foreign scum, but her children looked startled. (El Bezaz 2006, 152)

Across from me stood a true-born Amsterdam woman with a popular accent to abuse Moroccans.

'You have to piss off to your own country,' she cried. 'I wouldn't dare let my children play outside.'

The girl whom she shouted at wore a fashionable blue suit and a matching veil and spoke in the dialect of Aerdenhout: 'This is my country. Here, I was born. Here, I have studied and here I work as an economist. So don't call me a criminal, don't call me a foreigner. I am Dutch and I haven't killed Theo van Gogh and I don't know the murderer either. Morocco is not a village where everyone is related. I am a Muslim and killing is forbidden by Islam. Whoever did it is an ordinary murderer and therefore no real Muslim. I am disgusted that you don't have the intelligence to realize that. (El Bezaz 2006, 151)

In spite of the hate expressed against her, Amelie emphasizes her Dutch identity, which fits in perfectly with her religion, just like the colours of her suit and her veil. As a well educated resident of one of the wealthiest towns of the Netherlands – Aerdenhout is known for its villas – she represents the well-integrated, successful immigrant, so the over-simplified xenophobic statements are refuted.

Amelie's friend Elsa also has anti-Muslim sentiments and rants about Moroccans and Muslims, while she uses the words 'Moroccan', 'Muslim' and 'fundamentalist' as synonymous (cf. El Bezaz 2006, 156-157), and links them with 9/ 11:

'First New York and Madrid and now Van Gogh. Who's next?' [...] Elsa continued to rant and rave against the New Dutch citizens and against parents who did not know how to bring up their children and against the great danger of Islam. (El Bezaz 2006, 157)

Amelie tries in vain to add nuances and explains that she is also afraid of Islamic terrorism (cf. El Bezaz 2006, 156-158). Elsa's statements hurt her, but she is afraid to admit that she is of Moroccan origin:

But you just cannot pigeonhole the whole group. That is unfair and the level-headed Elsa I know is humanitarian and does not allow hate to come into her life. (El Bezaz 2006, 158)

Elsa might perhaps be regarded as a symbol of the Netherlands, respectively its political and social climate, which under the influence of current political developments has lost two characteristics – level-headedness and humaneness – which are perceived by many people as typically Dutch. Amelie begs: "Don't let this come between us." (El Bezaz

2006, 158). This could be seen as a contribution to current debates. It can be seen as a warning to the reader that anti-Islamism and xenophobia can cause a division of society like the split in the friendship between Amelie and Elsa.

In the course of the novel, Amelie suffers increasingly from depression and hopelessness:

> '[...] Who says that I will have a child? Maybe I don't want it. It's a fucking world, and perhaps it's better that I spare him this shit because I'm sure that there is a third world war coming.'
> 'Where did you get that idea? What nonsense!'
> 'Because history repeats itself.' (El Bezaz 2006, 251)

The novel *De verstotene* [The outcast] is an indictment of growing Islamophobia and discrimination against migrants. Moreover, even strict Islamic views have been criticized and it is shown that liberal currents of Islam also exist.

Sometimes the characters are confronted with anti-Islamic sentiments at very unexpected moments. The first-person narrator in *Goddelijke duivel* [Divine Devil] has just given a lecture on the subject of fear. During the subsequent discussion, a man begins to debunk Islam:

> The second question comes from a tiny old man, covered with pigment spots and with a great air of imagined superiority. He starts talking about the vicious religion that Islam is because it only wants to convert the others, or else behead them, you just need to watch the jihad and you just need to read in Huntington, who, in his *The Clash of the Civilizations,* said something similar; namely, that everything in Islam is bloody, with the result that a clash between the human West and the inhuman Islam is inevitable. Whether I should have the guts to contradict that. (El Haji 2006, 98)

By using the subjunctive and the words "imagined superiority" the narrator dissociates himself from these statements.

Growing mutual mistrust

In the novels you can observe a growing mutual mistrust, between immigrants and natives and between Muslims and non-Muslims.

When Amelie is sitting outside on a bench, three Moroccan-Dutch boys walk by on their way home from school:

Young people, certainly born here, but with the accent of immigrants, looked at me suspiciously, because I looked at them. Their eyes pierced me menacingly, an attack from foreigners on – what they believed themselves to see – a native. (El Bezaz 2006, 62)

The mistrust that Amelie feels, could also be due to a generation gap, a common mistrust that adolescents could feel against adults. And, perhaps in her perception she is also influenced by the generation gap. What she perceives as an inability to speak without an accent, could be a purposefully chosen substandard. In some forms of slang it is common practice to talk intentionally with a Moroccan sounding accent.[5] Furthermore, a hint is given to the reader that Amelie is also of foreign origin, which she is still hiding for some unknown reason.

Dutch Muslims become increasingly suspect and are often perceived in connection with terrorism and fundamentalism:

Rowanda rang while I was watching a broadcast of NOVA in which the famous columnist discussed with the eloquent lawyer about whether every Muslim Dutchman had to be screened as a potential terrorist. I was surprised. (Vuijsje 2008, 163)

A whole group of society is now in the focus of attention and is suspected in advance. When David returns from Memphis to the Netherlands by plane, he draws the attention of a Dutch couple:

In Memphis, I was already on my seat by the window when Henk and Ria arrived. Ria leaned before Henk and asked in English if I was a Dutchman. I pretended not to hear. I didn't want to have conversations about where I had been and how much it had cost.

Five minutes later, Henk asked. I said in English that I was not a Dutchman.

Ria asked Henk, in Dutch: 'Do you think he is a Muslim?'

Henk was not sure, but he thought so.

Ria asked if she had to warn the stewardess. She did not trust me. Later I would blow up the plane.

First, Henk thought that I was a Moroccan, but spoke no Dutch, only English. Then, he was not sure.

They agreed that Ria should keep an eye on me. If she saw anything

---

[5] Cf. René Appel, "Straattaal. De mengtaal van jongeren in Amsterdam," *Thema's en trends in de sociolinguïstiek 3. Toegepaste taalwetenschap in artikelen* 2 (1999): 52 and Peter de Langen, "Straattaal," *Onze Taal* 7/8 (2001): 189 and Hellen Kooijman, "Straattaal is van alle tijden," *0/25. Tijdschrift over jeugd* (Febr. 2001): 21.

suspicious, she should warn the stewardess.
Henk found that a good idea. (Vuijsje 2008, 264)

Because of the fact that other passengers see in him an al-Qaeda terrorist, David asks himself whether he may still feel at home in the Netherlands, and feels deeply hurt (cf. Vuijsje 2008, 264-265).

Being settled in Dutch society

While the characters experience suspicion and Islamophobia and while they are pushed into the position of the *other*, they are presented as people who grew up with literature and music from the Dutch and European canon.

The first-person narrator of *De verstotene* [The outcast] for example, began her reading experience with *De geheime tuin* written by Els Pelgrom, or with the translation of *The Secret Garden*, by Frances Burnett (cf. El Bezaz 2006, 162). As examples of the many books she has read she names Balzac and the Brontë sisters (cf. El Bezaz 2006, 164). She listens to music by U2, Mozart and Tchaikovsky (cf. El Bezaz 2006, 141, 154, 158) and in the Rijksmuseum she admires a painting by Rembrandt (cf. El Bezaz 2006, 228). Only in the culinary field might you sometimes recognize her roots, when she goes to the Islamic butcher to buy original Moroccan merquez sausages (cf. El Bazaz 2006, 186) or when she drinks a cup of mint tea with lots of sugar (cf. El Bezaz 2006, 12, 59, 113).

In *Goddelijke duivel* [Divine devil] the first-person narrator has Parson Weems, Lev Tolstoy, Oscar Wilde and Hermann Hesse in his cultural baggage (cf. El Haji 2006, 146-147, 197, 205) and listens to English pop songs (cf. El Haji 2006, 45, 78, 105). He sees himself as both a European and Moroccan-Berber (cf. El Haji 2006, 19, 168). And, while he speaks Dutch and English flawlessly, his knowledge of Tarifit is limited (cf. El Haji 2006, 214).

Fadil, the main character in *De gebroeders Boetkaboet* (2008), listens to songs by the Moroccan-Dutch rapper Ali B. (cf. Sahar 2008, 61) or 'Too hot to handle' by Coolio (cf. Sahar 2008, 148), but also to rai or chaabi (Sahar 2008, 12).

These characters are presented as people who are settled in the Dutch society, while they also have cultural links with their country of origin.

Identity crisis and feeling displaced

Something very different is going on with the main character David in *Alleen maar nette mensen* [Only decent people]. Because he is perceived as a Moroccan, he is often treated badly. He begins to feel increasingly displaced and wonders where he belongs. Partly for this reason he is looking for love affairs with women with particularly black skin, first in Amsterdam and later in Memphis.

This is reflected in his choice of music, and he even knows how to play with it when he is in the subway and tries to pick up a girl:

> She got in at the stop Van der Madeweg. There weren't any seats free, so she stood beside me. I leaned against the side by the door. She stood so close to me that she could hear through the headphones which music I was playing on my iPod.
>
> I had just put new songs on it. They were almost exclusively black songs from Donell Jones, Tupac and Jaguar Wright. But also a few white songs from André Hazes. I'm still from Amsterdam.
>
> Because I had done 'shuffle songs' all the songs were mixed. At the beginning of a song by André Hazes, I thought: does she think that I'm too white? I looked for the best song on the iPod to make her hear it through the headphones. I turned to Anthony Hamilton, then she could see that I was not just listening to black music. I was an expert. (Vuijsje 2008, 34)

David prefers 'black' music and he uses music to express his chosen 'black' identity. With the 'white' songs by André Hazes, he wants to underline that he also belongs to Amsterdam. But the native Dutch often perceive him as a foreigner, so he wonders ever more which group he belongs to. Because of his experiences with xenophobia and exclusion he suffers from an identity crisis.

His Jewish background also plays a role in his feeling of displacement. He says to Rowanda, his new black girlfriend:

> 'Grandma was not Jewish, she was able to go outside. In 1943 the Germans came to take away my grandfather. Grandma was not at home. She was pregnant with my father, but she didn't know that. [...]
> My grandfather was betrayed by the neighbours. He was taken to Auschwitz. [...] My grandparents' neighbours were the parents of the people who are now my neighbours. Or their grandparents. [...] I like black hair. I can only trust people with black hair.' (Vuijsje 2008, 52)

One day David discusses with his schoolfriends whether he belongs to the native Dutch:

According to Bass, I was a Dutchman, just like him. My grandfather said the same, when he was put on the train to Auschwitz. I'm a Dutchman, just like you. Why should I have to leave the Netherlands? (Vuijsje 2008, 275)

Then he draws a direct link between the persecution of the Jews during the occupation and the recent xenophobia against Moroccans:

Jews do not trust Dutchmen. What happened in the war, could happen again. But then it won't happen with the Jews, but with Moroccans. (Vuijsje 2008, 10)

This can be taken to reflect on the current debates about Moroccan-Dutch people.

Even the main character in *De gebroeders Boetkaboet* [The brothers Boetkaboet] often feels uprooted. At first glance, he seems culturally more orientated towards the country of his parents' origin. Fadil likes to listen to chaabi and rai:

Once again Fadil put on a chaabi-CD, because that nice mix of all kinds of music never bored him. He had bought the CD during a holiday in Morocco and he had almost turned it to pieces. And, when he put on the music now and laid down on his bed with his eyes closed, then he imagined himself in Morocco and saw the palm trees, the free people, the whole wonderful life over there. Then, he felt like Cheb Khalid from Algeria or Amr Diab from Egypt, through whose music you always got the feeling that you belonged, that you were in a different kind of life than in the daily hassle around you, in your own paradise of music. He rather listened to that than to Maroc-hop, because he was currently not in the mood for difficult topics such as politics, discrimination, attacks and so on. Although you shouldn't bury your head in the sand. (Sahar 2008, 12)

One reason for his preference is to evoke a holiday feeling by playing music from his holiday destination. But this music also fulfils his need for social affiliation, a feeling that he cannot have at home in the Netherlands, which indicates his personal experience of exclusion. So he just does not listen to Dutch-Moroccan hip-hop, because he can currently not bear the typical issues of politics, discrimination and 9/11.

But also Morocco does in reality not match his musical daydream:

He always found such a holiday an adventure, but it was not all couscous and roses there. There were lots of things which annoyed him; not the poverty, not the heat, but that he was a stranger in his own country. At home he felt homesick for Morocco and in Morocco he felt homesick for home. (Sahar 2008, 21)

In fact he is settled in the Dutch culture. When Fadil accidentally sees that his friend Najib is taking lessons to get a truck license, he jokes: "Are you busy with a truck license? Soon we will have `With the flame in the pipe´. I tear through the Brenner Pass..." (Sahar 2008, 88) He uses the famous Dutch trucker song 'Met de vlam in de pijp' by Henk Wijngaard as a frame of reference for his joke.

The brothers Fadil and Redouan are both acquainted with the popular Belgian comic book *Lucky Luke* and they have used this comic among other sources as inspiration for inventing a secret lingo that they sometimes speak among themselves (cf. Sahar 2008, 64). But the cartoon character Lucky Luke is also known as the restless lonesome cowboy who travels around, has no home and fights for the good.

Radicalisation and terrorism – a reaction to exclusion?

The novel *De gebroeders Boetkaboet* [The brothers Boetkaboet] deals with Islamic fundamentalism and terrorism as the main topics and examines why some people could become attracted to it or why they even could become involved in it against their will.

After he has served half a year in prison, the main character Fadil wants to improve his life and begins a job as a postman. To his astonishment, he notices that his friend and former accomplice Najib has also renounced crime and has converted to a religious life in quite a pious way (cf. Sahar 2008, 50-53). Fadil repeatedly states that he finds his metamorphosis very strange:

'You're like an imam', said Fadil, 'as pious as you talk. You are totally overdoing it, aren't you?' (Sahar 2008, 51)

'Well, well, you are laying it on thick! Don't make a fool of yourself, man! You are overdoing it!' (Sahar 2008, 89)

To his dismay he realizes that Najib (cf. Sahar 2008, 54-56), Najib's girlfriend Marlies (cf. Sahar 2008, 89-91), who is a converted native Dutch, and his brother Redouan (cf. Sahar 2008, 96, 105), adhere to Islamic fundamentalism and welcome terrorism:

Fadil sighed deeply. He looked at his brother closely, but was also desperate. Hopeless. What should one do with this? You read it in the newspaper or see it on TV, but if it's your own brother, and then in public as well without shame, then you're perplexed, astonished and dumbfounded. You might want to run away or scream, but that's not possible. (Sahar 2008, 107)

Fadil knew enough about it and left it at that. But it was all wrong. If Dad knew about this, he would never put up with it. And, then Redouan was not the favourite son any more. [...] Now he knew almost for certain that a sort of club existed, where Najib and Iman, and perhaps others belonged, and that they not only had a terrible hate against the Netherlands and the Dutch, but maybe even be up to something. (Sahar 2008, 108)

Fadil disapproves of Islamic fundamentalism and terrorism and knows that his father thinks the same way.

Thus he points out to Najib and Marlies that there are moderate and liberal movements within Islam:

'[...] I understand what inspires you. Well-intentioned all of it. But we are one million Muslims in the Netherlands and in Europe a good thirty million, and it can't be possible that they're almost all crazy and gone astray, and that only you and a small group of people have the monopoly on truth and wisdom. There are more than a hundred imams who came together recently to make a case for a good, positive Islam. They don't look in the Qur'an for hate and jihad, but rather for tolerance, for liberty and religious freedom, human rights, all those things. So that we will be better understood ...' (Sahar 2008, 91-92)

He remembers a fable that his grandmother once told him, in which a son receives a letter from his deceased mother, in which is written among other things:

You see that we go out of life as we came, naked. So be good to other people, care for those who have less, don't grieve your father, because if you should take something to paradise, it's kindness to others. That is the whole of Islam. (Sahar 2008, 135-136)

Fadil sees the imminent danger and tries repeatedly to persuade Najib, Marlies and Redouan that they are clearly wrong, but otherwise he undertakes nothing to stop them. He does not know which way to turn in this situation, because it is hard enough for him to shift his own life back on track and because he feels insecure (cf. Sahar 2008, 61-62, 108, 113-114). This kind of behaviour is very characteristic for an adolescent. Moreover, it is not an option for him to betray his friends or his brother (cf. Sahar 2008, 115).

He experiences the whole situation as very awkward and complicated; it feels like he is caught in a spider's web:

Fadil could hardly have an answer to this, but he felt like he was woven into a spider's web from where it is difficult to escape. The silk threads

surround you. You definitely know you don't want to be there, and that
you should find a way of escaping before it's too late. But how? (Sahar
2008, 91)

The metaphor of the spider's web underlines how hopeless the
situation seems to Fadil and what an immense effort it takes for him to try
to escape. When later against his will he has become involved in a failed
attack on the parliament building in The Hague, a similar metaphor is
used:

Together they had managed to let Fadil walk into a trap, like a fish, like a
cold-blooded animal, they had let him swim right into it. (Sahar 2008, 155)

A fish which ends up in a trap, is caught in a similar manner as a fly in
a spider's web. By this image the narrator creates understanding for Fadil's
situation. Like a fish, he is caught unintentionally and without significant
guilt in a trap, which is set by his friends Najib and Ab.

In *De gebroeders Boetkaboet* [The brothers Boetkaboet] we are given
an insight into the role of the first generation of immigrants. Fadil's father
also disapproves of fundamentalism and terrorism. He advises his son to
avoid Najib:

'[...] But I come to the mosque every week, and there they say he has
insulted the imam. He said that the imam doesn't preach the true Islam, but
worthless talk without obligations, because he's afraid that he wouldn't get
a Dutch passport. And, that he is paid by the Dutch government to keep the
Muslims stupid and backward... Well, that's insane, so that guy is
completely on the wrong track.'
    'Oh, Baba, let's be glad that the biggest criminal in The Hague is
improving his life.'
    'Yes, but formerly he did set you on the wrong path.'
    'No, I did it by myself.'
    'I don't want you to mix with him.' (Sahar 2008, 73-74)

He tries to correct his son and makes it clear to him (and the reader),
that crime and fundamentalism are in fact two ways of walking on the
wrong track, fundamentalism is just as wrong as crime. Again the novel
reflects on current public debates, which are dominated by the image of
Muslim parents who do not resist attempts to radicalize young Muslims.

Something similar happens in the novel *De verstotene* (The outcast) by
Naima El Bezaz. One day, the main character Amelie witnesses how
Moroccan-Dutch adults intervene when boys on the street shout slogans
about a known Muslim extremist, praising him:

A group of seven boys had formed in front of the flat. They shouted slogans and honoured Bouyeri. It took only a moment until a group of Moroccan men of the first generation came out of the Islamic butcher's and ran furiously to the group. The boys scattered like a bunch of pigeons. And, then there was silence. (El Bezaz 2006, 158)

Another example: an elderly Moroccan-Dutch neighbour makes a clear comment about a group of Moroccan-Dutch boys in the neighbourhood, who are rejoicing about the death of Theo van Gogh:

'Children down there are bad,' he said. 'They don't understand that it is haram to murder and haram to be glad about a man who has died.' (El Bezaz 2006, 154)

Also in this novel, the characters of the first generation are (with some exceptions) presented as being opposed to terrorism, and they intervene whenever they see how young Muslims applaud terrorism.

Islamic fundamentalism and terrorism are thus presented as an exception, which is refused by the majority of Muslim characters. Hence the novels under consideration here contribute to ongoing public debates. While Muslims in the media are often presented in a generalized way from an outsider's view on the basis of a dichotomy between the backward, strict Islam and the modern, free West[6], the novels write 'back' from an insider's view. The Muslim characters in *De gebroeders Boetkaboet* [The brothers Boetkaboet] are depicted as individuals in a heterogeneous, complex community, where the majority are moderate Muslims like Fadil's father Driss or Hafid and his wife Kadisha, who have raised their daughter Esra to be "a modern, emancipated Muslim woman" (Sahar 2008, 99) or atheist Muslims like Ab who likes to drink a pint of beer (cf. Sahar 2008, 16, 53).

The first generation is represented by the hardworking Driss (cf. Sahar 2008, 72v) and uncle Hafid, who is characterized as "a modern, fully integrated Moroccan" (Sahar 2008, 45). Driss points out the positive points of the Netherlands to his son Redouan:

Driss [...] said aloud to himself, while he was plucking at the fringe of his beard: 'I swore I would never want to see those people [in Morocco] again, never. I did not want my sons to grow up between people who cut

---

[6] Cf. W.A.R. Shadid, "Berichtgeving over moslims en de islam in de westerse media; Beeldvorming, oorzaken en alternatieve strategieën," *Tijdschrift voor Communicatiewetenschap* 33 (2005): 330-334.

one another's throats for the stupidest things: a wall, a piece of ground,
no...'
    Redouan said: 'But now we're in a country where they spit on us
Muslims and humiliate us, so what's worse?'
    'No, in this country, all people are equal before the law, and that law
applies to everyone, but in Morocco, there are different laws. Power and
money. Here, you can work hard and achieve something that no one can
take away from you.'
    'Nonsense, baba. Here, they don't like us, and I don't like them. [...]'
(Sahar 2008, 82)

Father Driss' words contrast sharply with the experiences of the second
generation. Redouan sees that his father is working very hard (c.f. Sahar
2008, 11, 72), nevertheless he can barely manage on his earnings. The
family lives in a poor flat (cf. Sahar 2008, 10, 97-98, 122) and the holiday
trips of Fadil and Redouan to Morocco are partially sponsored by uncle
Hafid (cf. Sahar 2008, 117), the best friend of Driss. Seen from an
insider's point of view, radicalized youngsters could be motivated to
choose fundamentalist beliefs. With this in mind, modern Dutch post-9/11
novels directly participate in current cultural and political discourses.
    Fadil, Redouan and Nahib represent a group of Moroccan-Dutch
youngsters of the second generation, who feel more or less excluded by
the growing anti-Islamism and racism.

It was not for nothing that a kind of unholy war had begun between the old
and the new Dutch. There was one riot after another and you always
thought that the storm would blow over. But it only got worse.
    Then there was someone who called Islam retarded and found that
Morocco and Turkey did not belong to the modern time. And, then there
was someone who called the Moroccans goat-fuckers and queer-bashers
[...]. At worst, he found the slanging-matches about the aggressive morons
of Allah, and the poison that the Koran produces. So it was said literally.
No, you never forget that and you never forgive that. And, that the
backward Muslims hate women. But worst of all was that someone made a
fool of the prophet and said that Mohammed had a sweetheart of eight or
nine years old and therefore he was a little-girl-fucker. In all hangouts in
Schilderswijk everybody was furious; and in all social studies lessons
heated discussions arose. But everyone, foreigner or not, agreed that this
was sowing hate. (Sahar 2008, 112-113)

Again the novel addresses current debates as the reader, who has
followed the news, recognizes immediately quotes and statements of right-
wing populists like Pim Fortuyn, Theo van Gogh and Geert Wilders. The
paragraphs reveal the possible effects of hate speeches. While Fadil

represents the majority of Moroccan-Dutch youngsters, who despite his feelings of frustration and uncertainty keeps on the right track (except for youth sins) and starts working as a postman, feelings of exclusion cause a few like Redouan and Najib to drift to terrorism via fundamentalism.

The novel seems to be a literary complement to the research of Slootman and Tillie on radicalization among young Muslims in Amsterdam. Their research has shown that a very orthodox religious conviction can play a role in radicalization (religious dimension). Besides, young people could be susceptible to processes of radicalization by experiences with discrimination and exclusion, and because of the feeling that society and policy behave unjustly toward Muslims (political dimension). Young people who combine religious and political dimensions show, according to research, an increased risk of being radicalized.[7] In the case of Najib, Marlies and Redouan, both dimensions play a role: they show a very orthodox religious conviction and they feel discriminated against and excluded (cf. Sahar 2008, 50, 160).

Fadil, who follows the news about the riots after the Danish Mohammed cartoons, the protests in Islamic countries and the indignant Western reactions to these protests, says: "Can all these people shut up for once? They just ask for hate and revenge." (Sahar 2008, 113) His words are a clear plea for all sides of society to break the vicious circle of prejudice, anger, fear, mistrust, hate and (Islamic or enlightened) fundamentalism.

A differentiated view and plea for mutual respect

The novel *De gebroeders Boetkaboet* (The brothers Boetkaboet) argues that an orthodox religious conviction need not necessarily pose a problem. This is underlined by linking orthodox Islamism with the orthodox Protestantism in the Bible belt. Father and sons Boetkaboet are visiting uncle Hafid and the families are sociably chatting with each other:

> It was about De meiden van Halal who had their own television program in which they, as Muslim girls, went looking around in Dutch society for interesting places. They came to very Christian families on Urk, strictly religious; it was always an island and through that isolation everything stood still and remained as it was, even the most conservative views. And those looked darned outmoded like many of the rules of Islam: praying regularly, clothing that covers, a God who is central on the way you walk,

---

[7] Cf. Marieke Slootman, Jean Tillie, *Processen van radicalisering. Waarom sommige Amsterdamse moslims radicaal worden* (Amsterdam: IMES, 2006), 92-94.

no sex before marriage, and so on. Esmaa, Jihad and Hajar found this quite
remarkable, because Urk had been included in the Noordoostpolder a long
time ago, so the modern time would also intrude there. (Sahar 2008, 102)

The characters talk about the episode 'Urk' of the television program
De meiden van Halal [The girls of Halal], which is broadcast on 14 May
2006 via NPS[8]. This clearly shows that the difference between orthodox
Islam and orthodox Protestantism is hardly noticeable. And as the majority
of the Dutch population do not have a problem with the pious religious
conviction of many Protestants on the former island of Urk, there is also
no reason for being concerned about devout Muslims. Whoever has a look
at the home page of the program *De meiden van Halal*, sees three smart
girls with a red, white and blue headscarf, with which they show that they
consider themselves to be Dutch of Islamic faith. The message of their TV
program is that their emancipated life and modern views go effortlessly
hand in hand with their Islamic faith and mode of living. With their
program the Moroccan-Dutch directors want, according to an interview in
the journal *Intermediair*, to stimulate mutual understanding between
people of different opinions and cultures.[9]

By referring to similarities between orthodox Protestantism and
orthodox Islam and by creating an intertextual relation with the television
series *De meiden van Halal*, the narrator makes a plea against Islamophobia
and for mutual respect.

Although the novel *De verstotene* [The outcast], where the main
character was cast out by her strictly Islamic mother and sister, at first
glance looks like an indictment of Islamic fundamentalism, on second
glance there is a clear nuance noticeable. Amelie remembers that when she
was a schoolgirl, she delved into literature on Islam and saw that a liberal
interpretation of the Koran was possible (cf. El Bezaz 2006, 210-212).
Now as an adult and after she has been abandoned by her boy-friend and
her experiences with Islamophobia, she is depressed and often has suicidal
thoughts. When she decides to continue her pregnancy, she says to her
unborn child:

---

[8]   Cf.   http://www.nps.nl/nps/mix/welcome.html?../meidenvanhalal/mainframe_
meidenvanhalal.html~main.

[9] Cf. Maaike Bos, "De meiden van Halal: 'Wij zijn Hollanders, een product van dit
land,'" *Intermediair* (May 9, 2007), http://www.intermediair.nl/artikel//43999/de-
meiden-van-halal-wij-zijn-hollanders-een-product-van-dit-land.html   (accessed
May 5, 2012).

I'd like to bring you up to be a Muslim, but an enlightened one. With respect for all faiths and with the awareness that there are different truths and that these can coexist side by side. (El Bezaz 2006, 253)

This is a strong message to the Dutch society and religious fundamentalists for tolerance and mutual respect.
Amelie promises her unborn child:

And when you grow older, I'll show you the land of my mother and father because that's also a bit of your country. You'll be happier, if you know who you really are, because perhaps, then you'll understand yourself a bit better. (El Bezaz 2006, 254)

These sentences are a plea for the acceptance of transcultural identities and against demands for the assimilation of immigrants, which now dominates the debates. Indirectly, Amelie shows that she particularly regards herself as Dutch.

Unfortunately, it appears that in the recent political climate there is no room for well integrated immigrants, who also want to cherish their own cultural and religious roots. Neither does there appear to be space for differentiated views. Amelie, who has decided to continue her life as Mina, that is her complete identity, falls off her balcony. The reader must assume that she has not survived this accident and is left with a pensive feeling.

Conclusion

The novels that have been examined contribute more or less to current debates in the aftermath of 9/11. Both Islamophobia and discrimination are exposed as fundamentalist movements in Islam. The main character of *De verstotene* was cast out by her strictly Islamic mother and sister and some minor characters in *De gebroeders Boetkaboet* have converted to a religious life in a pious way. Many characters with migrant roots who travel by plane after 9/11 experience thorough security checks of passengers and their luggage. While other passengers are checked randomly, they are almost always picked out from a crowd of travellers and are searched more carefully. 9/11 has caused a change of the social climate. Dutch Muslims are confronted with anti-Islamic sentiments, become increasingly suspect and are often perceived in connection with terrorism and fundamentalism. While the Moroccan-Dutch main characters are presented as settled in the Dutch culture and with characteristics of a hybrid identity, they are victimized by a growing mutual mistrust and xenophobia. Sahar's novel shows how experience with discrimination, Islamophobia and exclusion can cause radicalization and terrorism in a small minority of young Muslims. The majority of the Moroccan-Dutch characters disapprove of fundamentalism and terrorism. Via a kind of writing back, the Islamic characters are shown as individuals with different religious convictions. The novels plead against Islamophobia and xenophobia, and for more mutual respect.

Bibliography

Primary Sources

Benali, Abdelkader. *Feldman en ik.* Amsterdam: De Arbeiderspers, 2006.
Bezaz, Naima El. *De verstotene.* Amsterdam/ Antwerpen: Contact, 2006.
Haji, Said El. *Goddelijke duivel.* Amsterdam: Prometheus, 2006.
Sahar, Hans. *De gebroeders Boetkaboet.* Amsterdam/ Antwerpen: De Arbeiderspers, 2008.
Vuisje, Robert. *Alleen maar nette mensen.* Amsterdam: Nijgh & Van Ditmar, 2008.

Secondary Sources

Appel, René. "Straattaal. De mengtaal van jongeren in Amsterdam." *Thema's en trends in de sociolinguïstiek 3. Toegepaste taalwetenschap in artikelen* 2 (1999): 39-55.
Bos, Maaike. "De meiden van Halal: 'Wij zijn Hollanders, een product van dit land.'" *Intermediair* (May 9, 2007), http://www.intermediair.nl/artikel//43999/de-meiden-van-halal-wij-zijn-hollanders-een-product-van-dit-land.html (accessed May 5, 2012).
Kooijman, Hellen. "Straattaal is van alle tijden." *0/25. Tijdschrift over jeugd* (Febr. 2001): 20-21.
Langen, Peter de. "Straattaal." *Onze Taal* 7/8 (2001): 189.
Schouten, Rob. "Nederlandse schrijvers mijden maatschappelijk engagement." *Trouw* (September 4, 2011), http://www.trouw.nl/tr/nl/4468/Schrijf/article/detail/2890821/2011/09/04/Nederlandse-schrijvers-mijden-maatschappelijk-engagement.dhtml (accessed September 8, 2011).
Schulpé, Liesbeth. "Vader en een zonnekoningin." *Recensieweb. Nieuwe Literatuur. Nieuwe Gidsen* (October 31, 2007), http://www.recensieweb.nl/recensie/2283/Vader+van+een+zonnekoningin.html (accessed September 8, 2011).

Shadid, W.A.R.. "Berichtgeving over moslims en de islam in de westerse media; Beeldvorming, oorzaken en alternatieve strategieën." *Tijdschrift voor Communicatiewetenschap* 33 (2005): 330-346.

Slootman, Marieke and Tillie, Jean. *Processen van radicalisering. Waarom sommige Amsterdamse moslims radicaal worden.* Amsterdam: IMES, 2006.

http://www.nps.nl/nps/mix/welcome.html?../meidenvanhalal/mainframe_meidenvanhalal.html~main

MICHAEL CHABON'S
THE YIDDISH POLICEMEN'S UNION
AS A 9/11 NOVEL

BRYGIDA GASZTOLD

Michael Chabon's *The Yiddish Policemen's Union* (2007) employs multi-genre code-switching: the author combines a noir detective story with the Holocaust narrative, and counterfactual history with the 9/11 novel. Chabon's narrative evokes a time and place that is above the Yiddish language speaking community and the controversies connected with the establishment of the state of Israel. The author explores American, Jewish and Arab relations, interrogating the issues of loyalty and national identity, with religious fanaticism at its background. The events of 9/11 made these categories visible in new ways; mainly the issue of racial identity acquired a new reading after a period of multiculturalism, which tended to obfuscate the nature of ethnic differences. The present day agenda seems to lean towards the view that:

> [t]he many hopeful claims of globalization which were significant to much cultural theory (Appadurai, 1966; Radhakrishnan, 2003) now appear to be in question since 9/11 in a world that seems to be finding a new agenda and where theories of cultural hybridization sit uncomfortably alongside nationalism and ideas about goodness and evil.[1]

Literature after 9/11 exhibits tensions between border crossing and border protection, and between the requirements of multicultural diversity and the need for national security. It was after the traumatizing experiences of the 9/11 terrorist attack that such critical discursive structures were prompted into existence.

Literature is often a place where cultural and moral conflicts are presented and analyzed. Since September 11, 2001, a new context has emerged,

---

[1] Jo Lampert, *Children's Fiction About 9/11. Ethnic, Heroic and National Identities* (New York and London: Routledge, 2010),30.

which set in motion various cultural forces. The body of literature which answered, consciously or not, to the anxieties resulting from the event came to be known as the 9/11 novel. Examples of such literature are: Lynne Sharon Schwartz's *The Writing on the Wall* (2005), Jonathan Safran Foer's *Extremely Loud and Incredibly Close* (2005), John Updike's *Terrorist* (2006), Don De Lillo's *Falling Man* (2007), Joseph O'Neill's *Netherland* (2008), Teju Cole's *Open City* (2011), and *The Submission* by Amy Waldman (2011). Examples of Hollywood's response to the events of 9/11 are: Spike Lee's "25th Hour" (2002), Oliver Stone's "World Trade Center" (2006), and Paul Greengrass's "United 93" (2006). As much as these projects all differ in terms of content and presentation, they all refer, directly or not, to the 9/11 attacks.

> One of the most significant trends in the political aftermath of 9/11 is the emergence of new discourses about what it means to be a good and responsible citizen and about the nature of national identity. Also emerging have been complex notions of ethnicity including how ethnicity is (or is not) related to good and evil, questions about racial profiling, and talk about border protection.[2]

As the terrorist attacks rarely target the assailant's own community and generally involve, at least, two different groups, it happens that it is usually religion, ethnicity, and politics that seem to be the areas where the problem of terrorism is located. However, these three issues are indelibly connected to the economic and social situation in the countries that the terrorists are recruited from. An unstable economy, a corrupt political system, the unequal division of labour, production, distribution and consumption of goods, a low level of education, and ineffective social policy are among the key factors that may trigger waves of social unrest. The poorer and more underdeveloped the country is, the easier it is to find desperate volunteers who feel neglected and excluded and who, consequently, can be craftily manipulated into sacrificing their own lives for illusionary causes. Yet, this popular myth that poverty and inequality are root causes of terrorism is challenged by a more complex hypothesis, which enumerates other variables such as a repressive political regime, which is an instrument to maintaining the monopoly of political power, or the structure of party politics, which encourages various discriminatory policies, and the ethno-religious diversity of the population, which triggers the emergence of a class-ridden society.[3] Regimes which sanction political

---

[2] Ibid., 2.
[3] James Piazza, "Rooted in Poverty?: Terrorism, Poor Economic Development, and

discrimination, often combine politics with religion in an attempt to control all anti-regime activities. As long as the spheres of political authority and religious power overlap, such a state's dominance is unharmed.

Although not explicitly, Chabon's narrative explores the 9/11 context. It is stated to be a:

> 9/11 novel in that it has internalized the post-9/11 sensibilities of shadowy government meddling in the Middle East and the feeling of an impending global and religiously motivated conflict. To expect a novel to explicitly place 9/11 into a context that offers us all some greater understanding of it is to misunderstand how fiction works.[4]

There are several traces, which link Chabon's story to the traumatic events which shook America and the whole world. Since 9/11 is an essentially American narrative, *The Yiddish Policemen's Union* tells a story which also takes place in the United States. The narrative presents an alternate version of the Jewish history, in which the United States, in 1948, provisionally gives the Federal District of Sitka in Alaska to the Jews, who have just been driven out of Jerusalem by the Arab armies. The arrangement involves the condition that in sixty years, that is, in 2008, the Americans would get the area back. The procedure, which sets the Jews on their quest for their homeland once again, is called the Reversion. The author relies on documented plots of history, such as the 1939 political activity of the United States Interior Secretary Harold Ickes, who promoted the idea of Alaska as a place of Jewish refuge. The familiar concepts, however, are presented with newly drawn borders and are set in a transformed space of the predominantly Jewish-inhabited Alaskan island of Sitka.

In 1939, the Interior Secretary Harold Ickes, a close advisor to President Roosevelt, came up with a plan to resettle a growing number of Jewish refugees on the Alaskan frontier. As Alaska is an American territory, but not part of the mainland, Ickes thought it might be set apart from the quota system. Then, it would allow the extra Jewish refugees to be admitted, in addition to the regular quota. After the tour of Alaska, Harold Ickes advocated this idea and supported the Slattery Report of 1939/1940, whose official title was "The Problem of Alaskan Development." The report was signed by the Under-secretary Harry Slattery, because none of the Federal Bureau officials in Alaska wanted their own name to be

---

Social Cleavages." *Terrorism and Political Violence* 18, no.1 (2006): 174-177.
[4] C. Max. Magee, "The Myth of the 9/11 Novel," last modified Sept. 11, 2007, http:// the millions.com.

associated with the plan. The Slattery Report considered raising private money to support the Jewish refugees in Alaska until they could sustain themselves. President F. D. Roosevelt, who had already considered Angola and the Dominican Republic as possible destinations for the Jewish resettlement schemes, failed to support the Alaskan plan. So too did the Alaskan governor, Ernest Gruening, even though his parents were German Jews. Harold Ickes' idea also encountered local opposition in The Alaskan Chamber of Commerce, which objected to the idea of bringing Jews to Alaska, as they would take away the jobs of the local people. Other opponents pointed out the fact that non-quota immigrants might end up as second-class citizens of Alaska, a situation which would only in time destabilize the unity of the Alaskan community. Strong anti-Semitic attitudes in the United States, which were fuelled by radio priests such as Charles Coughlin, who defended the anti-Jewish pogroms as a means to eradicate communism, did not create a favourable environment for the Jewish cause among Americans.

The dialogic relationship between history, cultural values and the text results in the meaning of the novel ,which is mediated between the text and the reader. Allusions to the Jewish history of diaspora, international politics, and the Holocaust place the novel in a context which allows two collective identities, ethnicity and national identity, to be analyzed. As 9/11 has become a discourse related to race-politics, the pressure to identify as "us" or "them" was crucial. "The attacks on 9/11 became associated with ethnicity almost immediately, by precipitating discussions of racial targeting following closely on the heels of speculation about the motivations of the 'ethnic' terrorists".[5] Similarly, Chabon's novel introduces the groups which have long been identified as hostile. In terms of religion there are Jews and Muslims, which signal the conflict in the Middle East, Jews and Christians, which present the United States as a scene of the Diasporic struggle, and Orthodox and Reform Jews, which represent different interpretations of the same tenets of faith. Then, there are Jews and Palestinians who argue about the legitimacy of the independent State of Israel and Palestine. Their land dispute combines the whole array of political, religious, and territorial issues, making it impossible to pin down a single cause of the conflict. The Jewish experience in Alaska triggers not so much religious as territorial claims with the Native Indians, in which the perpetrator-victim dichotomy becomes even further blurred. Whether it is North America or the Middle East, the novel launches a debate whose outcome is not readily predictable

---

[5] Lampert, *Children's Fiction About 9/11*, 28.

as the truth depends on who tells the story. The intricate web of global and personal interrelations presented by the plot mirrors the inability of man to find meaning in the surrounding world. Hence, Chabon's novel is a comment on the human condition in the modern world through the lens of an ethnic and religious conflict.

In the case of the 9/11 attacks both sides of the conflict were instantly recognized. Chabon's novel, however, uses the characters' ethnicity not to clarify, but rather to obfuscate the truth. Majority-minority, Western- non-Western world, or the Christians-Muslims polarity is no longer binding, but interrogates the questions of individual and communal responsibility.

> How one aligns oneself with ethnic community and with a sense of national loyalty or how solidarity contributes to the sense of personal duty to perform in what comes to be seen as a proper, just, and heroic manner are interrelated in complex ways.[6]

Chabon's protagonist-detective Landsman represents individual heroism, which is not corrupted by ethnic bias. He pursues all criminals regardless of their ethnicity and his own affiliation to the Jewish community. Being a law officer on Sitka, his aim is to enforce justice, whatever it might take. He will find the solution to the mystery murder even if it might jeopardize the interest of his own people. "Landsman tries to weigh the fates of Berko, of his uncle Hertz, of Bina, of the Jews, of the Arabs, of the whole unblessed and homeless planet, against the promise he made to Mrs. Shpilman, and to himself, even though he had lost his belief in fate and promises".[7] By choosing to fulfil the promise given to the victim's mother and, more importantly, by staying true to his own convictions, Landsman highlights the importance of individual choice in the chaos of the modern world. When "a global or totalizing cultural narrative schema which orders and explains knowledge and experience"[8] fails to deliver a coherent whole, one can always rely on one's own beliefs. Since "[h]eroism, post 9/11, is more than ever bound up with ways to perform as citizens of the nation"[9], Landsman, who is a policeman by profession, thus somebody who guards the nation's feeling of safety, embodies what comes to be seen as American values: honesty, persistence and integrity. By way of contrast,

---

[6] Ibid., 24.
[7] Michael Chabon, *The Yiddish Policemen's Union* (New York: Harper, 2008), 410.
[8] John Stephens and Robyn McCallum, *Retelling Stories, Framing Culture:Traditional Story andMetanarratives in Children's Literature* (New York and London: Garland Pub.,1998), 6.
[9] Lampert, *Children's Fiction About 9/11,* 33.

the protagonist, with an ethnic background, becomes the paragon of a loyal and law-abiding citizen for Americans, who are represented by corrupt and fraudulent officials. By subverting the official hegemony, which promotes the domestic (mainstream) over the alien (minority), the author redefines the roles of a perpetrator and a victim. The novel's message conveys the claim that the "us' and "them" logic, which is based on the binary divides such as mainstream – minority, secular – religious, reason – fanaticism, is no longer adequate enough to define social groups in a modern society. In America, for example, the Jews have gone a long way from their immigrant beginnings and are no longer regarded as an ethnic minority. A similar claim is echoed by Michael Rothberg who calls for a new kind of literature: "what we need from 9/11 novels are cognitive maps that imagine how US citizenship looks and feels beyond the boundaries of the nation-state, both for Americans and for others."[10] An outsider's lens may help to rewrite the vision of pluralist America by addressing two conflicting issues: how "to provincialize the claims of 'the first universal nation' and to mark its asymmetrical power to influence world events."[11]

There are other similarities which link Chabon's narrative to the genre of the 9/11 novel. The story culminates in the planting of a bomb and the destruction of the place which is important for the nations of the Middle East. The obliteration of the Dome of the Rock is a step in the direction towards the Jewish repossession of Palestine from the Arabs. Just like an ancient Jerusalem temple stands for the cradle of national identity, the World Center Towers were viewed as secular temples of modern capitalism. The target in both attacks is thus connected with the fundamental symbols which help to define American, i.e. Western, and Middle Eastern identity. There is, however, no polarity which, otherwise, might be suggested by this juxtaposition, as the narrative reveals a much more complex plot. What Chabon's detective-protagonist discovers is that Mendel Shpilman was murdered, because he threatened to expose the U.S. government-backed plot to supply armaments to religiously fanatic Jews. What is more, the secretive deal is done through evangelical Christians. After the attack, the Jewish religious extremists plan to rebuild the Temple and restore the sacrificial service. Their overall goal, however, is to seize Palestine from the Arabs and re-establish the state of Israel. Thus, Chabon's novel presents the act of terrorism as a reversed analogy to a

---

[10] Michael Rothberg, "A Failure of the Imagination: Diagnosing the Post-9/11 Novel: A Response to Richard Gray," *American Literary History* 21, no.1 (2009): 158.
[11] Ibid., 158.

9/11plot: Westerners are the perpetrators whose actions are directed towards Muslims. With Christian fundamentalists portrayed as villains, the author evades simplistic conclusions and, instead, presents all sides of the conflict as wicked. Wherever there is bloodshed, the narrative argues, no party involved can be exonerated for the act of aggression. There is a purpose to *The Yiddish Policemen's Union*'s open-endedness and the avoidance of taking sides, as this rhetoric mirrors the fluidity and ambivalence of real-world crises, in which good and evil no longer mean what they used to.

The most crucial parallel, which can be drawn between the 9/11 discourse and the themes that alternate to the norm history novels such as *The Yiddish Policemen's Union* engage with, is the concept of religion, or more precisely, religious fanaticism. Religion motivated actions, whether by a biblical sense of entitlement or ushered in by radicals of any hue, constitute the background of the narrative. The Hasidic dynasty of Verbovers are the gangsters who rule Sitka and despise all infidels and the whole secular world. Convinced of their own righteousness, they perpetrate the acts of violence in the name of God – whom they regard made them privy to the secret truth. Their aim is to drive the Arabs away from Jerusalem and, consequently, restore the Jewish state of Israel. With help from their American allies, they commit an act of terrorist violence. According to Matthew J. Morgan:

> there is a considerable segment of international Jewry that supports the state of Israel in alliance with evangelical Christianity, in a manner that appears to subvert the geopolitical imperative of U.S. foreign policy – which otherwise might prefer to back less ambiguously Arab client states and secure peace in the Middle East.[12]

The choice of Jerusalem as the target of the terrorist attack – the place where Christians, Jews, and Muslims have been historically doomed to meet – is not a coincidence. Places like this, with a long history of warfare and hostilities, attract religious extremists and, if the strike is successful, it usually affects more than one community. By choosing Jerusalem as the target of the attack instead of a place somewhere in the United States, the narrative also perpetuates "the [Jewish] myth of the US as the land of escape from European horror and misery."[13]

Chabon's narrative warns the readers against the threat of religious

---

[12] Matthew J. Morgan, *The Impact of 9/11 on Religion and Philosophy. The Day That Changed Everything?* (New York: Palgrave Macmillan, 2009), 91.
[13] Ibid., 92.

fanaticism in the contemporary world, the danger that has been well known and documented in human history. It has been observed that "religious political activism is directed away from social improvement (which was an overwhelming priority for an earlier generation of liberal or else neo-orthodox American Protestants) toward geopolitical military strategy."[14] The novel's criticism is aimed at Zionists who are portrayed as fanatic mobsters who unethically exploit messianism. Religious zealotry, however, is not the primary motivation of the attack, but rather creates a favourable climate for such an action to arise. Religious fanaticism fuels terrorism by creating no rationale other than the expression of hatred. The introduction of a massive terrorist threat to what starts as a typical noir fiction shifts the reader's focus from the local to the global. Even if a lone detective-protagonist discovers an international conspiracy, he is not able to prevent the disaster, because it turns out that there are more powerful forces in play, namely, the U.S. government: "We knew our limitations. And we called that a choice. But we didn't have any choice."[15] Thus, the author constructs a plot in which religion is strictly connected with the world's politics: "God damn them all. I always knew they were there. Down there in Washington. Up there over our heads. Holding the strings. Setting the agenda."[16] The use of religious scriptures and apocalyptic images of destruction to justify the acts of violence, which are in fact financed through illegal methods, questions the whole idea of morality. With the world of business and international politics saturating religious practices it is extremely difficult, the author suggests, to distinguish between religious and political terrorism. Invoking the imagery of global terrorism, the novel interrogates the question of individual responsibility. What Chabon's protagonist illustrates is what can be done in the immoral world – one can try and retain one's own moral integrity.

Another central tenet of Chabon's novel is the danger of territorialism, the term which originally denoted a political movement of the Jewish Territorialist Organization (1905-1925) whose aim was to create an independent Israeli territory. Territorialists used the East European experience of pogroms and forced emigration as reasons for locating the Jewish home outside Europe. There had been plans to establish a Jewish settlement in various parts of Africa, Asia, Australia, and America until the Balfour Declaration in 1917, which led to a gradual dissolution of the territorialist agenda. However, there continued disputes between Zionists, who insisted on the Land of Israel as the Jewish home, and those who

[14] Ibid., 92.
[15] Chabon, *The Yiddish*, 410.
[16] Ibid., 375.

sought to establish a Jewish state wherever the Jews were granted the territory. History has shown that the Zionist path proved successful and led to the establishment of the State of Israel in 1948. Throughout the novel, the author reiterates the theme of uprooted peoples and disputed territories. The history of the Jewish Diaspora is permeated by experiences of dislocation and territorial claims, the growth of fascism, World War II, and the tragedy of the Holocaust and the annihilated East European Yiddish-speaking communities and displaced millions of people, not only of Jewish origin. The establishment of the state of Israel in 1948 not only aggravated the Arab-Israeli conflict but affected world politics. The Jews in Chabon's novel engage in a bitter feud not with Palestinians, which would be historically believable, but with the Native people of Alaska. Yet, the nature of the controversy remains the same and is connected with the possession of land. Looking at a political map of the world with its apparently neatly delineated contours, one might come to a conclusion that the problem of territory is no longer relevant to the contemporary world. However, a closer look at how and where the national borders were established reveals a multitude of unresolved controversies, which simmer under the guise of current politics. Chabon's novel evokes important moments in the world's, and Jewish history – thereby signalling the problem of territorial claims as a potential trigger for terrorist attacks.

Alternate history novels are based on a rupture of history, which becomes the starting point for various alternative versions of the past and/or present. Similarly, what happened on 9/11 is also understood to mark a rupture of history in the sense that it was a local event, which initiated global political, social, and cultural consequences. Correspondingly, the fictional terrorist plan, which begins in a remote area of Alaska called Sitka, culminates in Jerusalem: no place is safe from a terrorist mindset, the narrative seems to claim. In *The Yiddish Policemen's Union's* case the rupture happens at the end of the story, whereas the whole narrative is devoted to the unravelling of the terrorist plot. But throughout the narrative the readers are confronted with events whose bearing on the characters is similar in nature to the rupture of history. Large-scale conflicts are mirrored in local and personal tragedies. World War II and the Holocaust not only destroyed many lives but left the survivors homeless and disillusioned. The diasporic experience and attempts to find alternative homes raise questions connected with loyalty, both ethnic and religious. The storyline revolves around a murder, always a traumatic event in itself, of a man who was viewed by some as the future Messiah. The belief in a Messiah, who will finally come to redeem his people, lies at the bottom of Judaism. His appearance will mark the end of the Jewish exile, will restore peace, religious justice and prosperity to Jerusalem, and to the lives of traditional Jews – the so called messianic age will commence. This idea is echoed in the protagonist's vision:

> [T]he Jews will pick up and set sail for the promised land to feast on giant grapes and toss their beards in the desert wind. That the Temple will be rebuilt, speedily and in our day. War will cease, ease and plenty and righteousness will be universal, and humankind will be treated to the regular spectacle of lions and lambs cohabiting.[17]

The narrative maps events which are global and local, asserting the validity of both. By demonstrating how the public realm of history overlaps with the private realm of memory, the author asserts their mutual interdependency. In other words: "Like a work of literature, terrorism is a public act that defines its success or failure by its ability to penetrate into the private sphere."[18] Avoiding promoting either perspective, Chabon illustrates how fictional stories may function as allegories for current world anxieties.

Another aspect of the novel that parallels the 9/11 plot is the idea of mass destruction. The use of force in the form of murder, violence, abuse, alcoholism, and the terrorist attack, which involves a multitude of casualties, are all elements of Chabon's plot. Events which involve individuals (a murder, a plane crash, an assault) are placed alongside the ones which signal the greater scheme of things (the Verbover's gang operations, the terrorist network, the corrupted government officials and police officers). Spectacular actions draw public attention better than a local, small-scale incident, especially when they target the enemy's territory. As Rothberg claims: "Terrorist acts today, and especially the attacks of September 11, are, among other things, a form of spectacle: they are intended for a global, mass audience of media consumers."[19] The annihilation of the commercial heart of New York or an ancient religious place of worship aims at generating a widespread public response, which is intensified by the fear instigated by the scale of the attack. "Rather than focusing on conventional goals of political or religious movements, more and more terrorists are using the purity of religious motives to adopt eschatological goals: they often seek destruction and chaos as ends in

---

[17] Ibid., 406-407.
[18] Michael Rothberg, "Seeing Terror, Feeling Art: Public and Private in Post-9/11Literature," in *Literature After 9/11*, ed. A. Keniston and J. F. Queen (New York: Routledge, 2008), 125
[19] Ibid., 123.

themselves."[20] Attacks, which target civilian populations are more lethal in their scope and, moreover, they sanction indiscriminate violence. Providing a fictional insight into one such plot, Chabon's novel is both the response to and the representation of the era of mass terrorism.

The mass media involvement in the mass destruction is another focal point in Chabon's novel. Despite the horror and trauma of the terrorist attack described in the novel, the way it is broadcast throughout the world appears similar to the real media coverage of the events on 9/11. In both cases television has become the main source of information:

> "I saw it on the television […] At first they said it was a mistake. Some Arabs making bombs in a tunnel under the Temple Mount. Then they said it was deliberate. The ones fighting the other ones."
> "Sunnis and Shiites?"
> "Maybe. Somebody got careless with a rocket launcher."
> "Syrians and Egyptians?"
> "Whoever. The President was on, saying they might have to go in. Saying it's a holy city to everybody".[21]

The viewers around the world followed the events on 9/11 first with disbelief and then with horror. Chabon's narrative similarly reflects the observer's confusion and awe, which accompanied the shocking news. But what the narrative divulges is the fact that the response to and the understanding of the conflict varies depending on one's worldview: while some were crying over the loss, others were cheering the victory over the hateful enemy: "The young believers hug one another and jump up and down in their suits. Their yarmulkes tumble from their heads. Their faces shine with tears."[22] The varied reaction to the news about the attack mirrors the 9/11 coverage, which also showed those who cried in pain and those who laughed with joy. The mixed response to the tragedy shows how complicated the modern world is and how impossible it is to get to the truth. Instead of telling what truth is, the narrative asks whose truth it is. The author claims that such terms as absolute truth, good, and evil have lost their referentiality and, in the contemporary context, have become arbitrary. However, the very acknowledgement of the media's biased participation in the tragic event starts a process which calls for the redistribution and reintroduction of basic ethical principles into human lives.

---

[20] Morgan, *The Impact of 9/11 on Religion and Philosophy*, 1.
[21] Chabon, *The Yiddish*, 370.
[22] Ibid., 358.

The unscrupulous image of the mass media, which are solely focused on generating profit, is mirrored by presenting the anti-heroic attitudes of those who, amidst the horror and destruction, sense a good business opportunity:

> [s]ome hustler, inevitably, will work the thing up as a full-size poster, two feet by three. The hilltop in Jerusalem, crowded with alleys and houses. The broad empty mesa of paving stone. The jagged jawbone of burnt teeth. The magnificent plume of black smoke. And at the bottom the legend, in blue letters, AT LAST! These posters will sell at the stationers' for between ten dollars and $12,95.[23]

The author illustrates how traumatic events may defamiliarize and pluralize the meaning of such key terms as heroism, honesty and decency, and how they may stimulate the whole spectrum of public attitudes, from the most to the least desirable. Chabon's narrative redirects these issues and demonstrates how they shape a discourse about contemporary identity. Although the author pronounces judgement on the questionable value of the public, political, and religious realms, his "solution to the crisis unleashed by the attacks and 'the war on terror' does not involve a reworking of the corrupt public realm, but rather its abandonment."[24] The way his protagonist "has come to reject any dream of territorial belonging"[25] and, as an alternative, he has chosen to assert the importance of basic human relations, reveals what is really important in life:

> Landsman has no home, no future, no fate but Bina. The land that he and she were promised was bounded only by the fringes of their wedding canopy, by the dog-eared corners of their cards of membership in an international fraternity whose members carry their patrimony in a tote bag, their world on the tip of the tongue.[26]

The uninhibited and sincere contact with another person is where the source of strength to withstand the outside world is to be found. That is why Meyer and Bina decide to remain silent over their knowledge about an international conspiracy, promoting the idea of self-preservation over a sense of global justice. Their final reconciliation signifies "the need to

[23] Ibid., 358.
[24] Rothberg, *A Failure of the Imagination*, 154.
[25] Sarah Philips Casteel, "Jews Among the Indians: The Fantasy of Indigenization in Mordechai Richler's and Michael Chabon's Northern Narratives," *Contemporary Literature* 50 no.4 (2009): 796.
[26] Chabon, *The Yiddish*, 411.

reinvent the public realm as a response to the brutalization of politics,"[27] locating the notion of Jewishness not in terms of geographic coordinates, but in the valorization of familial ties.

The term 9/11 has become a metaphor not only for an unprecedented attack on American symbols and the vicious destruction of many innocent lives, but also for the lack of control over one's own fate. What happened on 9/11 demonstrated how arbitrarily people's lives can be affected by outside forces, such that they can neither predict nor control. A traumatic accident, which ruptures one's life, declares willpower meaningless. But the attack on 9/11 was not aimed at destroying an individual's life, but the spirit of the whole nation, just like the destruction of the temple in the novel is directed against the Palestinians with a view to crushing their self-confidence. A successful annihilation of a carefully chosen target, whose importance is both material and symbolic, entails a sense of finality. That is why a heroic identity, such as a Yiddish detective's, is crucial as such identities "provide a kind of tangible (albeit imaginary) truth, not only about what is possible, but about what can be hoped for."[28] Not everybody was directly affected by the attack but, whether they wanted or not, they participated in the public discourse that was dominant after 9/11, and Chabon's novel is one of the voices in this debate. The end of *The Yiddish Policemen's Union* brings the alternate history to a close equivalence with ours – the United States, a group of Jewish fanatics, and the Arab world engage in a struggle for ideological and political supremacy. Juxtaposing a sense of individual justice against the need for self-preservation, the narrative criticizes religious fanaticism, demonstrating how it exploits individuals out of short-term political necessity. Yet, the novel's final words: "I have a story for you"[29], which are directed to Landsman's friend who is a journalist, carry a promise that the truth will finally be revealed. By touching upon the problems which still smoulder under the guise of global politics, Chabon's novel is an important voice in the literary discussion of national terrorism. In spite of the novel's relevance to the peculiarities of the Jewish historical context, it manages to convey global concerns connected with the questions of historical rootlessness, the intensity of religious observance, and the conflicts over authority.

---

[27] Rothberg, *A Failure of the Imagination*, 154.
[28] Lampert, *Children's Fiction About 9/11*, 33.
[29] Chabon, *The Yiddish*, 411.

Bibliography

Appadurai, Arjun. *Modernity at Large: Cultural Dimensions of Globalisation*. Minneapolis: University ofMinnesota Press,1966.

Chabon, Michael. *The Yiddish Policemen's Union*. New York: Harper, 2008.

Casteel, Sarah Philips. "Jews Among the Indians: The Fantasy of Indigenization in Mordechai Richler's andMichael Chabon's Northern Narratives." *Contemporary Literature* 50 no.4(2009): 775-810.

Lampert, Jo. *Children's Fiction About 9/11. Ethnic, Heroic and National Identities*. New York andLondon: Routledge, 2010.

Magee, C. Max. "The Myth of the 9/11 Novel." Last modified Sept. 11, 2007. http:// the millions.com.

Morgan, Matthew J. *The Impact of 9/11 on Religion and Philosophy. The Day That Changed Everything?*NewYork: Palgrave Macmillan, 2009.

Piazza, James. "Rooted in Poverty?: Terrorism, Poor Economic Development, and Social Cleavages."*Terrorism and Political Violence* 18, no.1 (2006): 159-177.

Radhakrishan, Rajagopalan. *Theory in an Uneven World*. Oxford: Wiley-Blackwell, 2003.

Rothberg, Michael. "Seeing Terror, Feeling Art: Public and Private in Post-9/11Literature." In *LiteratureAfter9/11*, edited by A. Keniston and J. F. Queen, 123-142. New York: Routledge, 2008.

—. "A Failure of the Imagination: Diagnosing the Post-9/11 Novel: A Response to RichardGray." *American Literary History* 21, no. 1 (2009):152-158.

Stephens, John, and Robyn McCallum. *Retelling Stories, Framing Culture: Traditional Story andMetanarratives in Children's Literature*. New York and London: Garland Pub., 1998.

THE AMBIGUITY OF THE "OTHER" IN THE POST-9/11 NOVELS *THE RELUCTANT FUNDAMENTALIST* (2007) BY MOHSIN HAMID AND *HOME BOY* (2009) BY H.M. NAQVI

KAROLINA GOLIMOWSKA

> *"[T]he ultimate threat does not come from out there, from the fundamentalist Other, but from within, from our own lassitude and moral weakness, loss of clear values and firm commitments"*
> (Slavoj Žižek *Welcome to Desert of the Real*)

Post-9/11 binary oppositions and the construction of the "evil other"

This paper aims at discussing two novels and the ways in which they address the changing image and perception of America after 9/11 among Muslims living in the United States. The main characters of these two texts, Changez and Chuck, both go through a certain development that eventually leads to personal disillusionment with the American life and the American Dream. These disappointments and confusions play an important role and become a motivation to determine one's position within the extremely risky, vague and also dangerous "us vs. them" dichotomy so strongly encouraged and imposed by George W. Bush's administration, as demonstrated in a quote from one of Bush's public speeches: "Either you're with us or you're with the terrorists"[1] indicating that if one does not support the US, one automatically becomes its opponent. This approach of the U.S. government was triggered by tremendous fear of an enemy difficult to define, characterize or even assign or locate geographically. It is also a desperate attempt at self-defence. It sets a binary opposition that

---

[1] Bush, George W. Address to a Joint Session of Congress and the American People on September 20, 2001. The White House. http://georgewbush-whitehouse.archives.gov/news/releases/2001/09/20010920-8.html

excludes all forms of the in-between and therefore requires great simplifications, so inappropriate to a multicultural society. It attempts to locate and name the enemy by trying to force everyone to position themselves within this dichotomy – both on the individual as well as the national and political level. This brings to mind structuralists' ideas on culture based on Saussures's *Cours de Linguistique Générale*. According to these theories, difference is essential to meaning; without it, meaning would not exist. Stuart Hall applies this standpoint and argues that meaning is relational: we know what "black" means only if we can contrast it with "white."[2] Accordingly: we know what "us" means only if we can contrast it with its opposite, i.e. "them" or "not-us". There is no essence of blackness or of the notion of "us"; only the difference between the opposites of a binary opposition counts. Mikhail Bakhtin claims that we need difference, because the only way of establishing meaning is through a dialogue with the "other". If meaning is dialogic, Hall argues further, then we need the "other" to be able to construct it. In conclusion: we need to know the "other" or "them" in order to know who "we" are and what "we" means. We need to know the difference, which in this particular dichotomy is a very difficult task. Poststructuralism has shown that all binary oppositions are simplifications; they are always imposed by the stronger pole, the unmarked upon the marked (white on black, male on female etc.) and are therefore never neutral. The end of the novel *The Reluctant Fundamentalist* follows this argument and shows that wanting to set such dichotomies, not only after 9/11 but in general, is pure hypocrisy.

After 9/11, some mass media propagated an imagined identity of the "other", who has had to be identified, scrutinized and either rejected or changed – Muslims were portrayed as dangerous "subjects", the unknown "others". This process and its consequences are visible in both of the books *The Reluctant Fundamentalist* and *Home Boy*. Possibly 9/11 was not a milestone or a "watershed moment", but a catalyst to escalate existing stereotypes.

I am going to focus on the two main characters and narrators of these two novels, two young Muslim men educated in the U.S. whose lives change drastically after 9/11. I want to point out their different roles with regard to pinning down the power relations between the seemingly clearly divided groups that are supposed to be enemies and that stand in binary opposition to one another. I also want to show how differently these characters are portrayed; how they see and perceive the U.S. before and

[2] Hall, Stuart ed. *Representation: Cultural Representations and Signifying Practices*. London: Sage, 2003: 234.

after the attacks. Finally, I am interested in the way the idea of American exceptionalism, the propagation of which has also been part of the U.S. politics after 9/11,[3] is discussed and questioned in the context of the post-9/11 politics and social changes.

Polite and reluctant

The Reluctant Fundamentalist, published in 2007 and written by Mohsin Hamid, a Pakistani writer born in Lahore, who has lived in New York and London, is a dramatic monologue. It is told in the second person, by Changez, a Pakistani native, and addressed to an American man who is visiting Lahore and agrees to have dinner with the narrator. The characters transcend any representation of real individuals. The representational mode is not realistic but rather allegorical. These two men become universal and symbolic agents of the opposites of the highly problematic and questionable "us vs. them" or "the West vs. the rest" dichotomy. Hamid's idea is to approach it by entering an allegorical meta-level.

Changez's story of his life in America, narrated chronologically by himself, shows him as a young, talented and ambitious student at Princeton who is well received among his mostly white American peers and who is known for his hard work and politeness. Straight after graduating he begins a professional career in a management consultancy firm, which lifts his spirits even more: "I was in my own eyes, a veritable James Bond – only younger, darker, and possibly better paid." (73) According to Anna Hartnell, the management consultancy firm called Underwood Samson, and abbreviated U.S., reflects American state power and represents its "pragmatic face."[4] The company propagates the philosophy of "sticking to the fundamentals", something that Changez becomes reluctant towards after 9/11.

Changez feels like a British spy and hero – a character he had most

---

[3] American exceptionalism served as part of the post-9/11 politics: "America was targeted for attack because we're the brightest beacon for freedom and opportunity in the world. And no one will keep that light from shining."(…) "This is a day when all Americans from every walk of life unite in our resolve for justice and peace. America has stood down enemies before, and we will do so this time. None of us will ever forget this day. Yet, we go forward to defend freedom and all that is good and just in our world." (Fragment from Bush's speech to the nation on September 11, 2001).

[4] Hartnell, Anna. "Moving through America: Race, place and resistance in Mohsin Hamid's The Reluctant Fundamentalist." *Journal of Postcolonial Writing* 46, 3-4, July/September (2010): 340.

likely been confronted with back in Pakistan. This, together with his accent in English that is more British than American and perceived by Americans as elegant, posh and polite, brings up Pakistan's colonial past and its legacy. Changez represents an individual whose life has always been influenced by a political and economic empire, first Great Britain and then the United States. Both of them, among other aspects, impose on him the English language, the imperial *lingua franca* that possibly makes him confuse American and British imperial features. The difference between "colonial" and "postcolonial" becomes very vague and their influences confused. Contributing to this issue is also the fact that Mohsin Hamid, who similarly to Changez studied at Princeton and started a career in a management consulting company, chose to write *The Reluctant Fundamentalist* in English.

Changez, having a well-paid and lucrative job, pictures himself as a perfectly assimilated Pakistani immigrant. He loves New York, a city in which he immediately feels at home and where his (American) dreams come true: "This is a dream come true (…) [with] the feeling that my life was a film in which I was the star and everything was possible."[5] His girlfriend Erica introduces him to the upper class of American society, in which he feels comfortable. He does not seem to have much in common with other Muslim Americans, who appear in the book as shop owners or taxi drivers, generally a lower, poorer class. Although Changez develops a sense of belonging and a very personal relation to the city of New York, watching the World Trade Center towers collapse (on a TV screen in the Philippines where he is on a work-related project) makes him feel "remarkably pleased."[6] The way the tragedy is broadcast live makes it impossible for Changez to think about the victims and identify with them as individuals or as symbolic Americans. He rather has the impression of watching a staged, planned and accordingly fulfilled, highly symbolic act of performance that does not even seem to be real at first, since real tragedies are not supposed to be *acted*.

> I realized that it was not fiction but news. (…) at the moment my thoughts were not with the victims of the attack – death on television moves me most when it is fictitious and happens to characters with whom I have built up relationships over multiple episodes – no, I was caught up in the symbolism of it all, the fact that someone had so visibly brought America to her knees.[7]

[5] Hamid, Mohsin. *The Reluctant Fundamentalist*. London: Penguin Books, 2007:3.
[6] Ibid., 83.
[7] Ibid., 83.

Hamid's description of his character's feelings and reactions can be seen as an answer to or as an application of the phenomenon of this tragedy, which Jean Baudrillard in *The Spirit of Terrorism* calls the "performance of cruelty", indirectly referring to Antonin Artaud's notion of "the theatre of cruelty"[8]. Baudrillard first calls the attacks on the World Trade Center a "spectacle" in which reality and fiction are inextricable. He claims that terrorist violence is not real but symbolic, which is far worse, since:

> only symbolic violence is generative of singularity […] It is the radicality of the spectacle, the brutality of the spectacle, which alone is original and irreducible. […] This is our theatre of cruelty, the only one we have left – extraordinary in that it unites the most extreme degree of the spectacular and the highest level of challenge.[9]

Mohsin Hamid in his novel gives Changez the intuitive insight to see this symbolic importance of the attacks in the moment of watching them for the first time – he sees and names something that witnesses in real life could only name and discuss long after it was over and after the first shock had passed. Only when Changez realizes that his girlfriend Erica is in New York, does he start feeling the terror and fear all his American colleagues share. This personal link to a living individual has a more powerful effect on Changez than the images he is confronted with. This stresses the power of fiction, which makes it possible for a literary protagonist to be simultaneously confronted with both: the material and symbolic meaning of the tragedy. The ability to distinguish between the symbolic dimensions viewed when approached from the perspective of his home country, and the material, emotional aspect shown through his love for Erica, leads to an internal conflict of the character. This puts Changez in a slightly different position in terms of awareness, cognition and perception to real witnesses.

At this stage in the book a very strong link between America and Erica becomes obvious. Sometimes they are confused with one another, the way America is often personified and Erica's actions and feelings, sound remarkably over-symbolic, almost universal and provide a certain unexpected pathos:

---

[8] In "The Theatre and its Double" (first published 1938), Antonin Artaud describes a theatre that operates with cruelty as a "tool" of getting to the spectator. This acted and staged cruelty must never leave the theatre and is always controlled by someone (the director, the actors) who as a consequence also controls the viewers' emotions.

[9] Baudrillard, Jean. *The Spirit of Terrorism*. New York: Verso, 2002: 29-30.

America was gripped by a growing and self-righteous rage.[10]

The destruction of the World Trade Center had, as she [Erica] said, churned up old thoughts that had settled in the manner of sediment to the bottom of a pond; now the waters of her mind were murky with what previously had been ignored.[11]

(Am)Erica and Erica are inseparable. When Changez leaves New York for the Philippines, he misses both and often cannot distinguish between their individual features. When the Twin Towers collapse, Erica's emotional world seems to collapse as well. Finally, near the end of the story, when Erica commits suicide and Changez leaves America for Pakistan, it seems irresistible to match the woman's suicide with the symbolic one of America that Jean Baudrillard in his *Requiem for the Twin Towers* refers to. He claims that the towers, which were the emblem of the United States' global power "still embody it in their dramatic end, which resembles a suicide. Seeing them collapse themselves, as if by implosion, one had the impression that they were committing suicide in response to the suicide of the suicide planes."[12]

Changez's love for New York is related and pictured through a tragic love story with an American woman – Erica. When the U.S. bomb Afghanistan, Changez feels betrayed and attacked personally: "Afghanistan was Pakistan's neighbour, our friend, and a fellow Muslim nation besides".[13] The political action undertaken and justified as a consequence of 9/11 becomes a trigger for Changez's decision to move back to Lahore, Pakistan. It is the political level, not a personal confrontation with racism, discrimination or violence as in Naqvi's *Home Boy*, discussed later, where trauma forces an escape from the country. In Hamid's novel, Erica has suffered from a personal trauma after the death of her boyfriend and life-long friend that she has had since her childhood – Chris. The feeling of irreplaceable loss resurfaces after 9/11 and Erica's (or America's) depression as a consequence returns and also touches, influences and occupies Changez.

Stories that surround Changez about Arab-looking men being persecuted, discriminated against or humiliated, and finally reactions to his beard among his colleagues at work, radicalize his attitude towards this

---

[10] Hamid, Mohsin. *The Reluctant Fundamentalist*. London: Penguin Books, 2007: 106.

[11] Ibid., 94.

[12] Baudrillard, Jean. *The Spirit of Terrorism*. New York: Verso, 2002: 47.

[13] Hamid, Mohsin. *The Reluctant Fundamentalist*. London: Penguin Books, 2007: 113.

possibly "new" post-9/11 American reality.

> I prevented myself as much as was possible from making the obvious
> connection between the crumbling of the world around me and the
> impending destruction of my personal American dream.[14]

A story about Janissaries told by Juan Bautista, a character who works at a
publishing house that Underwood Samson is consulting, makes Changez
feel like a traitor and makes him re-evaluate his life in the United States:

> 'They were Christian boys', he [Juan Batista] explained, 'captured by the
> Ottomans and trained to be soldiers in a Muslim army, at that time the
> greatest army in the world. They were ferocious and utterly loyal: they had
> fought to erase their own civilizations, so they had nothing else to turn to.
> They were always taken in childhood. It would have been far more
> difficult to devote themselves to their adopted empire, you see if they had
> memories they could not forget.'[15]

Changez feels like a Janissary himself; he also calls himself a product
of an American university and a "servant of the American empire at a time
when it was invading a country with a kinship" to his own.[16]

Changez develops an extreme desire and need for a sense of belonging
that is partly released and encouraged by the "us vs. them" dichotomy
mentioned in the beginning. In post-9/11 America, living the American
Dream as an immigrant from Pakistan seems no longer possible.
Individual success, so important in the construction of the American
Dream, is neither relevant nor satisfying in the context of the new political
setting and power relations. Changez feels that he cannot function as an
individual without being socially connected. He needs to determine and
protect his identity. According to Anna Hartnell, post-9/11 sentiments in
the US resulted in an attack on multiculturalism; the terrorist actions, as
she says, revived negative attitudes and problems that had been present in
the society for a long time if not always. Changez is confused with the
changed America and alarmed by its determination to idealize its past:

> …it seemed to me that America, too, was increasingly giving itself over to
> a dangerous nostalgia at that time [...] I had always thought of America as
> a nation that looked forward; for the first time I was struck by its
> determination to look back [...] What your fellow countrymen longed for

---

[14] Ibid., 106.
[15] Ibid., 172.
[16] Ibid., 173.

was unclear to me – a time of unquestioned dominance? of safety? of moral certainty? I did not know – but that they were scrambling to don the costumes of another era was apparent. I felt treacherous for wondering whether that era was fictitious...[17]

It is only after Erica's disappearance that Changez does not seem to confuse her with America anymore. What follows is a great disillusionment with the country and its politics. The concept of American exceptionalism is ridiculed:

'It seemed to me then – and to be honest, sir, seems to me still – that America was engaged only in posturing. As a society, you were unwilling to reflect upon the shared pain that united you with those who attacked you. You retreated into myths of your own difference, assumptions of your own superiority. And you acted out these beliefs on the stage of the world, so that the entire planet was rocked by the repercussions of your tantrums [...]. Such an America had to be stopped in the interest not only of the rest of humanity, but also in your own.'[18]

It is remarkable how the myth of American exceptionalism is being twisted here. This America is not a hero that helps the oppressed and supplies them with democracy; this America becomes more and more lost in its own mental disease and needs to be saved from itself. Changez also points out to his American listener in Lahore the high degree of hypocrisy that he finds in the official United States reactions after 9/11, something that very much recalls the writings and speeches of critics of the U.S. government. Noam Chomsky in his very controversial statement describes the degree of subordination to power after 9/11 in the U.S. as astonishing and adds:

If anyone were to say *invading Iraq is like what the Nazi war criminals were hanged for* – which happens to be correct – you are out of the debate, because some truths are not allowed. You have to say *it was blundering efforts to do good*. In fact, you say that in the face of the most awesome counter-evidence.[19]

Paul Smith in his essay *Why We Lovehate You* makes a significant

---

[17] Ibid., 130-131.
[18] Hamid, Mohsin. *The Reluctant Fundamentalist*. London: Penguin Books, 2007: 190.
[19] Endler, Tobias. *After 9/11: Leading Political Thinkers abort the word, the U.S. and Themselves*. Opladen & Farmington Hills: Barbara Budrich Publishers, 2011: 56. (emphasis original)

contribution to the discussion about hypocrisy in the divided new world after 9/11 and questions its newness. George W. Bush in his discourse differentiated between the so called 'Western World' as opposed to the 'rest' of it, including Muslim fundamentalists who then became this partly imaginary and symbolic enemy of the United States, sticking, unlike Underwood Samson, to the 'wrong' fundamentals. Smith makes the distinction between the U.S. ("you") and the rest of the world including the non-U.S. citizens living within the borders of the U.S. ("we"). Smith identifies himself as a part of the "we", i.e. non-U.S., like Changez and Chuck – the narrator and main character of Naqvi's *Home Boy* – and at the same time takes the side of the citizens of all non-western countries. His argument is that 'we' have to count on 'you' because 'we' depend on 'you' (to different degrees of course, but 'we' all do). What 'we' know though is "[t]hat 'we' cannot forever be the sufficient suppliers of the love that the narcissist finds so necessary."[20] Consequently, both Changez and Chuck eventually leave the United States and return to Pakistan.

A stranger in a suspicious environment: The study of fear

We hardly know anything about the listener of the monologue in Hamid's novel, apart from the fact that he is white, American, male, and that he used to be in the army but is now in Lahore "on business". He is scared and his anxiety is based on stereotypes about Muslims. He is reduced to these few mentioned features and therefore generalized. While reading the book one can get the impression of being addressed directly or of identifying with the symbolic white American portrayed as a stranger in a suspicious environment. This literary mechanism introduces and imposes a certain connection with the nameless listener and paradoxically, on the allegorical meta level, motivates the seemingly absurd "us vs. them" discourse. It shows reactions and fear based on stereotypes as behaviours clearly associated with either of the antipodes: West vs. Muslim. On this abstract level the presence of binary oppositions can be justified, differently to real life, that hardly ever is based on allegories. The relation between the two men talking is marked by a constant power struggle. The narrator seems to have full control over the situation, yet he is not forcing his American listener to stay, which means that the latter also does not feel entirely uncomfortable or threatened. Only sometimes he reacts abruptly to some moves, actions or sounds coming from outside or from within the

---

[20] Smith, Paul. "Why We Lovehate You." Accessed December 2, 2011. http://conconflicts.ssrc.org/USA/smith/.

conversation which betrays his self-confidence.

Changez provides descriptions of his listener's fearful reactions within the told story; they interrupt the plot, giving a feeling of constant insecurity, and consistently remind the reader of the monologue's context. Changez, in reacting to his listener's gestures and behaviours, compares his anxiety to that of an animal putting the American into a ludicrous situation:

> ...you, sir, continue to appear ill at ease. I hope you will not mind my saying so, but the frequency and purposefulness with which you glance about – a steady tick-tick-tick seeming to beat in your head as you move your gaze from one point to the next – brings to mind the behaviour of an animal that has ventured too far from its lair and is now, in unfamiliar surroundings, uncertain whether it is predator or prey![21]
>
> What bad luck! The lights have gone. But why do you leap to your feet? [...] Ah, they are back! It was nothing more than a momentary disruption. And you – to jump as though you were a mouse suddenly under the shadow of a hawk![22]
>
> I see that you have noticed the scar on my forearm (...) for I detect a certain seriousness in your expression, as though you are wondering what sort of training camp could have given a fellow from the plains such as myself cause to engage in these activities.[23]

The Reluctant Fundamentalist reveals a mutual anxiety that certainly pre-dates the attacks on the World Trade Center and the Pentagon, but 9/11 is doubtlessly an important turning point for this narrative. It is crucial for both levels of the narration: to what happens in Lahore when the two men meet, and for the story Changez tells the American while they are dining. Even if we assume that there are other (older) reasons for this vicious circle of anxieties between East and West, or Christians and Muslims, or empires and colonies, 9/11 still plays an important role in the process that Changez goes through (together with the story about Janissaries etc.). It acts as a kind of trigger or catalyst (also for the return of Erica's depression) that clarifies certain things for Changez and forces him to position himself clearly. It also physically 'eliminates' Erica from his life, making the decision of leaving the United States easier. He feels that he has to obey the new rules imposed by the new post-9/11 discourse.

Fear is one of many aspects that connect *The Reluctant Fundamentalist*

---

[21] Hamid, Mohsin. *The Reluctant Fundamentalist*. London: Penguin Books, 2007: 35.
[22] Ibid., 69.
[23] Ibid., 53.

and *Home Boy*. Chuck, the main character and narrator of Naqvi's novel experiences fear, similarly to both of the men in *The Reluctant Fundamentalist*. This fear that is a product and a method used by "them" who claim to be Chuck's enemies and who want to protect freedom with state terror, is portrayed as a specifically and exclusively American phenomenon.

The two plots complement each other; they show the dichotomy from both sides and in two different settings. One of the statements mirroring the post-9/11 fear in Naqvi's novel reads:

> What do you want me tell you, Ma? That life's changed? The city's changed? That there's sadness around every corner? There are cops everywhere? You know, there was a time when a police presence was reassuring, like at a parade or late at night, on the street, in the subway, but now I'm afraid of them. I'm afraid all the time. I feel like a marked man. I feel like an animal. It's no way to live. Maybe it's just a phase, maybe it'll pass, and things will return to normal, or maybe, I don't know, history will keep repeating itself.[24]

Hardcore Homeboys

Home Boy by H.M. Naqvi is set around the events of 9/11 and shows three young Pakistani New Yorkers, "hardcore homeboys", walking a fine line between the freedom and permissiveness of NYC and the rules of their conservative Pakistani immigrant families. They know New York like the backs of their hands, they go to parties, they are rappers and are "cool"; there is nothing here from the polite style of Changez's (self-)reflected talking. Chuck, the narrator of the story, like Changez, comes to the U.S. to study. His access to American society is through popular culture, hip-hop, slang, and being like everybody else. He comes over with dreams that after 9/11 "were turned to shit, like everybody else's."[25]

> ...but America was something else. The weather was mostly friendly, the people mostly warm, [...] you could as Mini Auntie told me once, spend ten years in Britain and not feel British, but after spending ten months in New York, you were a New Yorker, an original settler, and in no time you would be zipping uptown, downtown, crosstown, wherever, strutting, jaywalking, dispensing directions to tourists like a mandarin. "You see", you'd say, "it's quite simple: the city's like a grid".[26]

---

[24] Naqvi, H.M. *Home Boy*. New York: Shaye Areheart Books, 2009: 262.
[25] Ibid., 180.
[26] Naqvi, H.M. *Home Boy*. New York: Shaye Areheart Books, 2009: 19.

9/11 has consequences for all three of the boys in Naqvi's novel and possibly for the entire Muslim population in the United States, which is suggested by statements like the very powerful and significant opening of the novel:

> We'd become Japs, Jews, Niggers. We weren't before. We fancied ourselves boulevardiers, raconteurs, renaissance men, AC, Jimbo, and me. We were mostly self-invented and self-made and certain we had our fingers on the pulse of the great global dialectic.[27]

As a result of the post-9/11 crises, Chuck loses his job in an investment company. Lost and confused in a drastically changed America, he decides to become a taxi driver, joining the group of the "ordinary" Pakistanis, as Changez in *The Reluctant Fundamentalist* calls them. One day AC, Jimbo and Chuck take the cab and decide to visit Shaman, their friend in Connecticut whom they have not heard from for a long time. Arriving at their friend's place, the three protagonists realize that he is not there. They decide to stay anyway and wait for him. Anxious neighbours inform the FBI about "suspicious activity" going on in the house. It is the culmination point – when Chuck, AC and Jimbo are arrested and brought over to the Metropolitan Detention Center that has the ill-famed reputation of being Brooklyn's Abu Ghraib[28]. The dimension to which fear in America has grown after 9/11 becomes clear. Showing fear as a means of political and social manipulation that all U.S. citizens have been exposed to, Naqvi contributes to the previously mentioned picture of a changed and paranoid America that needs to be saved from itself. In prison, Chuck is tortured and humiliated only to eventually be released. The events of 9/11 cause a momentous shift in what it means to be an immigrant and in what it means to be a Muslim in the United States: "In prison, I finally got it. I understood that just like three black men were gangbangers, and three Jews a conspiracy, three Muslims had become a sleeper cell."[29] The multicultural society, the melting pot with all its principles, freedoms and tolerance seems to have fallen apart together with the Twin Towers. Chuck has never before been so conscious about his skin colour and general appearance; things are not 'normal' anymore: "Who then could have

---

[27] Ibid., 1.

[28] A discourse that dominated the US media around 2005. The MDC in Brooklyn has been called the local Abu Ghraib in e.g. "Democracy Now" http://www.democracynow.org/2005/3/1/brooklyns_abu_ghraib_detainees_in_post or in the New York Daily News.

[29] Naqvi, H.M. *Home Boy*. New York: Shaye Areheart Books, 2009: 153.

anticipated that it would soon not be possible for three brown men to drive across America in a rented car, even with a blonde in tow?"[30] Chuck's story could have been taken right out from the collection of non-fictional stories of Muslim immigrants edited by Tram Nguyen, who in the aftermath of September 11 decided to leave the US. All of them had been subjects to unjustifiable violence and cruelty and were examples of the US authorities violating human rights. Traumatized and shocked after the jail experience, Chuck feels homeless. Since his visa was to expire three months after he has lost his job, he is about to become an illegal immigrant or, in the language of national security, as quoted by Nguyen, a "clandestine transnational actor."[31] He decides to leave the United States.

After having been released from prison, AC and Jimbo remain in New York and there is an attempt at a partial happy ending with the conclusion that one always has a choice.

There is an interesting reaction towards the "us vs. them" dichotomy mentioned in the introduction, namely, one of complete refusal to accept it in the way it is being introduced by the government.

> AC: I care about this city. (…) Those bastards, they've fucked up my city! THEY FUCKED UP EVERYTHING![32]

After having heard one of George W. Bush's speeches on the TV, one of the boys raps:

> Yo, I thought this country was based upon freedom of speech/ Freedom of press, freedom of your own religion/ to make your own decision, now that's baloney/ Cause if I gotta play by your rules, I'm being phoney.[33]

Conclusion

Both of the novels contribute to the discussion of a changed post-9/11 America. They both question the idea of American exceptionalism and the American dream in relation to 9/11. Both offer a surprising and at the same time relieving twist at the end, proving that even in this changed world binary oppositions do not hold. In *Home Boy* it is the discovery of an obituary that explains the disappearance of Shaman: he was attending a meeting in one of the Twin Towers on September 11 and died in the

---

[30] Ibid., 87.
[31] Nguyen, Tram. *We Are All Suspects Now*. Boston: Beacon Press, 2005: XIV.
[32] Naqvi, H.M. *Home Boy*. New York: Shaye Areheart Books, 2009: 29.
[33] Ibid., 123.

catastrophe. In *The Reluctant Fundamentalist* it is the open ending that leaves the reader unsure as to whether either of the men really was honest or dishonest in his intentions. In his essay *My Reluctant Fundamentalist*[34], Mohsin Hamid writes: "People often ask me, if I am the book's Pakistani protagonist. I wonder why they never ask if I am his American listener. After all, a novel can often be a divided man's conversation with himself" — a statement that questions the legitimacy and applicability of all possible dichotomies, apart from the contradictions which we carry in ourselves.

In both novels, America is portrayed as a weak giant that invents its enemies and spreads paranoia and fear, trying to take revenge in a random and ridiculous way. Changez is mad, annoyed and disappointed with the US. He is capable of taking revenge, but also maintains a tactical distance and never stops being polite. Chuck is furious but also desperate. He leaves the U.S. and knows he is going to miss it. It is not his free choice; he feels forced to do it.

The literary power of *The Reluctant Fundamentalist* lies in its allegorical potential: it resembles a biblical parable which is meant to be re-read and discussed. It addresses a wide spectrum of individual experiences and collective tendencies and leaves space for various interpretations. It sets a universal frame or pattern that could be filled with all kinds of stories. As an allegory it retains binary oppositions as they are inscribed into the character of the story and the genre; they are "frozen", immune to time, social and cultural changes and are meant to exemplify. *Home Boy* by Naqvi complements this approach, focusing so much on individuals, their stories and personal confrontations with the changed America after the 9/11 attacks, without entering the meta-level of allegory.

Home Boy offers a complex and realistic portrait of a fictional character standing for a post-9/11 individual. In doing so, Naqvi decollectivizes the experience of 9/11 and its consequences. Changez in *The Reluctant Fundamentalist* is the universal (evil) "other" created by western dialectics. Hamid's novel criticizes unconditionally the entire new setting of post-9/11 reality. *Home Boy* tells one story and leaves hope that what happened to America is only temporary and will eventually get "sorted" and that living a dream will be possible again, even in the absence of the Twin Towers.

---

[34] Hamid, Mohsin. *My The Reluctant Fundamentalist*. http://www.powells.com/essays/mohsin.html

Bibliography

Artaud, Antonin. *The Theatre and its Double*. Grove/Atlantic Inc., 1966.

Bakhtin, Mikhail. *The Dialogic Imagination*. Austin: University of Texas Press, 1982. (Reprint) First published 1935.

Baudrillard, Jean. *The Spirit of Terrorism and Requiem for the Twin Towers*. New York: Verso, 2002.

Bush, George W. Statement by the President in His Address to the Nation. The White House. Address to a Joint Session of Congress and the American People on September 20, 2001. The White House. http://georgewbush-whitehouse.archives.gov/news/releases/2001/09/20010920-8.html

Endler, Tobias. *After 9/11: Leading Political Thinkers abort the word, the U.S. and Themselves*. Opladen &Farmington Hills: Barbara Budrich Publishers, 2011.

Flusser, Vilém. *Nachgeschichte : eine korrigierte Geschichtsschreibung*. Frankfurt am Main: Fischer-Taschenbuch-Verlag, 1997.

Hall, Stuart, ed. *Representation: Cultural Representations and Signifying Practices*. London: Sage, 2003.

Hamid, Mohsin. "My Reluctant Fundamentalist." Accessed December 2, 2011. http://www.powells.com/essays/mohsin.html. *The Reluctant Fundamentalist*. London: Penguin Books, 2007.

Hartnell, Anna. "Moving Through America: Race, Place and Resistance in Mohsin Hamid's 'The Reluctant Fundamentalist'." *Journal of Postcolonial Writing* 46, 3-4, July/September (2010): 336–348.

Kamboj, Kirti. "'The Reluctant Fundamentalist': The Assimilation Narrative Goes International." *Hyphen Magazine*. Accessed May 24, 2011. http://www.hyphenmagazine.com/print/3140.

Morey, Peter. "The Rules of the Game Have Changed: Mohsin Hamid's 'The Reluctant Fundamentalist' and Post-9/11 Fiction." *Journal of Postcolonial Writing* 47, no. 2 (2011): 135–146.

Naqvi, H.M. *Home Boy*. New York: Shaye Areheart Books, 2009.

Nguyen, Tram. *We Are All Suspects Now*. Boston: Beacon Press, 2005.

Saussure, Ferdinand de. *Course in General Linguistics*. Eds. Charles Bally and Albert Sechehaye. Trans. Roy Harris. La Salle, Illinois: Open Court. 1983.

Smith, Paul. "Why We Lovehate You." Accessed December 2, 2011. http://conconflicts.ssrc.org/USA/smith/.

Žižek, Slavoj. *Welcome to The Desert of The Real! Five Essays on 11 September and Related Dates*. London [u.a.]: Verso, 2002.

US AND THEM IN TERRY PRATCHETT'S PRE- AND POST-9/11 DISCWORLD NOVELS

DOROTA GUTTFELD

Politics and the Discworld

It is difficult to prove the existence of cause-effect links between specific real-life events and developments in Terry Pratchett's long-running series of Discworld novels. They discuss contemporary issues in a fantasy setting precisely so as to make them less clearly identifiable; according to the author, the distance engendered by the non-serious costume is necessary for them to be examined seriously[1].

Pratchett has definitely been influenced by current affairs; e.g. his Johnny Maxwell series reflects on the video-game quality of the broadcasts from the first Gulf War, trying to sensitize young readers to the humanity of the invisible victims, and the 2001 Discworld novel *The Last Hero* features what can be read as a discussion of terrorism[2]. It can be assumed that the subtext of Pratchett's later novels would also be informed by the war on terror. Yet, any interpretation of the portrayal of the Discworld as the author's response to current political situation is necessarily of a speculative character. After all, the chronology of the war on terror coincides with Pratchett's development as a writer and the natural development of his fantasy world.

With this reservation in mind, post-9/11 events could explain three noticeable changes in the way the series has been presenting the coexistence of Anglophone cultures and Others; specifically, the changes seem to include:

---

[1] John Connolly, "Terry Pratchett," interview. 2005. http://www.johnconnollybooks.com/int_pratchett.php. Originally published in *The Irish Times* as "Fantasies that deal with the real world" (December 6, 2005): 14.
[2] Eve Smith, "Civil discobedience or war, terrorism and unrest in Terry Pratchett's Discworld," *Comedy Studies*, Vol. 3 Issue 1, 2012: 29-39.

1) a new wave of radicalism and distrust between the two groups.
This is primarily presented in the stories centred around Ankh-Morpork's troubles with multi-ethnicity, featuring Vimes, the commander of the city watch. After a bumpy but essentially successful road to assimilation/acceptance that involved negotiating the identity of the immigrants and of the hosts, described in the pre-9/11 novels, in the post-9/11 books old divisions re-open between the locals and the immigrants.

2) abandoning transparently Arabic features in the portrayal of Others while transferring more abstract loci of conflict onto fantasy cultures.
During the supposed era of the Huntingtonian "clash of civilizations", Pratchett portrayed a thinly veiled and broadly painted pseudo-Arabic ("Klatchian") culture, featuring prominently in *Jingo*. Its virtual disappearance from later novels, without some threads being habitually resolved, seems an effect of 9/11; one can speculate that the portrayal lost whatever fantasy value it initially possessed as some remarks cut too close to the bone to preserve their universality. Post-9/11, the topic of cultural otherness is developed and continued in a more veiled way, for instance with the expansion of the dwarf tradition to include war-mongering clerics[3] and religious otherness.

3) introducing new characters who highlight the clash of civilizations as a fabricated conflict.
The re-examination of dwarfs and the introduction of other new groups of "Them" requires a new way of thinking about crimes and villains, progressively more difficult to handle for Vimes, the chief protagonist of the novels set in the city of Ankh-Morpork. As he grows in power to combat injustice, the power makes him (story-externally) too difficult to fit into the game without unbalancing it, and (story-internally) too much complicit in the city's politics. Thus, in some post-9/11 stories, his place is taken by characters who only have to be won over to Ankh-Morpork values – but not before they unmask some of the cynicism and evils inherent in the city's policies and values; for instance, the city's spirit of free enterprise is shown to work in the interest of the increasingly corrupt clacks company, whose wholesale destruction is imagined (but not put into effect) by Moist, the chief new protagonist. The new characters threaten

---

[3] Even if *grags* and knockermen have not been intended as such, they definitely have been read in this way; to name but one example, a review of *Thud!* mentions "the murder of 'grag' (think Ayatollah)" (Wright, Jerry. "Book Review: Terry Pratchett, *Thud!*", http://www.bewildering-stories.com/issue175/books.htm, DOA January 2013).

and renew the city's values, letting Pratchett stress his message of class rather than ethnicity being the main divisive factor we should examine.

In order to illustrate the above-mentioned changes in more detail, one needs to first depict the pre-9/11 co-existence of Discworld's "Us" and "Them" in Pratchett's earlier novels.

Discworld's "Us" and "Them"

Pratchett's Discworld has regions to mirror various parts of the real world, which allows the novels to discuss a range of contemporary socio-political issues. All kinds of enterprising or rejected "others" gravitate towards the world's equivalent of the "Big Apple"[4]. The city's resulting transformations lead Ankh-Morpork away from stereotypical pseudo-medievalism towards modernity, enhancing its potential to mirror real-life phenomena. One of the issues featured in the increasingly complex depiction of the city is immigration and the multicultural nature of the emerging future. The resulting diversity allows the author to discuss issues of racism, stereotyping, and ethnic and religious hostility, without directly referring to real-life identities.

Despite their fantastic character, Others in Ankh-Morpork are naturally defined by the series' origins as a thinly disguised parody of fantasy. Ankh-Morpork has its roots in the prototypical pseudo-medieval and pseudo-European fantasy setting, with ostensibly English-speaking inhabitants and a matching dominant culture. Only much later does the author begin the "development of Discworld's chief City [...] – initially perhaps no more than a nod to Fritz Leiber's Lankhmar – into an intricately sleazy metropolis with all the bustle and stench of Victorian London"[5]. Consequently, the standard represented by the first generation of Ankh-Morpork protagonists and by the city in general is human, white, European, Anglophone, and largely secular, while "otherness" may be defined as any departure from that mould – usually concerning the notions of law, religion and gender.

---

[4] Terry Pratchett and Stephen Briggs. *The Discworld Companion* (London: Gollancz, 1994), 24. All uses of italics in quotations from works authored or co-authored by Pratchett are original.

[5] John Clute and David Langford, "Pratchett, Terry," *The Encyclopedia of Science Fiction.* 2011-2012, accessed October 2012, http://sf-encyclopedia.com/entry/pratchett_terry.

Attitude towards immigration

In view of the correspondence between Ankh-Morpork and London/New York, one can read the "Others" migrating into the city as images of the real cities' various diasporas, including the substantial Arabic communities. Of the foreign groups appearing in the series, the most detailed and interesting portrayal is that of the race/culture of dwarfs, initially largely explained through the hybrid figure of Carrot, a human raised by dwarfs. Although the dwarf presence in the city grows from volume to volume, humans and dwarfs initially avoid interaction[6]. Immigrants are, simultaneously, vital to the city's development, and left to their own devices; expected to keep apart and under fire for being different. Difference is perceived from a double perspective of fear and superiority. Dwarfs are supposed to be, simultaneously, a burden to the city, but also inhuman in that they "work away like ants"; "incapable of any rational thought and so bloody shrewd at the same time" (*Men at Arms*, 118). Openly racist remarks are made less frequently by the growing non-human presence in the city and the visible support multiculturalism receives from the city's ruler, but a hypocritical version of political correctness emerges instead; the use of adjectives such as "ethnic" or "cultural" conceals the existence of racial tension and in fact reinforces a mental apartheid.

Faced with calculated detachment, the minorities develop separate social networks, granting support, work, communication and even jurisdiction. In *Men at Arms*, the parallel life becomes apparent to the policeman Vimes as he visits the family of a dwarf murder victim only to find himself powerless and redundant; the dwarfs have their own sources of information, and apparently trust their own means of ensuring security or enforcing justice (*Men at Arms*, 102-103).

The resulting feeling of humiliation and ineffectiveness makes the protagonist intensify his efforts to prove the city watch is neither as impotent nor as racist as believed. Vimes is moved by patriotism and unique devotion to the city, which overrules any racial prejudice; he is a character for whom the city "is a Woman" and his beloved woman, in turn, "was a city"[7]. A similar motivation to support multiculturalism is shared by two more characters: the idealist Carrot, a scion of the city's kings, bound to the city's fate, and his *realpolitik* counterpart, the city's Patrician (*Men at Arms*, 375), who requests the watch to take on

---

[6] Terry Pratchett, *Men at Arms* (London: Corgi, 1994), 50.
[7] Terry Pratchett, *Guards! Guards!* (London: Corgi, 1990), 94 and 407.

representatives of various minorities. Enforcing daily interaction proves a successful strategy: in personal contact with members of different groups, the citizens are gradually won over to the idea of integration by profit, the driving force of the city.

Changes in the host culture

A major incentive for interracial contacts comes from the spending and manufacturing power of the growing minorities. In *Men at Arms*, the city's notorious peddler, representing Ankh-Morpork's spirit, starts catering to dwarfs and trolls (*Men at Arms*, 190), whose combined impact on the city's economy is such that in time they become one of the most recognizable assets of the metropolis. In *Interesting Times* an Oriental despot dreams of subduing "Ankh-Morpork, with its busy dwarfs and its grasp, above all, of machinery"[8]. Generally, the "Ankh-Morpork way" (*Interesting Times*, 85) of dealing with immigrants seems to be a combination of self-interested materialism and the city's experience in converting newcomers to urban life. The qualities signalled by the term, used by the pseudo-Oriental tyrant, make the city difficult to rule and, specifically, to decree tolerance and equality, but they also enable true integration. While feudal lore rules the pseudo-Russian Uberwald, and hierarchical bureaucracy sustains the Oriental Agatean empire, the Western city of Ankh-Morpork derives strength from its social flexibility. Pratchett's protagonists, especially those ones whose life is closely bound to the city – Vimes, Carrot, and the Patrician – are occasionally frustrated by the irreverence, ingenuity, and fierce individualism of the city's inhabitants, but always ultimately embrace these qualities as the city's valuable heritage. In the later novels, especially with the emergence of post-9/11 protagonists, this approval for profit-oriented individualism is additionally often tempered with the demand for social responsibility.

As understood by the Oriental despot who attempts to emulate his enemies, "the Ankh-Morpork way" involves trusting abilities rather than social standing (*Interesting Times*, 85); indeed, one of the greatest recurrent evils in the volumes set in Ankh-Morpork is the idea of hereditary privilege, especially monarchy, as a dangerously appealing narrative that is nevertheless fundamentally at odds with the freethinking, critical, enterprising spirit of the modern metropolis. Since the city respects individual merit and success, it opens up chances for advancement to immigrants and those locals who are ready to note the

---

[8] Terry Pratchett, *Interesting Times* (London: Corgi, 1995), 85.

opportunities they bring. For instance, by *Feet of Clay* a human entrepreneur adopts a dwarf surname to capitalize on the popularity of the dwarf-made metalwork.

Soon, Vimes is ready to admit that the official policy that "alloys are stronger" seems to be effective[9], although the size and social mobility of the dwarf population still surprises him and some of his human colleagues. Colon, one of Vimes's oldest friends, is less eager to move with the times and would much prefer to withdraw to some imaginary rural idyll reminiscent of a simpler, golden age; the sergeant's version of good old white England, however, is humorously revealed to be entirely at odds with the man's actual urban lifestyle, demonstrating that there is no turning back from the future of constant transformation and adaptation.

Vimes himself is determined not to fall behind. It is painful for him to find there are some areas in the city and in the city's life where he feels awkward and uninformed but he starts learning "dwarfish" to keep up with the changing situation. In *The Fifth Elephant*, it comes as a shock to him that the character of the city to which he is married has changed forever. It is now "the biggest dwarf city outside Uberwald"[10]. By his effort to learn and insistence that "private dwarf things" are his concern too, Vimes asserts his responsibility for all Ankh-Morpork citizens (*The Fifth Elephant*, 22), while Carrot, the human-dwarf hybrid, is now uncharacteristically reluctant to reveal the inner life of the dwarf neighbourhoods.

The reversal of roles is symptomatic of the later stage in the relationship between humans and dwarfs. While WASP-like natives start to feel uncomfortable about the existence of the separate structures developed by dwarfs and require that dwarfs accept the same laws and obligations, immigrants have by now grown accustomed to their parallel life and sometimes resist integration from a position of power or the isolationism that will especially surface in post-9/11 novels.

Changes among immigrants

As the city of Ankh-Morpork is changed by its prolonged relationship with immigrants, the immigrants' culture is also changed by the Ankh-Morpork experience. This concerns not only the dwarfs actually inhabiting the metropolis, but gradually also dwarf communities abroad, as they are faced with changes in customs, religion, politics, and the very definition of being a dwarf.

---

[9] Terry Pratchett, *Feet of Clay* (London: Corgi, 1997), 224.
[10] Terry Pratchett, *The Fifth Elephant* (London: Corgi, 2000), 41.

In the first city watch volume, Carrot, raised as a model dwarf, on arriving in the city is shocked to learn the dwarf community conducts itself in a way unbecoming "proper standards of dwarf behaviour" (*Guards! Guards!*, 79) and immediately intervenes to end a brawl by reminding the fighters of their parents back home. The scene hints at several important features of dwarf immigration. First, the dwarfs in question are depicted as relatively young; second, they are apparently exploring new opportunities granted them by city life; third, and most crucially, as an invisible divide excludes them from the city community and emigration cuts them off from their homelands, they react by performing exaggerated versions of heroic-age dwarfishness, an an in-your-face re-enactment of a time when they would have been fearsome warriors rather than migrant workers. Using the time away from home to escape traditional roles enforced by parents and turning towards the mythologized identity of their ancient forebears do not seem to be contradictory but, as the narrator suggests, rather complementary reactions (*Guards! Guards!*, 77). The two responses to life in Ankh-Morpork – discovering new possibilities for enjoyment and self-fulfilment, and, contrariwise, trying to reassert traditional heritage in the face of surrounding otherness – surface in the changing perception of gender, and of the dwarf guardians of tradition.

The issue of dwarf gender is first seriously introduced by Cheery, a dwarf member of the city watch, who decides to proclaim her femininity, since ostensible genderlessness no longer seems tolerable once she discovers the many freedoms offered by the city (*Feet of Clay*, 113). Cheery works alongside a female werewolf officer, who – having migrated to the city in an attempt to escape bloody family heritage – is determined to live her own life as a girlfriend to the human/dwarf Carrot, regardless of expectations, stereotypes and upbringing. Influenced by this example, Cheery decides to proclaim her gender, although she is determined not to compromise her connection to dwarf heritage.

The issue of open femininity is closely connected to power relations within the dwarf community and the authority of the *grags* and knockermen, which also fluctuates due to pressures from the Ankh-Morpork lifestyle. These initially noble and spiritual occupations have been usurped by powerful dynasties and backed by the Discworld equivalent of petrodollars; consequently, any change that could undermine the traditional *grag*-mandated lifestyle is a political and financial threat to these fortunes. As Vimes learns in *The Fifth Elephant*, initially a knockerman's influence stemmed from visions experienced in mines and their reputation as a holy, self-sacrificing person, who performed the duty of clearing the mines of explosive gas, but with time the dynasties of knockermen gained hereditary political power (*The Fifth Elephant*, 236). The knockermen are still an important source of authority to the traditional, "deep-down" dwarfs. Their isolationist and impermeable attitude is symbolized by their traditional garb, originally devised to withstand explosions, but now worn by the traditionalists to prevent contact with the outside world (*The Fifth Elephant*, 232). The position of knockermen is jeopardized by an invention made in Ankh-Morpork, which renders their traditional services and the mystique surrounding their profession obsolete, leaving only unfounded authority, now increasingly resented by the more egalitarian city dwarfs (*The Fifth Elephant*, 237). *Grags*, dwarf lore masters wearing the same costume, are community leaders of quasi-religious authority, whose task is to interpret and preside over the application of dwarf law (*The Fifth Elephant*, 62). Like knockermen, they too constitute a privileged caste, their wealth based on controlling valuable natural resources (*The Fifth Elephant*, 61-62), although their chief power comes from the tradition they represent and, since their fields of expertise involve marriages and burials as well as contracts, from the power to impose their definition of a dwarf.

Cultivating a time-honoured lifestyle and wielding the power of traditional law, the deep-downers and their leaders not only appeal to that part of a city dwarf's psyche that still lives "back home" but also threaten the space of compromise that city dwarfs have developed over time. Ankh-Morpork dwarfs send money and letters to families abroad and strive to keep some of their parents' traditions in return for the myth of still being part of the homeland. The deep-down candidate for the office of Uberwald's dwarf king, plans to sever this umbilical cord and pronounce Ankh-Morpork dwarfs "non-dwarfs", excluding them from the symbolic community – an action which could be likened to excommunication, forcing the city dwarfs to rely on human law and give up their special double status (*The Fifth Elephant*, 244-245).

The Fifth Elephant, introducing knockermen, is the city watch novel following *Jingo*, and its description of the traditionalist dwarf culture, including the quasi-religious leaders, follows the earlier introduction and then virtual disappearance of the pseudo-Arabic Klatchians in *Jingo*. Although the Klatchian immigrants return to the city after the novel's political crisis has been resolved, none of them applies for work in the city watch, which is the typical scenario for other minorities. Indeed none of them ever appears as a major character again, and the issue of coexistence is never again discussed for the rest of the cycle. The detailed portrayal of the traditionalist dwarf country in *The Fifth Elephant* seems to inherit some characteristics previously attributed to the Klatchians or associated with their pseudo-Oriental culture. The resulting "re-othering" of the once assimilated dwarfs so that they take the place of the Klatchians continues in the post-9/11 *Thud!*, where it is the traditionalists who become a notable power in the city itself.

Paradoxically, in their eagerness to keep (or even over-perform) outward signs of dwarfishness, the generally progressive city dwarfs seem to empower deep-downers, whose conservative views now become a cause for concern. The definition of a dwarf for those who are traditionalists is much more restrictive than for those used to city life, as exemplified by the cases of Cheery and Carrot, the hybrid figure who no longer feels accepted as "a real dwarf" in the post-9/11 novel *Thud!*[11], when many young dwarfs, who have never seen their mythical homeland, prove to be particularly impressionable and eager to embrace radical manifestations of the traditional lifestyle – a desire that can be easily manipulated.

Post-9/11 estrangement

In *Thud!* Vimes investigates a crime by fundamentalist dwarfs and learns some of those involved were in fact city-born dwarfs manipulated by *grags*. One of the arrested, now sporting a deep-downer's costume, "went off to study in the mountains more than three months ago, against his parents' wishes" (*Thud!*, 298). Another, betrayed and left for dead to assure secrecy, "was [not] interested in the politics […] He just [...] wanted to feel like a real dwarf" (*Thud!*, 300). If deep-downers are viewed as representing radical Islam, the local dwarfs implicated in the crime could be equivalents of British and US-born terrorist suspects; by 2005, when the novel was published, the repatriation of Guantanamo detainees to the UK was a much publicized issue.

The *grag* influence causes unrest in the city and opens up issues the human populace, represented by Vimes, had considered long resolved. The beginning of *Thud!* describes how young dwarfs again try to re-enact a mythologized, larger-than-life version of dwarfishness in the circumstances of their diaspora life, and depicts *grags* stirring unrest, striving to undo what daily interracial contacts have achieved throughout the years (*Thud!* 36-38). The renewed tensions cause a backlash among the human populace. Watchmen once more voice resentments that were almost forgotten in two previous watch volumes (*Thud!* 67), and Vimes once more feels alien in his city, betrayed in his sense of tolerance and

---

[11] Terry Pratchett, *Thud!* (London: Corgi, 2006), 71.

open-mindedness (*Thud!* 77). In the days of growing radicalism, when it is "no time to be mostly a dwarf", Vimes finds some of his own officers believe loyalty to their dwarf community overrides that to the city and the chain of command (*Thud!* 70). Even Carrot, the model officer who used to insist the watch's responsibility is towards all citizens regardless of race, contracts some doubts about the legality of investigating murder in an isolationist community of deep-downers (*Thud!* 70-71).

By the end of the novel the status quo is recovered in that the culprits are revealed to have come from outside the city and Vimes's frustration to have been magnified by a supernatural entity. However, absolved by the magical nature of his anger, Vimes delivers a powerful rant not against the foreign fundamentalists themselves, but against the seemingly passive dwarf populace in general who let themselves be culturally, religiously and politically blackmailed into following the ideology promoted by the conservative *grags*. The watchman is temporarily convinced he has seen the real face of his dwarf compatriots, who have defiled the city's magnanimous offer to include them in the fabric of its society (*Thud!* 297-298).

For the ruler of Ankh-Morpork, such mounting frustration of human citizens is an important issue. With its growing size, the dwarf populace becomes not just an important factor in the city's economy, but also in its politics[12]. Ankh-Morpork relies on resources imported from abroad and often supplied by dwarf populations; any controversy between foreign and city dwarfs, or any accusation of racial oppression has the potential to disrupt these relations. The city's ruler himself is also hostage to the public perception of his support for multiculturalism. Any backlash against racial minorities can be used by the internal opposition to depose him and institute a less "progressive" regime – just as the issue of immigration is repeatedly used in British politics to muster the support of those opposed to "letting everything in".

Hegemonic power and imperial guilt

Vimes becomes aware of geopolitics as he gradually climbs the social ladder. As he becomes commander of the city watch, a duke, landowner and, of necessity, a diplomat, he discovers links between international issues and daily problems in his home city, learns how others perceive Ankh-Morpork and develops mixed feelings about the city's use of its military, economic, and cultural power.

---

[12] Terry Pratchett, *The Truth* (London: Corgi, 2001), 45.

The first international case investigated by Vimes is the crime of staging an assassination of a Klatchian prince on a visit to Ankh-Morpork to provoke a war in *Jingo*. Vimes observes how chauvinism is used in both countries involved to engineer not just support for war, but to effect internal coups; he also discovers his city's imperialist past and feels responsible for preventing another attempt at a military hegemony[13], a vision resurrected to divert the public's attention from internal problems. Opposing it, Vimes reasserts the responsibility of his watch for all Ankh-Morpork's citizens, including the Klatchian immigrants, and his responsibility as a citizen for the policy of his city. However, in attempting not to yield to the negative stereotypes promoted by the city's warlords, he falls into another mental trap. Driven by postcolonial guilt, he refuses to think badly of Klatchians to the point of denying them individuality and full humanity (*Jingo*, 342) and at times is perceived as racist despite his efforts.

The fact that other nations might have a critical opinion of Ankh-Morpork's "unthinking arrogance" (*Jingo*, 345) is impressed on Vimes on his first official foreign assignment. At the beginning of his ambassadorial trip to Uberwald he needs to be reminded that not all "good guys" have to be supporters of Ankh-Morpork's policies (*The Fifth Elephant*, 216-217). Faced with open criticism of Ankh-Morpork, Vimes reacts with "patriotic" exhortations of the freedoms offered by the city: freedom from feudal violence perpetuated by werewolves (*The Fifth Elephant*, 324), and freedom to pursue individual happiness in ways impossible in the traditional dwarf society, in response to the accusations of the dwarf king, who objects to Ankh-Morpork's cultural hegemony and the brain drain affecting his country (*The Fifth Elephant*, 231). Vimes cites immigration as proof of his homeland's redeeming features, suggesting the dwarf king is out of touch with the real needs and interests of many of his countrymen (*The Fifth Elephant*, 232). For all intents and purposes, Vimes practically claims his city, like the US, will accommodate "your tired, your poor, your huddled masses yearning to breathe free".

Nevertheless, Vimes experiences moments of dismay as the city's ambassador. He expected diplomacy to be about values, but instead his mission gains Ankh-Morpork a monetary reward in natural resources, just as the dwarf king suspected (*The Fifth Elephant*, 407). Inside his embassy, Vimes is shocked to find a secret chamber filled with documents suggesting that access to natural resources is the driving force behind foreign policy (*The Fifth Elephant*, 271-272). Vimes also experiences

---

[13] Terry Pratchett, *Jingo* (London: Corgi, 1998), 28-29.

imperialist guilt about introducing changes that, he expects, will destroy the proud, ancient dwarf tradition (*The Fifth Elephant*, 395). However, like in the case of the Klatchians, he seems overprotective – and, in fact, patronizing – towards the Other. When he believes an artefact made in Ankh-Morpork will undermine the foundations of the dwarf culture, he denies this culture the very adaptability known from the Ankh-Morpork diaspora. While the dwarfs might not like Ankh-Morpork's dominance, they are perfectly capable of adjusting and they give the representative of the proud power an allegorical lesson in flexibility (*The Fifth Elephant*, 446) by embracing the "grandfather's axe" paradox: though each part of the weapon be replaced, the whole may, spiritually, retain its identity.

In comparison to these pre-9/11 stories, *Monstrous Regiment* offers a change in perspective, as Vimes, the city's special envoy to a war-torn region, is relegated to the role of a mastermind behind the scenes. Previously Vimes, representing the virtuous side of Ankh-Mopork, would learn about others but ultimately bestow them with the city's values; this time, the focal characters are natives of a fiercely chauvinistic country whose suicidal politics the metropolis needs to oppose for the sake of regional stability. Although Vimes is in a position of power, the new characters seem to have more faith in the newly discovered "Western" values, and demand that the city follow what it preaches. The envoy has grown cynical about his mission; he realizes his task hinges on a regime change in the third-world state and is not motivated by noble sentiments, but rather by the city's financial and political interests[14]. In the end, he is able to offer a solution for their country that his conscience can accept and withdraws the city's support for a "Western-educated" local despot, whom Ankh-Morpork has previously helped to arm (*Monstrous Regiment*, 205). However, although he might have been personally moved by the courage of the local protagonists, Vimes bluntly explains his decision in terms of geopolitics and public support generated by the media (*Monstrous Regiment*, 460-461).

To summarize, the post-9/11 solution for Borogravia depends not just on Vimes, the story's puppet-master, but on local protagonists refashioning their own country. Some features of the war in Borogravia can be interpreted as pertinent to Iraq and Afghanistan during the US interventions (e.g. the media dominating the perception of the war, or the Western powers overthrowing leaders they had previously supported); interpreted in this light, the novel's conclusion would be that "Western" standards cannot be successfully brought on bayonets. Vimes can act

---

[14] Terry Pratchett, *Monstrous Regiment* (London: Corgi, 2004), 32.

behind the scenes, but it is up to the new Borogravian characters to introduce order, depose their belligerent god, and achieve gender equality, resolving three main loci of conflict with the West.

Loci of conflict: law, religion, gender

Despite the obvious differences between the dwarf states, the Oriental Klatch, and the rural Borogravia, the three cultures with which Vimes is confronted on his foreign missions share a number of characteristics enabling a distinction between Us and Them. Vimes is an obvious representative of the metropolis, his watch embodying the city microcosm, characterised by three features: jurisprudence, secularity, and gender equality. Indeed, issues of law, religion, and gender, feature prominently in the image of the West's Others.

In Uberwald, the law is substituted by feudal lore and custom granting rights to the powerful and leaving the lowly unprotected. In Klatch, Vimes is highly critical of the law of the desert, which requires quick justice rather than formal trials; it is to his Klatchian counterpart, too, that Vimes wishes to prove the independence of law from the political authorities. In Borogravia, apart from committees of "[p]rodnoses, curtain-twitchers and vigilantes" imposing religiously understood virtue, there is no civilian system of justice (*Monstrous Regiment*, 32). The description brings to mind the *mutaween*, police squads enforcing *sharia* morality in countries such as Saudi Arabia, or Afghanistan during the Taliban rule, and links the issue of law to the issue of religion.

Another crucial difference between Ankh-Morpork protagonists and the local cultures is the attitude to religion. While dwarfs deny being religious, the mysticism and ritual permeating their traditional lifestyle and the role of laws derived from the *deus otiosus* called Tak suggest otherwise; importantly, since the post-9/11 *Thud!* dwarfs have been explicitly attributed with a reverence towards the written word and advanced to the position of 'people of the book', as if to substitute for the vanished quasi-Arabic Klatchians. As for the Klatchians themselves, their religious zealotry is signalled as two immigrants start a sectarian fight (*Jingo*, 160), ultimately harking back to different translations of a single word in their religion's holy text. A similar religious war is mentioned in a footnote referring to "the Schism of the Turnwise Ones and the deaths of some 25,000 people in the ensuing jihad"[15].

---

[15] Terry Pratchett, *Mort* (London: Corgi, 1988), 128.

Since Borogravia's society is the only one of the three to be described from within, the country's religion receives the most detailed description. It is extremely oppressive, with a constantly expanding number of phenomena viewed as "abominable". Borogravia's god dislikes "pictures of living creatures" (*Monstrous Regiment*, 76), gender equality (*Monstrous Regiment*, 80), and modern technology, such as the clack's telegraph (*Monstrous Regiment*, 191). A resolution of Borogravia's problems is only possible once the old querulous god is pronounced dead and the harsh commandments are attested to have come not from him, but " [f]rom your fear [...] from the part that hates the Other, that will not change. They come from the sum of all your pettiness and stupidity and dullness. You fear tomorrow, and you've made your fear your god" (*Monstrous Regiment*, 362). Vimes, in his capacity of an envoy representing Ankh-Morpork, which used to be an abomination (an equivalent of Khomeini's "the Great Satan"), offers to help the country find a new god that will ensure stability and, presumably, suit Ankh-Morpork's interests (*Monstrous Regiment*, 458).

All the three cultures contrasted with that of Ankh-Morpork, represented by Vimes, are also depicted as conservative about gender roles. The dwarf attitude to femininity has already been discussed above. In Klatch, in a city comparable to Ankh-Morpork, the women are expected to keep to themselves and out of the way of men. In *Monstrous Regiment*, gender inequality is motivated by religious fundamentalism, which prevents women from wearing trousers (*Monstrous Regiment*, 80), a seemingly marginal question of clothes translated into social dependence (*Monstrous Regiment*, 120), by a similar token as the *burqa* has become a highly political topic.

Similarities between dwarfs, Borogravians and Klatchians are visible whenever they come into conflict with Ankh-Morpork standards. Indeed, some conversations and incidents in the novels featuring these cultures seem exact counterparts. For instance, in climactic scenes both dwarf and Borogravian women are revealed to perpetuate gender discrimination themselves. Also, the argumentation used by the Borogravian military to revile Ankh-Morpork and the counter-argument used by one of the recruits closely mirror the exchange between Vimes and the dwarf king in *The Fifth Elephant*. Crucially, the argument arising from mass immigration, once raised by Vimes, is now voiced by representatives of "Them", whose actions ultimately promise to change their oppressive culture from within (*Monstrous Regiment*, 70-71). Symmetrically, some of the arguments used against Ankh-Morpork are identical to grievances voiced by those city inhabitants who are opposed to "letting everything in" and forming a multiracial society. Indeed, the mentality of the Borogravian god is likened to the bigotry and racism of the Ankh-Morporkians writing to the local newspaper (*Monstrous Regiment*, 29). In this way, the author stresses that real divisions do not run along ethnic or religious lines, but across them, between those who "will not change" and wish to regulate the lives of others, and those who are open to compromise and ready to consider the "grandfather axe" scenario of adaptation.

Temptations of control

Confronted with obstinate, uncompromising individuals at home and abroad, and invested with considerable authority and a strong moral sense, Vimes faces numerous temptations to abuse his powers. Though he has the means to intervene in the name of what he sees as progress and stability, he repeatedly refuses to encroach on his self-imposed code of conduct and overstep his function as the keeper of peace.

It is difficult not to see Pratchett's 1997 decision to confront Vimes with stereotypes about the Klatch and growing nationalism as a reaction to popular theses about the supposed clash of Western and Oriental civilization. The later virtual disappearance of Klatch from Pratchett's political map might be a move to substitute fantasy Others for an imagery that suddenly became too obvious and direct. Given that the Discworld lacks an equivalent for America and Ankh-Morpork seems an image of New York as well as London, the city's intervention in Borogravia in the 2003 novel *Monstrous Regiment* might to a certain extent illustrate the author's attitude to American missions in Afghanistan or Iraq, as some of the jokes suggest (e.g. "shock and awe", *Monstrous Regiment*, 140). By the same token it is difficult not to read Vimes's temptations and the limitations to his peacekeeping role as a political issue, related to the role of the West, and most prominently the US, as a global policeman, and the related discussion on the justifiability of torture, the shifting balance of security and freedom visible in the Patriot Act of 2001, and the appropriate response to terrorism. Pratchett's novels examine the difference between law enforcement and military action, the treatment of suspects and convicts, and the curtailment of citizens' rights.

Regarding the first issue, in *Jingo* and *Night Watch* Vimes insists on distinguishing policing from the military, i.e. political, action (e.g. in *Jingo*, 165-166). While soldiers take orders from political authorities, the rule of law should be a way to check political power. Throughout the sub-series the watch progressively extends the rule of law while avoiding solutions based on violence or authoritarianism, repeatedly opposing powerful interest groups, including political and military leaders. Vimes believes "there must be a policeman, even for kings" (*Jingo*, 345) as war does not suspend the law; indeed, it is itself the ultimate crime, and the mighty who benefit from it, including politicians, should be brought to justice (*Jingo*, 346-247).

However, as his influence grows in later novels, Vimes himself sometimes wishes for a power to disregard the law so as to closely monitor and approve of or prevent actions of the city's inhabitants likely to destabilize the situation in the metropolis. In *The Truth*, he is dissatisfied with the newly invented press and would like to effectively introduce censorship (*The Truth*, 156-157). In *Thud!*, whose publication coincided with the controversy surrounding *Jyllands-Posten's* Mohammad cartoons, the murder of the director Theo van Gogh, and the related discussion of censorship, Vimes objects when memorial post stamps threaten to cause unrest among the city's minorities, although their printing is perfectly legal (*Thud!* 39), and feels an urge to preventively arrest dwarf hate clerics. Such impulses to curtail civic rights appear in the post-9/11 novels, although it is difficult to tell apart the effects of real-life inspirations and of the fictitious character gradually rising in power. Regardless of their origin, the temptations are always countered either from the outside, or by Vimes's internal policeman – his conscience.

Finally, Vimes is vehement about the letter of the law when it comes to the treatment of criminals. In *Making Money*, the watch are shown to maintain a strict procedure for prisoner handovers, and in *Feet of Clay* Vimes states: " [o]nly crimes could take place in darkness. Punishment had to be done in the light" (*Feet of Clay*, 393-394). The stress placed on transparency is best visible in *Night Watch*, where Vimes opposes political arrests and torture used to force confessions of conspiracy. He insists that the police document and track the handovers of all the arrested, so that nobody can disappear from custody records[16] in a Discworld equivalent of a black site. Although the same message is present throughout the series, in later novels it becomes more pronounced: if the policeman is to maintain peace and protect the law, he must first police himself and set limits to the authorized use of violence. Translated into real-world terms, this could be read as a statement on the role of the West, and most likely the United States, as an exporter of democracy and the rule of law.

---

[16] Terry Pratchett, *Night Watch* (London: Corgi, 2002), 135.

Temptations of expansion

The urge to expand the reach of "Western" values can be symbolized by the image of the clacks. The system of semaphore towers plays an ambiguous role in the series, and Vimes enters into an uneasy relationship with this visible sign of his city's hegemony. The array of towers, stretching across the continent, represents values associated with the metropolis brought into what seems the heart of darkness, or otherness:

> There was a line across the map: the progress of the semaphore towers. It was mathematically straight, a statement of intellect in the crowding darkness of miles and miles of bloody Uberwald. (*The Fifth Elephant*, 100)

Clacks are a means of exporting the Ankh-Morpork way of life; they are also synonymous with modernity and progressiveness, and used to distinguish between "us" and "them". In the description of a local autocrat who initially enjoys the city's support, backing the clacks system appears side by side with education, secularism and modernization (*Monstrous Regiment*, 31). In terms of real world phenomena, semaphores could be read as representing the media, technology and business complex used to export Western values, but also capable of doubling as tools of cultural and monetary hegemony.

Both the werewolf supremacist movement and the nationalistic/theocratic Borogravia declare war on the values of the Ankh-Morporkian globalization, free trade and progress by destroying the clacks towers. In both cases, representatives of the city, although not uncritical of their homeland, experience a rush of pride when faced with opponents. In *Monstrous Regiment*, the Ankh-Morpork journalist boldly approaches Borogravian soldiers and asserts his city has gone to war to stop "bandit activity" endangering communication (*Monstrous Regiment*, 246). For Vimes in *The Fifth Elephant*, the clacks come to embody a sense of belonging and support, reaffirming the existence of values that he tries to stand up for (*The Fifth Elephant*, 387).

Indeed, the semaphores become associated with the equality, relatively democratic standards and the spirit of free enterprise that the city itself represents. The history of the semaphore's development depicts Ankh-Morpork as a land of opportunity where "everybody who could put together a pole, a couple of gargoyles and some second-hand windmill machinery was in on the business" (*The Fifth Elephant*, 121), where cooperating with a gargoyle would be perfectly natural, and where any "bright young man" can make a difference (*The Fifth Elephant*, 78). The description of the semaphore stresses that it is used by individuals and in the interest of individual profit rather than by the state and for matters of the state alone; by individuals who are free to rationally choose from a number of options; and by the middle class rather than the aristocracy (*The Fifth Elephant*, 120-121).

However, the aim of the " [k]nowledge, information, power, words... flying through the air, invisible" (*The Fifth Elephant*, 78) is not necessarily innocent. They fly above the heads of local people, in the interest of "the whole world" that has "never cared. [...] And now it wants to rip the top off the country and take what's underneath" (*The Fifth Elephant*, 183). The political meaning of power represented by the clacks is implied in a scene where Vimes imagines the ripples caused by his actions, the image of kneeling Uberwald dwarfs juxtaposed with the notion of an Ankh-Morpork influence spreading by means of the semaphore system (*The Fifth Elephant*, 390).

Although the values transmitted and symbolized by the clacks include law as opposed to the rule of force, the clacks company itself functions largely outside the city and seems to have adapted to the lawless surroundings. They employ a private army and are prepared to make an example of anybody who could threaten the system (*The Fifth Elephant*, 261). This ambiguous nature of the clacks is highlighted with the introduction of another, post-9/11, protagonist into the series, an immigrant from Uberwald who becomes an accomplished conman in the big city. The clacks company is described in more detail and revealed to be a financial empire based on crime and the exploitation of its workers, run by a ruthless tycoon. If the clacks used to be an epitome of the city's power, this sense of power is now shown to, at least partially, result from "greed, arrogance, and wilful stupidity"; the company's apparent omnipotence comes from the position of an unregulated monopolist, able to use corporate-speak to cover up offences committed in the name of profit[17] in perversion of Ankh-Morpork freedoms.

Temptations of violence

Once Moist, himself a reformed anti-social egoist, embraces a more responsible lifestyle, he is immediately scandalised by the injustice represented by the clacks company. The new, post-9/11 protagonist considers the idea of destroying the towers. Having contacted a group of anti-system hackers, he learns of the possibility of turning the clacks technology against itself; the technology heretofore described as a product

---

[17] Terry Pratchett, *Going Postal* (New York: Harpertorch, 2005), 307.

of Ankh-Morpork's multicultural genius, a sign of progress in the wilderness of nature and barbarity, that now serves "a monster, eating people" (*Going Postal*, 338). He envisions the destruction of the semaphore towers in a vision that must be striking if read in the post-9/11 context:

> Fire from the sky... […] One after another, the towers failed. Some burned when the shutter boxes broke free and smashed on the cabin roofs, spilling blazing oil. There was no hope of fighting fire in a wooden box sixty feet up in the air; you slid down the suicide line and legged it to a safe distance to watch the show.
>
> Fourteen towers were burning before someone took their hands off the keys. And then what? […]
>
> Moist awoke, the Grand Trunk burning in his head. (*Going Postal*, 343-344)

However, like so many immigrants before him, the protagonist has become co-opted by the Ankh-Morpork society and in its interest he finds "a way to destroy the company but leave the towers standing" (*Going Postal*, 364) and expose the crimes of the clacks magnates without indiscriminate destruction (*Going Postal*, 365). He hands the towers, which corporate bosses previously hijacked, back to the workers and inventors, a victory that heralds a new, socially responsible economy, where "profit turn up[s] spread around the whole of society" (*Going Postal*, 384).

The same message of reform rather than confrontation seems to concern the non-human minorities. Moist, an advocate of evolutionary change with respect to the clacks, becomes engaged to the head of a trust helping golems find a place in the Ankh-Morpork society, and his post office, which opposes the semaphore company, becomes an equal opportunities employer for the ostracized golems. One of the most radically "other" groups, the golems insist on liberating themselves from slavery by operating strictly within the legal system and refuse to "free their comrades by force and bloody revolution" (*Feet of Clay*, 407). If the golems have an enemy, it is the same one that Vimes and Moist encounter: the rich and privileged who wish to prosper by "cutting corners" and exploiting the underprivileged, native or immigrant. Ordinary semaphore crews, from whom corporate tycoons stole the clacks, have been worked to their deaths, and workers are exploited in sweatshops by the very men who also use golems and plot the overthrow of the city rule that promotes multicultural coexistence. The betrothal of two causes: freeing golems and reclaiming the clacks (i.e. the towers representing values perverted by big business), signals the true line of conflict in the novels.

Us and them: a class divide

Ultimately, in Pratchett's series, identification and loyalty come to be defined not by ethnicity, culture or religion, but mostly by class. While initially many problems, like the crimes unfolding before Vimes, seem to be caused by racial or cultural Others, the protagonist always discovers that the crime at the bottom is one by an aristocratic and/or financial group of interests, and blame lies with greed, class inequalities, politics or, possibly, individual vices, not ethnic or racial differences. Rather than a "clash of civilizations"[18], where culture and religion are perceived as the main forces, Pratchett's vision of world conflict seems closer to "Jihad vs McWorld"[19], where instead of cultures as such, the values of global capitalism clash with the local, "tribal", traditional values of "jihad". However, Pratchett puts emphasis on the class component of the struggle, suggesting all the values in the conflict are actually hostage to power and the economy. Representatives of traditionally underprivileged classes can reclaim their rights if they look beyond cultural differences, through the narrative of civilizational conflict, and develop solidarity with the seemingly "other" immigrants sharing a similar social niche.

In *Men at Arms*, Vimes is initially quite indifferent to dwarf and troll sensitivity, and the problems of multicultural life in the city do not particularly concern him, as he is about to enjoy a "happily ever after" with his wealthy, upper-class wife. The breakthrough in his attitude comes when he sees prejudice against non-humans presented by aristocrats who combine racism with disdain for lower classes, complaining in one breath about "uppity dwarfs and trolls and rude people" (*Men at Arms*, 116); evidently, they see immigration as a facet of social mobility and gradual empowerment of the masses, who now also enjoy basic rights, as citizens. Originally a working-class man himself, the protagonist then realizes his class solidarity with the non-human immigrants. Apart from a fire-forged camaraderie, it is the class aspect, the shared experience of street life, that makes Vimes firmly take the side of the non-humans and go beyond stereotypes to learn about their cultures (*Men at Arms*, 129). Fittingly, the book's villains prove to be aristocrats attempting to restore monarchy in

---

[18] Samuel Huntington, *The Clash of Civilizations and the Remaking of World Order* (New York: Simon & Schuster, 1996).
[19] Joseph Barber, *Jihad vs McWorld* (New York: Ballantine Books, 1996).

order to reclaim the "good old days" of feudal privilege; thus, cultural diversity becomes a symbol of a modern, more egalitarian society.

In *Feet of Clay*, aristocratic privilege, exploitation of others for profit, and a wish to overthrow the city's ruler are interconnected in a conspiracy plotted by a vampire authority based on peerage and heraldry. The villain resents the interracial relationship between the potential king, Carrot, and his werewolf girlfriend and, more generally, the social mobility offered by the modern metropolis (*Feet of Clay*, 289). The connection between vampires and the aristocracy seems a likely reason for Vimes's aversion towards these creatures (*Men at Arms*, 55), while he finds himself entrusting the life of the city ruler to working-class dwarfs and trolls (*Feet of Clay*, 146), in recognition of the fundamental opposition between the immigrants and the rich, with the latter most likely to benefit from a coup and the restoration of a puppet monarch. Vimes also decides to side with the golems after recognizing the relationship between the fate of non-humans and the exploitation of human workers. Visiting a factory where a golem has written "Workers! No masters but yourselves!" on the wall, he sees miserable human employees probably coming from the very class into which he was born (*Feet of Clay*, 350-351). On leaving, he learns that the factory is owned by a "resident in Park Lane, one of the most select addresses in the city" (*Feet of Clay*, 155), who has been demanding that his street be no longer patrolled by non-human guards.

Indeed, minorities present a problem to the city's powerful factions. Guild leaders and those traditionally "bred to lead" find it hard to impress their importance on the mixed populace. Remaining outside the city's power structures, immigrants could prove uncontrollable in the event of a coup; their very presence renders a return to absolutism impossible (*Feet of Clay*, 225). In *Jingo*, aristocrats are able to briefly grasp power by stirring anti-Klatchian sentiments, but have no place in their plan for non-human citizens. Neo-imperialist jingoism strives to present the city as a religious and racial monolith, and the non-human presence in Ankh-Morpork proves the vision to be outdated. Likewise, in *The Truth* the presence of non-humans in the city baffles hitmen hired by the aristocrats in yet another attempt to depose the city's ruler (*The Truth*, 93), whom they accuse of letting the city become a melting pot, "open to all and sundry" (*The Truth*, 260). Evidently, rather than a liability, the growing economic and cultural strength of the minorities has become a factor safeguarding freedoms enjoyed by Ankh-Morpork's commoners.

Even when non-natives occasionally do prove to be villains, it is possible and indeed necessary for the protagonists to reframe the conflict in terms of class. Even in *Thud!*, where dwarf assassins in deep-downer clothes attack Vimes's family on a suicide mission sponsored by fundamentalist *grags*, he finally manages to see the situation from a perspective other than a clash of civilizations. Most of the dwarfs following the radicals are in fact manipulated by wealthy mine-owners anxious to maintain their traditional privileges, and some are ultimately abandoned when they outlive their usefulness. It is the vision of such commoners falling victim to grand crimes of the powerful that repeatedly spurs Vimes into action.

McSheikhs vs the People

It would appear that Pratchett's novels (or at least their protagonists) arrive at a Marxist interpretation of the "clash of civilizations" as a false conflict, serving the interests of privileged groups. Many "Others" vote with their feet to partake in the values to which the West adheres or at least pays lip service: the "Ankh-Morpork way" that involves equality, individualism, the rule of the law, and an acceptance of diversity, including the spheres of gender and religion. Although some of these immigrants embrace fundamentalist versions of their identity in response to stereotypes, by and large both the host culture and the newcomers adapt to the new situation, creating a multicultural society – a feat which Pratchett holds possible under the supervision of an enlightened and pragmatic leader, with the support of a few key characters devoted to the good of the state.

In Pratchett's works it is the traditional elites who are often revealed to fuel prejudice, either deliberately, to divide the society and retain power, or out of instinctive fear for their position, which might be lost if the underprivileged discovered that "alloys are stronger". A hybridized society, containing a large admixture of immigrants, grows difficult to steer by means of old nationalistic mantras, and consequently needs to be discouraged. In the immigrants' home country the situation is very similar, and the traditional leaders have even less practice in dealing with rapid change; hence the pressure to resist "Western" influences and instead reinforce traditional standards when it comes to gender, law, and religion.

If we now decide to substitute "the West" for Ankh-Morpork and Muslims for the various Others (remembering that this is merely one of many possible pairings), Pratchett would seem to say that no "Jihad vs McWorld" conflict actually exists. What exists is a class conflict where the underprivileged are used as pawns against each other to further the interests of power elites on both sides of the barricade. Those who berate the influence of "Others" are happy to use and oppress their own compatriots in the name of profit. This is no justification for violence: the towers representing great business and neo-imperialism should not be destroyed, but rather handed back to the workers, so that the original virtues of the West may be recovered.

In Pratchett's series, it does not pay to deny that sometimes the values embraced by Us might become perverted, as in the case of the clacks company. In later novels, especially once dwarfs take over the role of a religious as well as an ethnic Other, conflicts between them and human characters seem to multiply; however, these post-9/11 parts of the series also present foreigners' perspectives on the city more often than before, with some novels casting as protagonists characters who have to be won over to the side represented by the city. Simultaneously, throughout the series, city characters realize that, even used with good intentions, essentializing and totalizing labels such as "Them" actually deny others and oneself a full, three-dimensional humanity. As Vimes realizes, applying an ethnic key to a case severely limits one's options for understanding and solving a problem, and the following passage seems true of both the racial and the class other:

> And *then* he realised why he was thinking like this.
>   He wanted there to be conspirators. It was much better to imagine men in some smoky room somewhere, made mad and cynical by privilege and power, plotting over the brandy. You had to cling to this sort of image, because if you didn't, then you might have to face the fact that bad things happened because ordinary people, the kind who brushed the dog and told their children bedtime stories, were capable of then going out and doing horrible things to other ordinary people.
>   It was so much easier to blame it on Them. It was bleakly depressing to think that They were Us. If it was Them, then nothing was anyone's fault. If it was Us, what did that make Me? (*Jingo*, 199)

Bibliography

Barber, Joseph. Jihad vs McWorld. New York: Ballantine Books, 1996.

Clute, John and David Langford. "Pratchett, Terry" in *The Encyclopedia of Science Fiction*. 2011-2012, accessed October 2012, http://sf-encyclopedia.com/entry/pratchett_terry.

Connolly, John. "Terry Pratchett" [interview]. 2005. http://www.johnconnollybooks.com/int_pratchett.php.

Huntington, Samuel. *The Clash of Civilizations and the Remaking of World Order*. New York: Simon & Schuster, 1996.

Manlove, Colin N. *Modern Fantasy*. Cambridge: Cambridge University Press, 1975.

Pratchett, Terry. *Night Watch*. London: Corgi, 2002.

—. *Men at Arms*. London: Corgi, 1994

—. *The Fifth Elephant*. London: Corgi, 2000.

Pratchett, Terry and Stephen Briggs. *The Discworld Companion*. London: Gollancz, 1994.

Pratchett, Terry. *The Truth*. London: Corgi, 2001.

—. *Guards! Guards!* London: Corgi, 1990.

—. *Pyramids*. London: Corgi, 1997.

—. *Interesting Times*. London: Corgi, 1995.

—. *Mort*. London: Corgi, 1988.

—. *Wyrd Sisters*. London: Corgi, 1989.

—. *Feet of Clay*. London: Corgi, 1997.

—. *Monstrous Regiment*. London: Corgi, 2004.

—. *Going Postal*. New York: Harpertorch, 2005.

—. *Thud!* London: Corgi, 2006.

—. *Witches Abroad*. London: Corgi, 1992.

—. *Making Money*. London: Corgi, 2008.

—. *Unseen Academicals*. London: Corgi, 2010.

—. *Snuff*. London: Corgi, 2012.

Smith, Eve. "Civil discobedience or war, terrorism and unrest in Terry Pratchett's Discworld" in: *Comedy Studies*, Vol. 3 Issue 1, 2012, pp. 29-39.

Stableford, Brian. *Historical Dictionary of Fantasy Literature*. Lanham: Scarecrow Press, 2003.

"TERRORISTS WIN":
IDENTITY, CENSORSHIP AND TERRORISM
IN POST-9/11 VIDEO GAMES

KRZYSZTOF INGLOT

When a tragedy as impactful as the 9/11 attacks befall a nation, the aftershocks are felt in many spheres of culture worldwide, including the interactive electronic entertainment medium. This article is a qualitative analysis of how mainstream modern video games handle the concept of terrorism in connection with player identity and how these concepts have altered throughout the last decade due to the terrorist threat.

This paper does not concern itself with the portrayal of terrorists as much as it analyzes the problem of player immersion within the context of terrorism. In other words, this paper does not analyze how exactly the terrorists are depicted in the electronic entertainment medium. After all, there already is a number of articles on that, and it seems that "the production of European and American mainstream video games exhibits a strong cultural bias when constructing and reinforcing stereotypical representations of Arabs and Muslims" and usually depicts these groups as terrorists.[1] What this paper does analyze, however, is how games portray the protagonist (hero/player) and the antagonist(s) – and, in some cases, the setting – in relation to terrorism. This article argues that the frequency of terrorism as a trope in video games has increased during the last decade, mostly due to 9/11, and that video game developers avoid depicting the gamer's controlled character as a terrorist.

Since video games studies, or Ludology, are a very recent academic field, still dependent on other fields and struggling to fully define itself[2], it

---

[1] Šisler, Vít. 2008. "Digital Arabs: Representation in Video Games." In *European Journal of Cultural Studies*, Vol. 11, Issue 2 (2008): 205. SAGE Publications.
[2] Aarseth, Espen. "Computer Game Studies, Year One." *The International Journal of Computer Game Research*. Vol. 1, No. 1 (2001). Accessed May 2, 2012. http://www.gamestudies.org/0101/editorial.html.

may be necessary to lay out the basic terminology and context commonly used within the studies. The protagonist of the game, the hero controlled by the player, is often labelled the "avatar".[3] The "locus" may refer to an area within a game, such as a room, hall or even building .[4] "Gamer" is synonymous with "video game player". "FPS" is an acronym for a First-Person Shooter, a type of game where the player views the world with the eyes of his or her avatar; "TPS" is a Third-Person Shooter, a game type where the avatar is mostly or entirely visible on the screen; "RPG" is a Role-Playing Game, a game which focuses on the role-playing aspect, i.e., on immersing the player into the fictitious world, or "universe" of the game. There are far more genres of video games, though the ones mentioned here are the focus of this paper. Also, in video games, there is a lot of genre-mixing, with fuzzy boundaries at work (cf. *Mass Effect* series). FPS, TPS and RPG can be labelled as Action/Adventure games, which in turn are the best-selling genre of video games.[5] The commercial significance of the electronic games medium is unquestionable, with many titles exceeding the popularity of such monumental franchises as *Batman*, *Lord of the Rings* or *Star Wars*.[6] For example, *Call of Duty: Modern Warfare 3*, a 2011 FPS game, earned nearly half a billion dollars in just its first 24 hours of sales.[7] In North America alone, the video game industry is

---

Raessens, Joost and Jeffrey Goldstein. 2011. *Handbook Of Computer Game Studies*. Cambridge, MA: MIT Press, 17-36.

Bogost, Ian. 2006. *Unit Operations: An Approach to Videogame Criticism*. Cambridge, MA: MIT Press, 172.

[3] Burn, Andrew. 2006. "Playing Roles." In *Computer Games: Text, Narrative And Play*, edited by Diane Carr, David Buckingham, Andrew Burn, Gareth Schott. Cambridge: Polity Press, 72.

[4] Flury, T., Gilles Privat and N. Chraiet. 2003. "A Model and Software Architecture for Location-management in Smart Devices / Ambient Communications Environments". In *Communication with Smart Objects: developing technology for usable pervasive computing sysems*, edited by Pierre-Noel Favennec, Claude Kintzig, Gerard Poulain, Gilles Privat, London: ISTE Ltd., 81.

[5] ESA. Entertainment Software Association. 2011. *Essential Facts About the Computer and Video Game Industry*. Accessed May 2, 2012: 8. http://www.theesa.com/facts/pdfs/ESA_EF_2011.pdf.

[6] Johnson, Robert. 2009. "Call of Duty: Modern Warfare 2 destroys records in first day sales rampage, pulls in $310M." *NY Daily News*, November 13. Accessed April 29, 2012. http://www.nydailynews.com/news/money/call-duty-modern-warfare-2-destroys-records-day-sales-rampage-pulls-310m-article-1.417049.

[7] Crecente, Brian. 2011. "Call of Duty: Modern Warfare 3 Shatters All Sales Records, Nears Half a Billion Dollars in Day One Sales." *Kotaku*, November 11. Accessed May 2, 2012. http://kotaku.com/5857400/call-of-duty-modern-warfare-3-shatters-all-sales-records-surprises-no-one.

worth more than $25 billion and is rapidly growing.[8] With such a vast audience, it is important to question how these games function and what the agenda of their creators is.

As far as terminology is concerned, one more term needs defining: "terrorist". Terrorism is considered a pejorative term and one quite difficult to define properly[9] but this paper uses the definition given by the European Union. According to the EU, a terrorist can be defined as a person whose activities "may seriously damage a country or an international organisation [which results in]: seriously intimidating a population; or unduly compelling a Government or international organisation to perform or abstain from performing any act; or seriously destabilising or destroying the fundamental political, constitutional, economic or social structures of a country or an international organisation."[10]

This article analyzes the problem of identity and terrorism within the context of American and Western European digital games, i.e., *de facto* the mainstream branch of the electronic entertainment market, barring some independent, small-sized developers. The Japanese video game market is a strong contender as far as electronic games are concerned, with many Japanese titles being sold by the millions worldwide, like *Resident Evil 5* (over 1.5 million copies[11]) or *Metal Gear Solid 4: Guns of the Patriots* (more than 3 million units sold, Konami 2008, 4[12]). The popularity of Japanese games notwithstanding, this article limits itself to video games produced within the so-called Western culture – the culture which was the main target of the al Qaeda terrorism (MI 5 – The Security Service[13]) and

---

[8] ESA. Entertainment Software Association. 2011. *Essential Facts About the Computer and Video Game Industry*. Accessed May 2, 2012: 11.
http://www.theesa.com/facts/pdfs/ESA_EF_2011.pdf.

[9] Hoffman, Bruce. 1998. *Inside Terrorism*. New York, NY: Columbia University Press, 32.

[10] *Council Framework Decision of Combating Terrorism*. 2002/475/JHA. Accessed May 2, 2012.
http://www.statewatch.org/news/2002/jul/frameterr622en00030007.pdf.

[11] Thorsen, Tor. 2009. "NPD: Resident Evil 5 infects 1.5 million, March game sales sink 17%." *Gamespot*, April 16. Accessed April 29, 2012.
http://www.gamespot.com/news/npd-resident-evil-5-infects-15-million-march-game-sales-sink-17-6208084.

[12] Konami Corporation. 2008. *FY2009 1st Quarter Financial Results Supplemental Material: April 1 – June 30, 2008.* Accessed April 29, 2012.
http://www.konami.co.jp/zaimu/0806/english/supplemental.pdf#page=4.

[13] MI5 – The Security Service. 2012. "Al Qaida's ideology." *MI5 – The Security Service*. Accessed April 16, 2012:4. https://www.mi5.gov.uk/output/al-qaidas-ideology.html.

which has changed the most due to the terrorist attacks at the beginning of the 21st century, including the 9/11 World Trade Center attack and the 7/7 London and the 11-M Madrid bombings.[14]

It needs to be noted, however, that there are several other game developers, outside of the above-mentioned regions, with many of them following the trends set by American developer studios. Many countries in Eastern Europe and a number in Asia and Africa house video game studios, e.g.: Poland – Techland (e.g., *Call of Juarez* 2006), the Czech Republic – Illusion Softworks (e.g., *Hidden & Dangerous* 2001), Finland – Remedy Entertainment (e.g., *Max Payne 2* 2003), Ukraine – 4A Games (e.g., *Metro 2033* 2011), South Korea – NCSoft (e.g., *Lineage II* 2003). Their material should not be discounted as insignificant, but the Western culture market favours titles produced by the Western culture, for a number of reasons, some of them obvious, whereas the Eastern European, Japanese and South Korean companies – the last two being home to the major game producers in Asia, both company-size-wise and product-sales-wise [15] – tend to ignore contemporary issues of American and Western European culture, at least as far as electronic games are concerned[16], with a few notable exceptions (*Metal Gear Solid 4: Guns of the Patriots* 2008). As Hirokazu Hamamura, the president of the company behind Famitsu,

---

[14] Forest, James J. F. 2007. *Countering Terrorism and Insurgency in the 21st Century: Strategic and tactical considerations*. Westport, CT: Greenwood Publishing Group: 90.

[15] Kanellos, Michael. 2004. "Consumers: Gaming their way to growth – Part 3 of South Korea's Digital Dynasty." *CNET News*, June 25. Accessed April 30, 2012. http://news.cnet.com/Consumers-Gaming-their-way-to-growth---Part-3-of-South-Koreas-Digital-Dynasty/2009-1040_3-5239555.html.
CESA, Nikkei Business Publications, Inc. 2010. "Tokyo Game Show 2010 Summary Report." Press release, September 27. Accessed April 15, 2012. http://expo.nikkeibp.co.jp/tgs/2010/pdf/tgs2010_20100927_e.pdf.
Game Press. 2010. "Lineage II: awesome views, rave reviews!" *MCV UK*, June 26. Accessed April 22, 2012. http://www.mcvuk.com/press-releases/read/lineage-ii-trade-awesome-views-rave-reviews.
Sinclair, Brendan. 2011. "Konami sales, profits slip slightly for full year." *Gamespot*, May 12. Accessed April 15, 2012. http://www.gamespot.com/news/konami-sales-profits-slip-slightly-for-full-year-6313439.
Capcom Corporation. 2010. "Capcom: History." *Capcom*, March 5. Accessed April 15, 2012.

[16] Cieslak, Marc. 2010. "Is the Japanese gaming industry in crisis?" *BBC News: BBC Click*, November 4. Accessed May 2, 2012. http://news.bbc.co.uk/2/hi/programmes/click_online/9159905.stm.

the most popular video game magazine in Japan, states, "The Japanese don't like shooting and war games very much" (as quoted in Cieslak 2010). Korean producers, in turn, usually centre more on fantasy-based massive multiplayer online games[17], not modern warfare or action titles. Thus, it is necessary to look westward for electronic entertainment products which take on the theme of terrorism.

The methodology for the analysis includes playing through each analyzed video game from start to finish and recording various linguistic constructs, especially names of in-game groups, during the process. The games have been played in English, which in most cases is the original language of the title. The *Resident Evil* and *Metal Gear Solid* series' original language is Japanese. The analysis also includes case studies on titles which have never been published, only announced and developed enough to gain publicity in the media. Additionally, the paper takes into account a number of so-called controversies connected with some of the analyzed material.

As it usually is the case when video games are analyzed, so does this article too face difficulties concerning references to specific instances within a game. Unlike books, recordings or movies, electronic games are not linear. It is pointless to write at which minute an instance within a game occurs, because each playthrough is different. The player is in control – more or less – and he or she decides on when or if an objective is completed, etc. Playing an electronic game more resembles going through a Petri net, with multiple conditions, trajectories, transitions and so on.[18] For the sake of simplicity, only the title of the game and the context of a specific instance is mentioned in the analysis.

Mainstream titles have been chosen for one important reason: they are the most popular and the most often played electronic games. Consequently, gamers in America (no small number; ESA 2011, 2) and multiple other regions have frequent contact with them. It can be said that mainstream games are nowadays piercing the Western and Eastern popular culture. The more popular they are, the larger the impact they have upon gamers, to the point where the players' opinions and attitudes may be influenced by some titles.

---

[17] Woong-ki, Song. 2010. "Midnight ban imposed on online games." *The Korea Herald*, April 12. Accessed May 2, 2012.
http://www.koreaherald.com/national/Detail.jsp?newsMLId=20100412000752.
[18] Cf. Natkin, Stéphane, Liliana Vega, Stefan M. Grünvogel. 2004. "A new methodology for spatiotemporal game design". *National Science Fundation*. Accessed May 2, 2012.
http://citeseerx.ist.psu.edu/viewdoc/download?doi=10.1.1.79.2030&rep=rep1&type=pdf.

The player within the avatar, the avatar within the player

One might ask: "Why does it matter whom we play as?" and that would be a valid question. After all, many may surmise that gamers playing shooters care only about killing enemies within a fictitious world or otherwise completing the game's objectives. Even if they were captivated by the game's story, setting, characters or context (all of which are very much present within most modern shooters), the in-game world is a world much different from the real-life one. As Peter Lunenfeld stated: "[video game players] live in an alternative universe, a solipsistic one scripted by designers."[19] Why should it matter whether a person plays on the Red team or the Blue team when the objective presents him or her with the same arbitrariness: go from A to B, defeat the enemy?

The point of multiple games, not only electronic ones, is to become a part of a different world or temporarily become someone else. The fact that video game developers try to build a world into the game, that there are a number of games with very rich fictitious worlds, that players grow attached to certain worlds loyally enough to buy the next instalments in the franchise, or that there are controversies about the story elements of games (more on them later) all prove the importance of the setting of the game and the significance of both playable and unplayable characters within.

Video games offer an immersion which grossly outstrips the immersion of all other media forms. Immersion is connected with a short-term loss of awareness of the real world and a sense of involvement into the game's world and its objectives and goals.[20] Playing a game often entails being briefly entrenched into its universe, forming an *ad hoc* personality or attaching one's persona to that of the avatar, some gamers would even say: becoming the avatar. "Unlike narrative, simulations are a kaleidoscopic form of representation that can provide us with multiple and alternative points of view [and] players can realize that there are many possible ways to deal with their personal and social reality."[21] Thus, games can teach

---

[19] Quoted in Wark, McKenzie. 2007. *Gamer Theory*. Cambridge, MA: Harvard University Press, 51.

[20] Jannett, Charlene, Anna L. Cox, Paul Cairns, Samira Dhoparee, Andrew Epps, Tim Tijs, Alison Walton. 2008. "Measuring and Defining the Experience of Immersion in Games." In *International Journal of Human Computer Studies*, Vol. 66, Issue 9 (2008). Duluth, MN: Academic Press, Inc., 5.

[21] Frasca, Gonzalo. 2004. "Videogames of the Oppressed: Critical Thinking, Education, Tolerance and Other Trivial Issues", 93. In *First Person: New Media As Story, Performance, and Game*, edited by Noah Wardrip-Fruin, Pat Harrigan, 85-

tolerance and construct a more objective view of certain realities. As desirable as this state may seem, it can also be potentially harmful. (To read more on immersion within electronic games and on subjective and objective ways of measuring it, see the study by Jannett et al 2008.)

In role-playing games (e.g., *Mass Effect*), players are even more entrenched into the character that they are playing than players of other types of games, as one of the key elements of RPGs is allowing the gamer to feel a better connection with his or her avatar. Such a phenomenon may occur since RPGs emphasize storytelling and interaction between characters more than any other game genre. Potentially, the player's and avatar's identities may intertwine, the player may feel sadness when the avatar is supposed to feel it, get angry when his or her avatar is also in such a state, etc. The gamer may feel responsibility and solidarity with the character he or she controls. In that case, what if the avatar is a mischievous character – will the gamer also be mischievous? Could a player learn from his or her avatar? Would a player playing a terrorist change his ideals? These questions lack definitive answers.

Moreover, it should be noted that video game designers' and publishers' decisions regarding game development are affected by contemporary real-world events and social contexts. The creators of *Metal Gear Solid 2: Sons of Liberty* (2001) removed a cut-scene where a ship hits the Statue of Liberty and changed the spelling of one key in-game character because it was reported to sound similarly to the name "Bin Laden".[22] *Syphon Filter 3* (2001), a game where terrorists plan to attack the United States with biochemical weapons, was delayed directly due to 9/11.[23] Its packaging and promotional material was significantly changed: the cover had its American flag surrounded by poisonous gas removed, and the term "terrorists" within the game was altered to "enemies", and descriptions like "deadly arsenal" were removed.[24] There are numerous similar examples. These kinds of modifications suggest that even though electronic games are set in fictitious worlds, their content is still subject to a (self-

---

91. Cambridge, MA: MIT Press.

[22] Leone, Matt. 2011. "How Japan's Earthquake Changed its Developers." *1UP*, November 21. Accessed May 2, 2012. http://www.1up.com/features/how-japans-earthquake-changed-developers?pager.offset=1.

[23] Ahmed, Shahed. 2001. "Sony delays Syphon Filter 3." *Gamespot*, September 20. Accessed May 2, 2012. http://asia.gamespot.com/news/sony-delays-syphon-filter-3-2813691.

[24] Dvorak, Jason. 2005. "The Filtering Process." *Game Rave*. Accessed May 2, 2012. http://www.game-rave.com/psx/playstation_perfect_guide/features/syphon_filter_3/index.html

)censorship related to the real-world. Changes implemented to certain games do not necessarily reflect some legal regulations or outside obligation, but can originate in the minds of the designers themselves. It is possible that "censorship is not primarily experienced as external pressure, but is generated from within."[25] With this point in mind, game developers may feel the urge to modify certain game elements which are potentially unwelcome or stigmatized by the society or audience. As the analysis will show, this self-censorship often uses a double standard.

Exposing the Other in terrorism

It is fitting to start with one of the most successful game franchises in the history of electronic entertainment, *Call of Duty*, a military FPS. The first instalments of the series, which were launched in 2003, were not concerned with terrorism in the slightest. The first three parts – and the fifth and seventh one – were set in the times of World War II, with their avatars being soldiers of the Allies, or the Cold War, with the British or Americans as avatars. Conversely, the *Modern Warfare* sub-series is set in modern times (cf. gameography). All instalments of *Call of Duty* are set in digital versions of real-world countries, players roam Pripyat, Ukraine, multiple American cities, the Middle East, Moscow, Russia and other regions. All personal names, however, are fictitious.

In the first part of *Modern Warfare*, the player controls agents from British Special Air Service and United States Marine Corps. Even though this part is to an extent set in a country in the Middle East, the name of the country is not disclosed. The decision to keep the name a secret is surprising, given that the names of other locations are clearly stated within the game. The theme of terrorism appears in *Modern Warfare* only in the epilogue of the game – the last stage is set in an aeroplane taken over by terrorists. Needless to say, the situation in many ways mimics the scenario of the plane take-over on 9/11. It needs to be stressed, however, that this level is short and optional, i.e., not required to complete the title and the gamer may opt out of playing through it. Also, the word "terrorist" itself is never used.

In *Modern Warfare 2*, the concept of terrorism is much more prevalent. The antagonist within the game is a terrorist, and the player's goal is to thwart his scheme. The game features a highly controversial level called

---

[25] Freshwater, Helen. 2004. "Towards a Redefinition of Censorship." In *Censorship and Cultural Regulation in the Modern Age*, edited by Beate Müller, 232. New York, NY: Rodopi.

"No Russian", where the player seemingly helps terrorists in an attack (killing civilians) at a Moscow airport. The game stresses, though, that the avatar is merely an undercover agent, not a terrorist himself. The stage does not require the gamer to kill any civilians and is optional, i.e., can be skipped entirely.

Modern Warfare 3, being a direct sequel to the series, continues the hunt after the terrorists from the second part. This instalment features terrorist attacks with the use of deadly biochemical agents on multiple European cities, including London. This time, the player does not infiltrate a terrorist cell. Throughout the series, the terrorists are depicted as despicable men.

It can be concluded that the developers of *Modern Warfare* tried to push the boundaries of what is culturally allowed to be depicted in a video game and what is not. On the other hand, one may also assume that Infinity Ward wanted to gain publicity through controversy. Either way, the series boldly presented Western real-world locations (London, Paris) devastated by terrorist attacks, crossing a line very few other mainstream game studios were ready to cross.

The idea of infiltrating a terrorist squad has been used in the electronic games medium long before *Modern Warfare 2*. In particular, the whole plot of *Tom Clancy's Splinter Cell: Double Agent* revolves around this kind of scenario. Even though Sam Fisher, the protagonist of the game, fills the ranks of a terrorist group, John Brown's Army [JBA], he still is a double agent working for the United States government. The gamer, through his or her avatar, is among the terrorists but never really becomes one him-/herself. Sam Fisher needs to use subterfuge to avoid suspicion; never can he familiarize with the JBA. The group always remains the Other. The player is rewarded with a better ending if he or she manages to complete his or her mission of betraying the terrorists.

Other parts of *Tom Clancy's Splinter Cell* revolve around assassinating terrorists. In some missions, the player needs to prevent attacks on American soil. In the latest instalment, *Tom Clancy's Splinter Cell: Conviction*, the avatar rebels against his earlier supervisors, but he does it for personal reasons and his targets turn out to be corrupt. In the end, Sam Fisher uncovers a terrorist threat among his previous superiors and fights them. Once again, the terrorists remain the Other, the enemy.

Additionally, terrorists in video games are often depicted as lunatics, madmen with incomprehensible goals and frantic plans, i.e., people who are not only unmanageable to relate to, but even impossible to understand. Such conclusions can be drawn after having played the series of *Metal Gear Solid* or *Resident Evil*. The former (or at least its first, second and fourth instalments) revolves in large part around fighting terrorism directed either against the United States or the West in general. Most – if not all – terrorists in the series are shown as mentally unstable: e.g., a psychic claiming to be able to read the future and wearing a military breathing mask at all times, a gunslinger with paranoid schizophrenia, a highly aggressive pyromaniac, a martial arts fighter who likes the taste of blood, and a number of other psychopaths. The plans of these enemies usually seem quite complicated, whereas their demeanour is almost maniacal.

However, a number of enemies in *Metal Gear Solid 1* and *2* (1998, 2001, respectively) may be presented in quite a different light, should the player decide to investigate. The profiles of multiple enemies from the series show that they were neglected as children by their parents or otherwise suffered in their youth. These bits of information are scarce and only available if the player actively searches for them: initiates optional dialogue, looks online for additional sources or plays other games from the series. Sniper Wolf, a female sharpshooter, was raised on the battlefield in Iraqi Kurdistan, constantly terrorized by never-ending gunfire and screams; Psycho Mantis, whose mother died giving birth to him, was resented by his father his whole childhood; Vamp, a close-quarters combat expert, lost his entire family to a bombing in Romania.

As far as the *Resident Evil* series is concerned, only its fifth part includes a terrorist theme. The main antagonist of the game, having a god complex, scientifically experiments on his own body, only to turn into a horrific mutation during the final showdown against the player(s). Never are the enemies in *Resident Evil 5* presented as likeable in the least.

Both *Metal Gear Solid* and *Resident Evil* were developed by the Japanese, a fact which perhaps explains why *Metal Gear Solid* offers some sympathy towards the terrorists. This kind of phenomenon was not observed in the analyzed American video games. Moreover, the first two parts of *Metal Gear Solid* were developed before the 9/11 attacks, when terrorism did not seem as large a threat. Interestingly, the third instalment of *Metal Gear Solid* (*Snake Eater* 2004), whose development started after 9/11, was a prequel to the first and second part and did not include terrorists and only vaguely touched upon the subject of the United States. Perhaps the Japanese designers felt that the September attacks warranted a break from the terrorism trope.

The video game *Counter-Strike* makes a curious reference point for the analysis. The title premiered in 2000, so before the 9/11 attacks, and was a quite successful FPS. The game allowed players to split into two teams, one explicitly named "terrorists" and the other – "counter-terrorists". The game mechanics even included the terrorists kidnapping hostages and setting up explosives. The game also includes the infamous notification "terrorists win" if the terrorists' objective is met. There was little to no controversy over these elements of the game back in 2000. However, never again would an American mainstream video game so overtly allow the players to play as terrorists, in large part, it would seem, due to the attacks of 2001.

The *Mass Effect* series can be treated as a small counterpoint to the trend so far observed in mainstream video games, but only from a certain – perhaps even far-fetched – perspective. The story revolves around a charismatic protagonist and is set many years into the future. At one point in the game, the avatar briefly joins a terrorist organization. This fact is in a way downplayed by the narrative, as the player's character is never called a terrorist him- or herself and the writing suggests the avatar does not like joining the group, criticizes the organization multiple times, accepts it only as a necessary evil, etc. Moreover, never does the avatar commit crimes which could be regarded as terrorist acts. Nevertheless, the character does not fight the organization from within, like in *Splinter Cell*, but accepts help from, and works alongside, terrorists. In the last instalment of the *Mass Effect* trilogy, the avatar leaves the organization, fights it and defeats its leader, reclaiming his or her integrity. It is also at this stage where the group is portrayed as cold, calculating and as inhuman as possible, with some of the members turning into machines.

The latest instalment of the American *Medal of Honor* series perfectly presents just how much the idea of gamers playing as terrorists is frowned upon. Only the part from 2010 is set in modern times, with the rest of the saga taking place during World War II. In *Medal of Honor* (2010), the player controls American soldiers during offensives in Afghanistan in 2002. The game tries to be loyal to the events of the War in Afghanistan, with real-world names for loci and factions, but fictitious personas. The Taliban are subjected to othering, and the Americans are depicted as heroes. What colours this video game interesting in terms of research, however, is the controversy which sparked shortly before the title's premiere.[26] Just as many contemporary FPS games have a multiplayer component, so does *Medal of Honor*. Players play matches against each other, and/or usually split into two teams. Very often these teams reflect the factions present within the game's single player campaign. Originally, gamers were to play as the Coalition forces or – and this gathered a large

---

[26] Thier, Dave. 2010. "New Video Game Will Let You Play as the Taliban." *AOL News*, August 13. Accessed May 2, 2012.
http://www.aolnews.com/2010/08/13/new-video-game-will-let-you-play-as-the-taliban/.

amount of criticism – as the Taliban. To allow gamers to play as the "Taliban" was called tasteless, callous, unpatriotic and disrespectful to the troops stationed in the Middle East. Also, "having U.S. children portray Taliban insurgents trying to gun down U.S. forces via the game"[27] was considered malicious, with many concluding that the title was meant for children, even though the majority of video game rating boards gave *Medal of Honor* a rating of "Mature/18+". After harsh comments from the media and politicians, some of whom even called for banning the game, Digital Illusions CE retracted the name "Taliban" and replaced it with a more neutral term, "Opposing Force".

In the case of *Medal of Honor*, controversial decisions foreshadowed a potential boycott of the game. The controversy concerning *Six Days in Fallujah* was far more damaging to its developers. The game, said to be near completion in 2009, was meant to be set in the Fallujah of 2004, during one of the harshest battles in American modern warfare. The creators were strongly criticized for both glorifying one of the "the worst of the war crimes carried out in an illegal and immoral war" and allowing players to experience these "horrific events".[28] In the end, the publisher, Konami, backed out due to this controversy, leaving the game unpublished, its development completion notwithstanding.[29] The controversy of *Six Days in Fallujah* should be considered not only in the context of video games, but of the whole "entertainment" industry.

There are numerous books and movies on the tragic events of the Iraq War, some of them quite brutal. Yet, such media usually gather critical acclaim instead of overwhelming criticism. *Six Days in Fallujah* was an attempt to bring the topic of contemporary real-life war into the industry of video games, but the right to do this was denied by American and British politicians, news media and activists. This might seem like only a singular occurrence, but since electronic game development costs rival those of film production, many game creators may see the case of *Six Days in Fallujah* as a strong deterrent to developing similar war-related or terrorism-related media.

---

[27] Ibid.

[28] GamePolitics. 2009. "Outrage Over Konami's 'Six Days in Fallujah'." *Game Politics*, April 7. Accessed April 14, 2012. http://www.gamepolitics.com/2009/04/07/outrage-over-konami039s-quotsix-days-fallujahquot.

[29] Reilly, Jim. 2009. "Six Days in Fallujah Developer Cuts Staff." *IGN*, August 6. Accessed May 2, 2012. http://uk.xbox360.ign.com/articles/101/1011452p1.html.

The decade behind, the decade ahead

It may be argued that the game designers do not want players to become criminals within the game. This argument, however, is quickly refuted by a number of video games which, indeed, not only allow but also reward – which is crucial – the player for committing a crime in-game. These include: the entire *Grand Theft Auto* series, with the avatar receiving money for killing pedestrians, points for stealing cars, taking part in illegal street races, supporting drug lords; *Manhunt*, with the player advancing levels for killing other people in gruesome ways; the *Saints Row* series, where the player receives rewards for a variety of crimes, including vandalism, murder, narcotics trade; the *Assassin's Creed* series, in which the avatar's main objective is assassination, and where killing guards (*de facto* the law enforcers) is rewarded with funds and equipment; and a number of others. Some of the titles mentioned here have been connected with controversies over brutality in games (mainly *Manhunt* and *Grand Theft Auto*), but further action against them was scarce. In other words, games allowing a player to wreak havoc and kill in-game people were more welcome than games portraying the player as a terrorist. Being immersed in the role of a terrorist is morally questionable, but so is being immersed in the persona of a drug-induced serial killer – yet the latter is a lot more prevalent within the genre than the former.

On the scale of "being abhorrently evil", the terrorist is at the very top, trumping any other criminal minds, including drug pushers and homicidal maniacs. The consumer can play as a gangster (e.g., *Grand Theft Auto IV: Lost and Damned* 2009), a serial killer (e.g., *Manhunt* 2003), but nearly never can he or she fill the shoes of a terrorist. The closest thing to playing as a terrorist would be *Splinter Cell: Double Agent* (2006), where the consumer can play as an agent infiltrating a terrorist cell. Even then, his or her ultimate goal is to destroy the organization from the inside. A similar scenario is available in *Call of Duty: Modern Warfare 2* (2009), where the player briefly controls an American agent who spies on a Russian terrorist group. Even then, the player only controls the character for one short mission and the mission itself is optional, a rarely seen phenomenon in the otherwise linear FPS genre.

At the same time, terrorism creeps into the electronic game genre in another way. The enemies in *Mass Effect*, *Splinter Cell*, *Call of Duty*, *Resident Evil*, *Medal of Honor*, *Army of Two*, *Metal Gear Solid*, *Syphon Filter* and *Grand Theft Auto* include terrorists. The gaming industry is not always afraid to have them in their products. In most cases, though, they are faceless, dehumanized, unmotivated, unreasonable, fully antagonistic, detached – and completely Other. The player is not to sympathize with them, or feel any connection or empathy for them. Even though terrorists are prevalent within electronic games, the standpoint of terrorism is not seriously considered, but introduced only to represent incomprehensible evil.

It should be considered what the reason for this trend is. One could argue that the target audience of video games is at fault. Common belief suggests electronic games are meant for children. If true, a child might indeed get the wrong idea if he or she is allowed to play as a terrorist. Arguably, the largest difficulty of the medium is connected with the stigma of being seen as a childish form of entertainment. This particular topic deserves its own dissertation, but should be briefly considered for the sake of the above-mentioned argument. In reality, the average gamer is about 37 years old[30], with only 18% of American gamers being under 18. Player demographics easily allow for serious and mature content within electronic games, let alone drama. Moreover, multiple games have a rating of "Mature", especially FPS titles.

Perhaps, the video game industry does not offer better insight into the ominous perspective of a terrorist because of the very nature of the electronic entertainment medium. After all, building a more intricate and noetic portrayal of a terrorist may be all but impossible, given that games tend to be all about fast-paced action. On the other hand, there are numerous games which both have achieved popularity (pierced mainstream) and touch upon more delicate or even contemplative matters, like loss and regret (*Braid* 2008), adulthood and companionship (*Limbo* 2010), deplorable self-sacrifice (*Persona 3* 2006), death of loved ones (*Mass Effect* 2007, *Persona 3* 2006), and other topics. It is true that a vast number of successful video games can be deemed shallow or uninspired, but there is also a strong niche for more sophisticated and elaborate products.

It may be that it is not the medium which is not ready, but the audience. It seems that a decade after one of the most devastating terrorist attacks on the Western world, society is still unable, in a way, to accept interactive electronic entertainment which centres on terrorism. As the numerous controversies mentioned above suggest, Western countries seek to treat terrorists purely as the Other, and allowing a gamer to play as one would break that unwritten rule. Looking at the potential of immersion, such a limitation may be plausible. Nevertheless, if the fact that gamers can fill

---

[30] ESA. Entertainment Software Association. 2011. *Essential Facts About the Computer and Video Game Industry*. Accessed May 2, 2012. http://www.theesa.com/facts/pdfs/ESA_EF_2011.pdf.

the virtual shoes of other criminals or murderers is taken into account, there is no question about a terrorism-related (self-)censorship at work within the video game industry.

What remains is to ponder about the future of this problem. If the past is any indicator of the future, it seems that, eventually, video game developers will start to embrace the topic of real-world terrorism more than they have done recently. Before war against fictitious terrorists gained a foothold within the industry (i.e., before 9/11), many – if not most – military FPS games had been set in the times of a real-world World War II (for example, the first instalments of *Call of Duty* or *Medal of Honor*), with little to no controversies. This past tendency suggests that society can accept depictions of real-life war within video games if the events in question happened a number of decades prior to the game.

As far as playing as terrorists is concerned, the situation presents itself as somewhat problematic. Once again, taking past titles into consideration may prove helpful. Mainstream electronic games with Nazi avatars have been few and far between, which may indicate, by analogy, that playing the role of a terrorist, or at least an Arabic terrorist, may remain unwelcome by the Western society for years to come. However, as the case of *Medal of Honor* (2010) proves, it may be enough to simply change names (here, from "Taliban" to "Opposing Force") to dodge a backlash from society. After all, censorship can be both "a debilitating impediment" and "an impetus to stylistic innovation"[31] for the writer. It is plausible to stretch this theory to include not only written media, but also electronic games, since these too contain numerous linguistic constructs and are subject to (self-)censorship.

However the game designers choose to deal with the problem, it may be summarized that the content of modern mainstream electronic games in a large part reflects the attitudes of the Western society. The designers tend to avoid the topic of the real-world Iraq War, and they do not overtly allow the player to become a terrorist in-game. In contrast, playing the role of a serial killer is allowed. Terrorists nearly always are depicted as the Other. If a studio tries to introduce a change to this trend, they often have to face strong criticism or are even left without a publisher. It seems that the Western society is still too sensitive to the topic of terrorist avatars and playing a contemporary war to include such themes into interactive entertainment. This in turn limits the artistic expression and options of video game creators and impoverishes the variety of available products

---

[31] Levine, Michael G. 1994. *Writing trough repression: literature, censorship, psychoanalysis*. Baltimore, : Johns Hopkins University Press, 2.

within the industry. In this way, it can be said that, indeed, "terrorists win".

Gameography

Games are listed alphabetically and with respect to the series to which they belong. Most games have both a developer (the creators, writers, programmers, etc.) and a publisher. The developer is listed first, the publisher second.

Army of Two (2008), EA Montreal, Electronic Arts.
Army of Two: The 40th Day (2010), EA Montreal, Electronic Arts.
Battlefield 1942 (2002), Digital Illusions CE, Electronic Arts.
Battlefield Vietnam (2004), Digital Illusions CE, Electronic Arts.
Battlefield 2 (2005), Digital Illusions CE 2005, Electronic Arts.
Battlefield: Bad Company (2008), EA Digital Illusions CE, Electronic Arts.
Battlefield: Bad Company 2 (2010), EA Digital Illusions CE, Electronic Arts.
Battlefield 3 (2011), Digital Illusions CE, Electronic Arts.
Call of Duty (2003), Infinity Ward, Activision.
Call of Duty 2 (2005), Infinity Ward 2005, Activision.
Call of Duty 3 (2006), Treyarch, Activision.
Call of Duty 4: Modern Warfare (2007), Infinity Ward, Activision.
Call of Duty: World at War (2008), Treyarch, Activision.
Call of Duty: Modern Warfare 2 (2009), Infinity Ward, Activision.
Call of Duty: Black Ops (2010) Treyarch, Activision.
Call of Duty: Modern Warfare 3 (2011), Infinity Ward, Activision.
Call of Duty: Black Ops (2010), Treyarch, Activision.
Counter-Strike (2000), Valve, Valve.
Grand Theft Auto IV (2008), Rockstar North, Rockstar Games. (NYC)
Manhunt (2003), Rockstar North, Rockstar.
Mass Effect (2007), BioWare, Microsoft Game Studios.
Mass Effect 2 (2010), BioWare, Electronic Arts.
Mass Effect 3 (2012), BioWare, Electronic Arts.
Medal of Honor (1999), DreamWorks Interactive, Electronic Arts.
Medal of Honor: Airborne (2007), EA Los Angeles, Electronic Arts.
Medal of Honor (2010), Danger Close, Electronic Arts.
Metal Gear Solid (1998), Konami, Konami.
Metal Gear Solid 2: Sons of Liberty (2001), Konami, Konami.
Metal Gear Solid 3: Snake Eater (2004), Konami, Konami.
Metal Gear Solid 4: Guns of the Patiots (2008), Konami, Konami.

Resident Evil (1996), Capcom, Capcom.
Resident Evil 2 (1998), Capcom, Capcom.
Resident Evil 3: Nemesis (1999), Capcom, Capcom.
Resident Evil 4 (2005), Capcom, Capcom.
Resident Evil 5 (2009) Capcom, Capcom.
Resident Evil 6 (unpublished) Capcom, Capcom.
Saints Row 2 (2008), Volition, THQ.
Six Days in Fallujah (unpublished), Atomic Games, no publisher.
Syphon Filter (1999), Eidetic, 989 Studios.
Syphon Filter 2 (2000), Eidetic, 989 Studios.
Syphon Filter 3 (2001), SCE Bend Studio, Sony. 2001.
Syphon Filter: The Omega Strain (2004) - SCE Bend Studio, Sony.
Syphon Filter: Dark Mirror (2006), SCE Bend Studio, Sony.
Syphon Filter: Logan's Shadow (2007), SCE Bend Studio, Sony.
Tom Clancy's Rainbow Six (1998), Red Storm Ent., Red Storm Ent.
Tom Clancy's Rainbow Six 3: Raven Shield (2003), Red Storm Ent., Ubisoft.
Tom Clancy's Rainbow Six: Vegas (2006), Ubisoft Montreal, Ubisoft.
Tom Clancy's Rainbow Six: Vegas 2 (2006), Ubisoft Montreal, Ubisoft.
Tom Clancy's Rainbow 6: Patriots (unpublished), Ubisoft Montreal, Ubisoft.
Tom Clancy's Splinter Cell (2002), Ubisoft Montreal, Ubisoft.
Tom Clancy's Splinter Cell: Pandora Tomorrow (2004), Ubisoft Shanghai, Ubisoft.
Tom Clancy's Splinter Cell: Chaos Theory (2005), Ubisoft Montreal, Ubisoft.
Tom Clancy's Splinter Cell: Double Agent (2006), Ubisoft Shanghai, Ubisoft.
Tom Clancy's Splinter Cell: Conviction (2010), Ubisoft Montreal, Ubisoft.

Bibliography

Aarseth, Espen. "Computer Game Studies, Year One." *The International Journal of Computer Game Research*. Vol. 1, No. 1 (2001). Accessed May 2, 2012. http://www.gamestudies.org/0101/editorial.html.
Ahmed, Shahed. 2001. "Sony delays Syphon Filter 3." *Gamespot*, September 20. Accessed May 2, 2012.
http://asia.gamespot.com/news/sony-delays-syphon-filter-3-2813691.
Bogost, Ian. 2006. *Unit Operations: An Approach to Videogame Criticism*. Cambridge, MA: MIT Press.
Burn, Andrew. 2006. "Playing Roles." In *Computer Games: Text,*

Narrative And Play, edited by Diane Carr, David Buckingham, Andrew Burn, Gareth Schott, 72-87. Cambridge: Polity Press.

Capcom Corporation. 2010. "Capcom: History." *Capcom*, March 5. Accessed April 15, 2012. http://www.capcom.co.jp/ir/english/company/history.html.

CESA, Nikkei Business Publications, Inc. 2010. "Tokyo Game Show 2010 Summary Report." Press release, September 27. Accessed April 15, 2012. http://expo.nikkeibp.co.jp/tgs/2010/pdf/tgs2010_20100927_e.pdf.

Cieslak, Marc. 2010. "Is the Japanese gaming industry in crisis?" *BBC News: BBC Click*, November 4. Accessed May 2, 2012. http://news.bbc.co.uk/2/hi/programmes/click_online/9159905.stm.

Council Framework Decision of Combating Terrorism. 2002/475/JHA. Accessed May 2, 2012. http://www.statewatch.org/news/2002/jul/frameterr622en00030007.pdf.

Crecente, Brian. 2011. "Call of Duty: Modern Warfare 3 Shatters All Sales Records, Nears Half a Billion Dollars in Day One Sales." *Kotaku*, November 11. Accessed May 2, 2012. http://kotaku.com/5857400/call-of-duty-modern-warfare-3-shatters-all-sales-records-surprises-no-one.

Dvorak, Jason. 2005. "The Filtering Process." *Game Rave*. Accessed May 2, 2012. http://www.game-rave.com/psx/playstation_perfect_guide/features/syphon_filter_3/index.html.

ESA. Entertainment Software Association. 2011. *Essential Facts About the Computer and Video Game Industry*. Accessed May 2, 2012. http://www.theesa.com/facts/pdfs/ESA_EF_2011.pdf.

Forest, James J. F. 2007. *Countering Terrorism and Insurgency in the 21st Century: Strategic and tactical considerations*. Westport, CT: Greenwood Publishing Group.

Flury, T., Gilles Privat and N. Chraiet. 2003. "A Model and Software Architecture for Location-management in Smart Devices / Ambient Communications Environments". In *Communication with Smart Objects: developing technology for usable pervasive computing sysems*, edited by Pierre-Noel Favennec, Claude Kintzig, Gerard Poulain, Gilles Privat , 71-90. London: ISTE Ltd.

Frasca, Gonzalo. 2004. "Videogames of the Oppressed: Critical Thinking, Education, Tolerance and Other Trivial Issues". In *First Person: New Media As Story, Performance, and Game*, edited by Noah Wardrip-Fruin, Pat Harrigan, 85-91. Cambridge, MA: MIT Press.

Freshwater, Helen. 2004. "Towards a Redefinition of Censorship." In *Censorship and Cultural Regulation in the Modern Age*, edited by Beate Müller, 225-246. New York, NY: Rodopi.

GamePolitics. 2009. "Outrage Over Konami's 'Six Days in Fallujah'." *GamePolitics*, April 7. Accessed April 14, 2012. http://www.gamepolitics.com/2009/04/07/outrage-over-konami039s-quotsix-days-fallujahquot.

Game Press. 2010. "Lineage II: awesome views, rave reviews!" *MCV UK*, June 26. Accessed April 22, 2012. http://www.mcvuk.com/press-releases/read/lineage-ii-trade-awesome-views-rave-reviews.

Hoffman, Bruce. 1998. *Inside Terrorism*. New York, NY: Columbia University Press

Jannett, Charlene, Anna L. Cox, Paul Cairns, Samira Dhoparee, Andrew Epps, Tim Tijs, Alison Walton. 2008. "Measuring and Defining the Experience of Immersion in Games." In *International Journal of Human Computer Studies*, Vol. 66, Issue 9 (2008). Duluth, MN: Academic Press, Inc.

Johnson, Robert. 2009. "Call of Duty: Modern Warfare 2 destroys records in first day sales rampage, pulls in $310M." *NY Daily News*, November 13. Accessed April 29, 2012. http://www.nydailynews.com/news/money/call-duty-modern-warfare-2-destroys-records-day-sales-rampage-pulls-310m-article-1.417049.

Kanellos, Michael. 2004. "Consumers: Gaming their way to growth – Part 3 of South Korea's Digital Dynasty." *CNET News*, June 25. Accessed April 30, 2012. http://news.cnet.com/Consumers-Gaming-their-way-to-growth---Part-3-of-South-Koreas-Digital-Dynasty/2009-1040_3-5239555.html.

Konami Corporation. 2008. *FY2009 1st Quarter Financial Results Supplemental Material: April 1 – June 30, 2008*. Accessed April 29, 2012. http://www.konami.co.jp/zaimu/0806/english/supplemental.pdf#page=4.

Leone, Matt. 2011. "How Japan's Earthquake Changed its Developers." *1UP*, November 21. Accessed May 2, 2012. http://www.1up.com/features/how-japans-earthquake-changed-developers?pager.offset=1.

Levine, Michael G. 1994. *Writing trough repression: literature, censorship, psychoanalysis*. Baltimore: Johns Hopkins University Press.

MI5 – The Security Service. 2012. "Al Qaida's ideology." *MI5 – The Security Service*. Accessed April 16, 2012. https://www.mi5.gov.uk/output/al-qaidas-ideology.html.

Natkin, Stéphane, Liliana Vega, Stefan M. Grünvogel. 2004. "A new methodology for spatiotemporal game design". *National Science Fundation*. Accessed May 2, 2012.

http://citeseerx.ist.psu.edu/viewdoc/download?doi=10.1.1.79.2030&re
p=rep1&type=pdf.

Raessens, Joost and Jeffrey Goldstein. 2011. *Handbook Of Computer Game Studies*. Cambridge, MA: MIT Press.

Reilly, Jim. 2009. "Six Days in Fallujah Developer Cuts Staff." *IGN*, August 6. Accessed May 2, 2012.
http://uk.xbox360.ign.com/articles/101/1011452p1.html.

Sinclair, Brendan. 2011. "Konami sales, profits slip slightly for full year." *Gamespot*, May 12. Accessed April 15, 2012.
http://www.gamespot.com/news/konami-sales-profits-slip-slightly-for-full-year-6313439.

Šisler, Vít. 2008. "Digital Arabs: Representation in Video Games." In *European Journal of Cultural Studies*, Vol. 11, Issue 2 (2008): 203-220. SAGE Publications.

Thorsen, Tor. 2009. "NPD: Resident Evil 5 infects 1.5 million, March game sales sink 17%." *Gamespot*, April 16. Accessed April 29, 2012.
http://www.gamespot.com/news/npd-resident-evil-5-infects-15-million-march-game-sales-sink-17-6208084.

Thier, Dave. 2010. "New Video Game Will Let You Play as the Taliban." *AOL News*, August 13. Accessed May 2, 2012.
http://www.aolnews.com/2010/08/13/new-video-game-will-let-you-play-as-the-taliban/.

Wark, McKenzie. 2007. *Gamer Theory*. Cambridge, MA: Harvard University Press.

Woong-ki, Song. 2010. "Midnight ban imposed on online games." *The Korea Herald*, April 12. Accessed May 2, 2012.
http://www.koreaherald.com/national/Detail.jsp?newsMLId=20100412000752.

CRITICISM OF AMERICA IN JAMES KELMAN'S NOVEL *YOU HAVE TO BE CAREFUL IN THE LAND OF THE FREE*

BARBARA POWAŻA-KURKO

The protagonist of James Kelman's novel *You Have to be Careful in the Land of the Free* (2004), is a man alienated from and critical of that society, America. Jeremiah Brown is a 34-year-old Scotsman in the USA, who has lived there for twelve years, and is leaving temporarily to visit his mother at home. The novel contains his confessions, effusions, reminiscences as well as observations and conversations conducted on the last night before his flight to Scotland.

The core of Kelman's endeavour, however, is an attempt "to write a novel that resists the enormous cultural pressure of America's defining narrative."[1] Yet if one expects a crushing criticism of America from a self-righteous European perspective, their expectations will soon be thwarted. The book does indeed contain criticism, but its political applicability to the US is subverted by two factors. Firstly, the narrator undermines his own credibility; secondly, the book does not present a veritable and realistic portrayal of contemporary America. Much of what is said is exaggerated and invented, thus presented in such a way that "Uhmerka" starts to resemble a kind of city of damnation in a modern morality play. Both these ploys actually add to the poignancy of the narrator's accusations in a more moral, universal sense, while lessening the possible political interventionist meaning. L. J. Lindhurst notices this larger-than-life convention of depicting America, calling it "an over-the-top metaphor in an over-the-top America," which "hits close enough to home to leave the reader wondering whether Kelman's novel is meant to serve as a warning

---

[1] Liam McIlvanney, "Give or Take a Dead Scotsman." *London Review of Books,* 26, No.14, July 22, 2004, accessed September 12, 2011, http://www.lrb.co.uk/v26/n14/liam-mcilvanney/give-or-take-a-dead-scotsman.

or a scathing indictment."[2]

The fact that the protagonist is a simple immigrant, whose views and judgements may be prejudiced saves the book from becoming "a caustic essay about the US global policy."[3] Kelman gives a voice to the type of character who is not usually given much authority, a simple working class man. Obviously, by doing so, he continues his own private apology for the right of indigenous people outside London to speak their language, which he started as the author of the notorious *How Late It Was, How Late*. When that novel, featuring a dropout who accidentally got in trouble with the police, was awarded the Booker Prize in 1994, the controversy seems to have been fuelled as much by the cruelty ascribed to the police as Kelman's use of the working class Scottish dialect. Its detractors claimed the novel was an act of vandalism on literature, while its supporters pointed to the fact it salvages the life experience and point of view of somebody who is far from the centre that determines literary taste and the linguistic norm. Neither book is an easy read for a cultured reader. It must be admitted that if any censorship imposed on *You Have to be Careful in the Land of the Free* had deleted all the variations of the "f-word" from Jeremiah Brown's stream-of-consciousness, the book would have shrunk dramatically. Yet it would have given no justice to the protagonist's idiolect. It is this kind of psychological and linguistic realism which seems to be the novelist's top priority. The main character does not merely tell the story of his life, but rather relives it as he thinks and talks about it. Confession in this novel does not entail ordering, as it usually does in an autobiography. Nor does it impose any meaning on his chaotic experience. Hence there is no division into chapters, units, and no consistent time framework. The book contains both retrospective and simultaneous narration, but the stream-of-consciousness technique makes the past and the present mix, as experience and memory equally constitute the world of the narrator.

The fallibility of the narrator is a skilfully used tool, which in fact adds to his criticism of America. Jeremiah Brown calls himself a failure. He is "a registerrred fucking non-integratit cunt with the wrang fucking politics, the wrang philosophy of life man, the wrang this and the wrang that."[4]

---

[2] L. J. Lindhurst, "Book Review: *You Have to be Careful in the Land of the Free*," accessed September 12, 2011, http://www/themodernworld.com/reviews/kelman-free.html .

[3] Anna Battista, "Book Review: James Kelman's *You Have to be Careful in the Land of the Free*," accessed September 12, 2011, http://www.erasingclouds.com/0922kelman.html.

[4] James Kelman, *You Have to Be Careful in the Land of the Free* (Orlando:

This very description of his life as a failure raises many questions, the paramount one being: What must one adjust to, into what system of values must one assimilate to be able to call oneself a success? Jeremiah Brown's life is the opposite of the American Dream, the conglomerate of beliefs, expectations and values, which is one of the major myths, or grand narratives, shaping the American mentality. Jeremiah Brown is unable to follow the rags-to-riches story because he has not invested everything in the pursuit of this aim. He has not shed his convictions, his critical thinking and his love of independence and even his national identity. At the same time he does not cling to any coherent identity which he would like to impose on his life experience to impress the reader, appear a better person and to make sense of his life. That is, paradoxically, what makes this unreliable narrator so credible. Being aware of the fragmentary nature of the truth communicated by Jeremiah, the reader is open to his confession and ready to take his judgements as they come to him: in all their crudity and subjectivity. That has, after all, always been the strength of the first person unreliable narration, as opposed to the omniscient narration, which orders the world for the reader and imposes the objective truth.

The first person narrator is unmistakably a Scotsman. He sticks to his idiolect even at the cost of distorting the correct spelling of many words, which he presents in their phonological form. He is a man from "Scallin," going "hame" to visit his "poor auld maw" (2) and pouring scorn on "Uhmerka," yet at the same time well aware that it was staying away from home that kept him sane (33). Thus he avoids a shallow identification of virtues with his own compatriots while ascribing all the vices only to Americans. He seems to shun all ideology or heroic narratives. What occupies him, for example, is his anorak, which he is very unwilling to lose, even if "It wasnay a faimly heirloom" and "a relic of bygone etceteras" (174). The lack of any discipline in his stream-of-consciousness, which seems to be a corollary to his neurotic disposition, results in unintentional humour. By dwelling on the topic of the anorak as a garment devoid of any historical significance, he ends up discussing Scottish history and starting a polemic with the opinion that "le bonné Prance de Charlee," who incidentally was not then wearing his anorak, crossed over the sea from Skye in 1745, as somebody else was certainly rowing for him (174). Despite this confusing rejection of ideology and national heritage, he still clings to his national and linguistic identity, which exposes him as

Harcourt, Inc., 2004), 135. Henceforth I include the page numbers of the quotations from Kelman's novel in brackets in the main text.

a foreigner and makes it necessary for him to repeatedly present his ID card according to new regulations, displayed in the forms of notices in public places.

This in turn leads to a more serious exposure as he presents his "Class III Red Card" (355), which marks his place in the hierarchy of this partly American, partly dystopian society. The Red Card, unlike the Green Card, which is the proof of full approval, is given to people who pose a threat to the accepted social order, i.e. socialists and atheists, including the Glaswegian hero of the book.

Jeremiah's attitude to his place as an outsider is in fact ambiguous. On the one hand he relishes his defiance and flaunts his imperviousness to the American dream ideal (113). He refers to a perfect exponent of the American Dream, Andrew Carnegie, who immigrated to the States from Scotland to make both a fortune and a name for himself as a philanthropist, but he remains unimpressed. For him Carnegie was just one of those who "finish up hurting millions and making billions" (69). At the same time he rejects the subtlety of political correctness, which makes some concepts more palatable and acceptable by making them more vague. He prefers to call a spade a spade, to be "an unassimilatit unintegratit alien socialist" rather than "a decadent post-christian secularist with agnostic leanings" (355). One may wonder if it is honesty that makes him reject hypocrisy or some kind of innate aggression, to which he occasionally gives vent. At one point he throws a snowball at a rottweiler, and then abuses its owner, who seems partly angry at such behaviour and partly concerned about the attacker's safety. Jeremiah is neither attacked nor even threatened by the dog, so his aggression is utterly gratuitous, and so is his scathing judgement on the owner, whom he calls "ya ku klux klan bastard" (387).

On the other hand, despite his rebellious nature, he sometimes gives in to dreams of happiness. More stability, which is epitomized by the Green Card, would have certainly helped to cement his relationship with Yasmin, whom he calls his "ex", even though they were never officially married (269). Without full citizenship rights his private life could not be successful. But even thinking about the painful break-up of his family and the separation from his four-year-old daughter, he realizes that losing his domestic happiness may mean preserving something important spiritually, for otherwise he could have become "a right-wing fascist bastard" (122). What is more, the very word "success" is ambiguous for him. On the one hand, it may have implied stability and domestic happiness; on the other hand, however, it is part of the hated jargon of American pop culture. It is "the psychology experts on these crazy talk-shows" who teach one: "Don't let life pass ye by! Grab the bull by the horns! Don't be a wilting flower!"

(49), and whose advice he did try to follow, even if only half-heartedly.

Ambiguity is an organizing principle in the novel. The narrator's sympathy lies with the individual against the state; he loves specific people and hates Americans as a nation. He finds it hard to believe how nice people can create the monstrosity of the allegedly free land, in which a thinking man must be on his guard. Theo Tait calls the book a "rant novel,"[5] which is a very adequate term indeed, for the protagonist either condemns or at least questions everything: American politics, their attitude to foreigners, work, religion, their ignorance and their handling of property.

He points to uncritical acceptance of capitalism as if it were the only viable option for mankind to live in a structured and profitable society. Of course, the critical stance he takes towards it is the only option for a Red Card holder. Very often he himself trots out clichés and trite propaganda and his criticism turns into mere outbursts of anger, for example when he provides a somewhat oversimplified diagnosis of the state of the country: "This land was good land. But these capitalist fuckers and their money-grabbing politico sidekicks had turned it into a horror" (3). One can treat these bombastic tirades and clichés disparagingly as symptoms of his own failure and frustration. Yet there is something very poignant in his criticism of American politics and the economy, namely, the observation he makes that Americans are very unwilling to discuss politics with him. Even with his beloved Yasmin politics was a taboo subject. (97, 110). When Americans raise such topics, it is only when they feel comfortable in their own company and there is no one to challenge their views. Surprisingly, fashionable artists and designers, who in Europe might be expected to hold less conservative views, here prove to be stalwart supporters of the regime. In the bar where he used to work he heard their praise of the system, which was considerably enhanced by the influence of alcohol. Apart from this context politics crops out in his conversations with Americans only in a playful, joking way. His colleague, an airport security operative, Sharifa, called her dog "Queenie," hoping for his approval, but she missed the mark. The stereotype has it that as a representative of Scotland, he must be dissatisfied with the reign of the English queen. Sharifa cracks a joke thanks to which he can take his little revenge on the English. But he is not interested in it. He treats his convictions with the utmost seriousness. It is "the very air I breathed," he claims (188). But his interlocutors cannot understand such radicalism as they are afraid to share serious views and debates with him, an alien, a foreigner.

---

[5] Theo Tait, "Tales of a wild-eyed loon," *The Telegraph*, May 30, 2004, accessed September 12, 2011, http://www/telegraph.co.uk/culture/books/3617979/Tales-of-a-wild-eyed-loon.

Critics notice that, although the novel was written after 9/11, the terrorist attacks are never openly mentioned. Yet fear and distrust pervade the society the novel depicts. One learns that the sense of insecurity increased after some specific events which are called "recent furnir disturbances" (90). It may be the very vagueness of the statement that makes it very foreboding for all non-Americans, all foreigners, who, as I have already-mentioned, have to carry their ID at all times and present it on request. Because Jeremiah Brown's speech gives him away as a foreigner, he has to do it repeatedly, which, of course, stigmatizes him in front of other people. There is no chance of escaping his suspicious status as an alien. He will always be different, and not just in the ordinary way: the barman suspects that the difference between them is "planetary" (10).

Jeremiah Brown's indictment of the "Uhmerkin" society is obvious here, but, interestingly enough, he is just as biased and prone to jump to conclusions as the others. Seeing a man on the train reading a Spanish newspaper, he forms a judgement which one might call extremely unfair or prejudiced, but which is first of all hilarious in its mixture of spite and sheer ignorance. For him the man "looked like Franco's politics would have been okay by him" (98). Meeting a third-generation Arab, he presumes he must be interested in algebra (216). But he is paid back in kind when his colleagues express surprise that he is not wearing a kilt (245). He shares ingrained stereotypes with the Americans, so the reader is not thoroughly convinced by his outrage when the barman implies he thinks all Italians belong to the mafia (16). Of course, the barman's defence of the Italians is ridiculous, because no accusation has been voiced, but it is also very sad, as it seems to be part of the discourse of stereotypes, which is going on irrespective of the interlocutors' actual contributions. Here one comes across another paradox. On the one hand people are capable of hurting each other's feelings with blunt, inconsiderate comments; on the other hand the ideology of political correctness makes a normal conversation very hard. One has to be constantly on one's guard. Talking to black people, Jeremiah Brown very consciously avoids mentioning their African roots. For example, having a conversation with a cab driver from Ghana, he does not refer to his possible status of a one time immigrant, even if he thinks about it at once. He simply introduces himself as an immigrant. But this does not change the reality, nor does it change the mentality. It merely makes conversations "fraught, deadly dangerous" (6). Although the narrator participates in the game, he is aware of the pitfalls and limitations and this wisdom establishes his intellectual superiority. The very awareness of his own failure provides him with a vantage point. The kind of irony with which he refers to his only life success, namely, giving up smoking, which he now regrets, testifies to his wisdom. He is even aware of his own propensity for paranoia. His fear and sense of persecution makes him see America as a place where babies are especially vulnerable to attacks from racists on beautifully mowed lawns in quiet and affluent suburbs (314).

There is a price to pay for wisdom, though. He suffers from a sense of oppression, a lack of air to breathe. And it is then that he wants to go in search of the Promised Land south, out of the States altogether, to "a land where people cared" (65). For they do not care here. They control, watch out, implement rules and regulations and keep up the appearances.

The protagonist's experience belies all talk of the melting pot or multiculturalism, the two major sociological concepts generally associated with the United States. Despite the coexistence of people from different continents and backgrounds, they hardly ever meet. Jeremiah, an immigrant from Scotland, is the first foreigner Yasmin has ever met (79). The seemingly mixed society in fact consists of very homogeneous communities, which do not come into much contact.

The status of an alien is thus not only a part of bureaucratic jargon, but it determines the protagonist's place in the society even on a very local scale as Yasmin's partner. He is sent away from the performers' table when he goes with her to her gigs (295). The other musicians do not like his Celtic origins. Sometimes, while driving, they tell him to lie down on the floor of the car so that he is not seen from outside (315). It seems they do not treat him seriously as a helper or an interlocutor.

He notices that, despite his rebellious convictions, as an "alien" he is excluded from serious debate about people who also fought for their independence against a regime or a stereotype. Yasmin's cousin was a great fan of Nina Simone, a jazz musician and a fighter for equal rights in the US, but she was very reluctant to talk about her idol's life and performance to Jeremiah (72). One can only speculate about the reasons, but it seems that any mention of racism or the need to struggle for independence poses a serious threat to the myth of America as the best possible state, the Promised Land, in which problems no longer exist.

People fear not only to find cracks in this monolithic vision of their country, but even to acknowledge that it is not the only one. The mere sight of a map is disturbing as it suggests the existence of the wider world, of some beyond (144). The sense of insecurity certainly derives also from the lack of knowledge about the world. The almost clichéd American ignorance is mentioned several times in the book almost always ironically, not to say sarcastically. Not only do they fear the map, but they even do not know how to use it. Those who place Scotland "in Germany, which they guessed was 'to the left hand side' of Australia" are ironically praised as those whose grasp of geography is "a wee bit better than the usual Uhmerkin deal" (71). They keep asking him if he has e-mail or basic technological appliances back at home. A bookshop in an American town is such a rarity that the narrator comments on it and imagines it was opened by some "enthusiast" (3).

This ignorance can have more far-reaching consequences. They do not know the price of the political system they uphold. Rita and Norman, a nice couple Jeremiah talks to on his last night in the States, have never heard about Domestic Retaining Camps and when the conversation becomes too risky, they simply refuse to talk about them. They would rather not know (351). This lack of knowledge combined with a total unwillingness to learn is bred by hypocrisy and at the same time makes hypocrisy thrive. It is a typical vicious circle of fake innocence based on ignorance.

The ideal is to follow procedures, work hard and obey. Workaholism is one of the serious faults Jeremiah finds with the American society. He has gained work experience in bars and the airport security. He did not find either very gratifying. Work made him too tired to think clearly and to write his book. Even the very basic, economic motivation for work was discouraged by the meagre salary. What is more, it is another alienating experience as his attitude to work is not generally understood in the world which is "gripped by a psychotic masochism", whereas he himself is "in favour of a universal strike, an eternal strike" (296). He mentions many drawbacks of the system, like the unwillingness of the employers to acknowledge a sick leave, the low salary on offer or the non-existence of the trade unions, which were replaced by the institution of the Shop Steward, who was more of a nurse or an agony aunt than a serious defender of the employees' rights. Work is seen as exploitation, depriving man of his creative powers. He barely has the time for sleep; writing is out of the question.

Both his jobs appear pointless. The first one consists in enabling people intoxication in a country where the general impression one gets is that the barman needs customers in order for them to listen to his sad life story. The second one is even worse, even if we treat his own description of his duties with a pinch of salt. This is how he describes his duties:

> "We were expected to bash the heads of demonstrating peace persons and attend high-risk pre-emptive-strike areas, often on the same day; then if it was Mardi Gras we could be rounding up highschool terrorists, plastic bullets obligatory, or else bodyguarding worldbank pickets at the entrances to anarchist conferences, and of course inside the local immigration

complex we were herding and strip searching bunches of pregnant ladies with full internal exploration. And that's just the white people" (351).

One of his duties is to incarcerate unwanted foreigners in the so-called Patriot Holding Centres and to deport native down-and-outs from the airport so that they would not spoil its attractiveness for the passengers who have just arrived in the country of freedom, democracy and prosperity. The poor were considered guilty of "flaunting of one's poverty in public" (185), which is, of course, frowned upon in the land of prosperity and dreams that come true. By their very existence they questioned the whole American system of values. If the very thought of wearing second-hand clothes is beyond comprehension for Yasmin, how could the authorities put up with people in rags that never turn to riches?

Interestingly, the influx of tramps to the airports was motivated by a kind of perverted version of the American Dream. People were driven by their hope of winning money in the so-called "Persian Bet." It is explained in the novel that the name is a distorted version of its original name, i.e. "Perishing Bet," which consists in betting on the chances of one's survival on board of an American airplane. The reference to 9/11 and its aftermath are very clear here. The narrator imagines what advantage practical money-makers could have taken of the phobia for flying. If it is seen as risky, let the risk be enticing, and, what is more, let it be profitable, too. It is a peculiar reversal of the American Dream as the money is to be won only in the case of death. A survivor does not gain anything, except for his life. Ticket lotteries came into being, offering the poor their last chance of winning money for their families. If they were unsuccessful in this respect, as most of them were, they stayed on and crowded the airports, suffering the odium of the better-off society and the authorities.

The narrator, working in the airport security, has to deal with such people who either have lost their Persian bet or were never given a chance to fly. He is on friendly terms with some, even though all "hobnobbing" with the riff-raff is strictly forbidden (196). Paradoxically, despite the repulsion and spite the tramps evoke, one of them gives rise to a quasi-religious movement. This exceptionally ugly "Being" as he (or she) is known, is believed to have disappeared into thin air when s/he was about to be captured. Nobody had ever seen the person's face or spoken to him (her), which intensifies the religious speculations surrounding this Being. It seems to be the utmost form of hypocrisy: the less people care for the human being that lives next to them, the more prone they are to invent great metaphysical and religious theories. In this sense the Being, who is in fact a destitute outcast, is elevated to the status of some symbol as a compensation for the neglect he suffers as a human being. Jeremiah is too perceptive not to see through this ramshackle revelation. His disparaging attitude to all forms of religion and belief in the supernatural estranges him even further from his colleagues, whom he would be glad to meet on the common ground of humanity. Yet ideology, religion, some beliefs that tower over man and suppress his individuality, always interfere and make natural, warm relations between people impossible.

What makes it worse is the fact that people do not even subscribe to these metaphysical theories and beliefs consciously. To Jeremiah's great distaste, religion is ubiquitous as a form of opportunism. His daughter is baptized "by default" (94), and his views were not considered at all. His is, to give his opponents their due, an extreme form of atheism. He finds the very concept of a unity with God laughable (407); he questions the validity of any religion in the world of such a multitude of beliefs and creeds (119). Even though he loses disputes with Yasmin's friends, who are creationists, he still imagines his own conversion to Christianity only in terms of satire or travesty: Freezing and lost in the unfamiliar town, completely drunk, he imagines he could promise conversion, if some taxi driver helped him to find the way on condition he sang a psalm (402). Even when he comes to the conclusion that gods are not merciful but revengeful, and are now punishing him for not praying by letting him freeze, he does not treat this seriously. He is simply giving vent to his bitterness, not to his belief that he is pursued by some divine powers (396).

Brown's deprecation of all metaphysics is certainly aggravated by the link he notices between religion, wealth and power. He watches with distaste how the rich "all toadied up to presidents, popes, politicians, mafia godfathers and priests, and any auld fucking monarch" (399). He also realises that to rise in the peculiar hierarchy established by the system of three colours of identity cards, he would have to not only found his own church, but also "ye've got to hold the inaugural service on primetime television dressed in top hat and tails, with a pair of army surplus jackboots" (167). It is a very spiteful comment on religion, laying bare what seems to Jeremiah its basic foundations. First of all it is a kind of herd instinct, which makes individuals comply with the requirements of the authority. Ironically, this latter-day American authority is the media. What is broadcast acquires prime importance: the medium creates the message. It also caters for the needs of the herd. Secondly, religion is the preserve of the upper strata of society, which is illustrated by the "top hat and tails" required of a church founder. And the last but not least constituent of religion is coercion, symbolized by the jackboot.

As has been demonstrated, Jeremiah Brown is an embittered, disillusioned, intelligent but also excessively critical observer of the quasi-

American reality. He deprecates its politics, religion, culture, employment conditions, and all the possible aspects of society one can imagine. At the same time he is not less paranoid than the society he so unfavourably describes. He often hallucinates that he is observed by agents who want to arrest him. Not only does he feel observed, but he also sees conspiracy in mere coincidences. He even suspects that the sign that the toilet was closed, which made him look for another one and eventually get lost in the town, was part of a plot against him. As with all the other aspects of his rant, it is his exuberant imagination that makes it not only bearable, but highly enjoyable for the reader, who is, for example, encouraged to imagine how the protagonist is attacked by "pentagon pricks in Frank Sinatra wigs" (312).

A sense of humour does not seem intentional on the part of the protagonist. He seems so preoccupied with his narrow vision and so engrossed in the exaggerated condemnation of practically everything that as a consequence he also shares in the absurdity of what he criticises. Against an undoubtedly absurd "Uhmerkin" background, he cuts a figure of a ridiculous crab. The lack of any objectivity or even attempt at the fairness of judgement on the part of the narrator is a useful tool in the hands of James Kelman. Whereas it does not make the reader reject all the criticism, it nevertheless leaves him some space to think and judge for himself, that is, it allows for the space for independence the protagonist wishes he himself had in "Uhmerka."

It seems that after all the reader is treated with respect as an intelligent individual, who can judge for himself without being inundated by the indiscriminate enumeration of American vices and foibles. The importance attached to individual judgement is visible both in the narrative structure and in the protagonist's professed hierarchy of values. The book Jeremiah Brown intends to write, but never actually does, is to be his personal response to this inhuman reality. Sadly enough, it is more a revenge than a positive programme of renewal. It is a protest of an individual who feels lost in a country of fear and suspicions and excessive regulations, which are still ineffective as means of curbing the ubiquitous anxiety. Dreaming of the book, he hopes to salvage his individuality.

It is individual people he appreciates. He mentions some quite ordinary conversations he has had with people who were able to relate to him simply as another human being. There is openness and genuine interest, for example, in the way he is treated by Lindy, the barman's wife, who joins the musicians at the table after the concert. She is a writer and treats him as her equal. She asks him straightforward, practical questions about the laptop he works with, and does not trot out old jokes about Scotsmen not having computers. It is about his girlfriend and daughter that he talks with tenderness and it is separation from them that makes him suffer. The break-up of his marriage is traumatic (490). One scene is exceptionally moving: being lost in the unknown city and almost frozen to death, he starts to have hallucinations. He imagines he sees Yasmin walking in front of him. The cruel sense of reality soon overtakes this image, but he seems strangely grateful for this sight and treats it almost as a privilege, for "Hallucinations are better than nothing" (394).

The elevated language of politics and ideology is very often juxtaposed with the subdued, simple idiom of a human story. There is some truth in the bombastic language, though. A second generation immigrant, Riçard, who introduces himself as coming from West Virginia, not Kenya, is surprised to hear Jeremiah is so critical of the country where he has "sought refuge". He asks him a rhetorical question:

> "You don´t think it is a good country that has taken you into its warm and tender bosom and will provide succour for your family and family's family? What don´t you admire about it?" (169).

As it is a rhetorical question, there is only one correct answer. And Jeremiah provides it. He says he does admire everything. Yet there is a sense of dishonesty, of something enforced on the protagonist. Riçard is the opposite of Jeremiah. He accepts his new American identity wholeheartedly and cuts himself off from his Kenyan roots. Jeremiah, on the other hand, admits to being torn in between the two countries. It is certainly easier for Riçard, who is a second generation immigrant, to feel at home in America. He seems not only to have taken root in America, but also to have incorporated its creed and propaganda. The rhetorical question posed by Riçard is a kind of trap. It is impossible to deny its claim, and yet one feels it does not do justice to the actual existence of man. It is vague and irrelevant to refer to the opportunity the country provides for the future generations when one's ties with the family are severed and one hovers in a kind of vacuum. Human existence eschews the easy categories ideology thrives on. That is why the bombastic language of Riçard's question seems so inadequate.

The underlying motto of the book seems to be the sentence uttered quite early in the book by the narrator: "If it wasnay for the individual population naybody would stey in the dump" (125). The whole narration is a rejection of utopia and an attempt to come to terms with the individual experience. The criticism of the USA, generally considered to be the paradigm of a liberal, democratic state, is so crushing, one suspects its purpose is not to direct the reader's eyes to some alternative, but to reject unrealistic expectations of an organised, political paradise on earth. The whole novel is a vindication of the individual, who does not resort to any idealisation. All myths that have traditionally served man to organize and find meaning in life are shattered by the relentless narrator in his peculiar search for the truth. It is the truth of the individual experience that matters. Overwhelmed by the demands of living in American society, Jeremiah was unable to write his book. Thus he is a crippled, unfulfilled man. By choosing Jeremiah as the narrator of his novel, James Kelman has lent an ear to all those Jeremiah-like defeated individuals whose voice would otherwise have remained unheard.

At the same time the book is far from being a masochistic celebration of failure. It vibrates with humour, even if it is dark humour and sarcasm that predominate. The comic character of the novel is prominent throughout, but it is mostly interwoven with sadness and bitterness. At times, however, the protagonist's tirades are so ridiculous that laughter dominates over all pensive reception of the book. His rants about American toilet paper and the quality of American television, where the best drama to be had is the weather forecast, belong to this category of humour.

The comic mode becomes subdued towards its end. Jeremiah remembers passing through different small towns and wondering what it would be like to live in one of them. It seems that the barriers between him and the inhabitants may be insurmountable: "You couldnay even talk politics never mind get involved. Then if they knew ye didnay gie a fuck for the supernatural and aw that stuff, Plus if ye were an alien. Just nay place to hide." (324). It is interesting to notice that he perceives lack of anonymity to be the main obstacle. He would feel exposed, noticed, without being welcome.

As his pub crawl progresses, his mood becomes more and more lugubrious. Afraid of death, suffering from solitude, he poses bitter questions about the meaning of life. His language starts to depict not only his origin and background, but also his decrepitude. The consonants in his narration become doubled or tripled as a sign of his shivering with cold: "Maybe ttonight was gauny be ththe night, mmmaybe that auld gguy with the long bbblack cloak and the ssscythe was a-gonna come lukkin fir me" (399).

It is not to say that he does not proceed with his criticism of America. He does it to the very end, even if he denies it on the very last page: "This is no polemical diatribe against the evils of imperialism, colonialism, capitalism, and all the rest of it" (410). Well, it is! It is a criticism of America as a "City of Damnation", not because of godlessness, but because of the lack of human warmth, trust and love, because of the surplus of control, regulation and prejudice. There is simply no "us", in the US created by Kelman. The society is so hostile to all forms of otherness that it starts to resemble a kind of self-regulatory prison compound, where no guards are necessary as all surveillance is carried out by the inmates. Thus, striving for perfect security, people forgo freedom, the value they originally set out to defend. The only sense of real belonging for Jeremiah Brown was lost as the ties with his wife and child were severed, leaving him lonely and disappointed. It is possible that the choice of the protagonist's name is not haphazard and the novel is a kind of modern jeremiad, lamenting the downfall of the "chosen people."

Bibliography

Primary source

Kelman, James. *You Have to be Careful in the Land of the Free*. Orlando: Harcourt, Inc, 2004.

Secondary sources

Battista, Anna. "Book Review: James Kelman's *You Have to be Careful in the Land of the Free*." http://www.erasingclouds.com/0922kelman.html, accessed September 12, 2011.

Lindhurst, L. J.. "Book Review: *You Have to be Careful in the Land of the Free*." http://www/themodernworld.com/reviews/kelman_free.html, accessed September 12, 2011.

McIlvanney, Liam. "Give or take a dead Scotsman", review of *You Have to be Careful in the Land of the Free* by James Kelman. *London Review of Books* 26, No.14, July 22, 2004. http://www.lrb.co.uk/v26/n14/liam-mcilvanney/give-or-take-a-dead-scotsman, accessed September 12, 2011.

Tait, Theo. "Tales of a wild-eyed loon", review of *You Have to be Careful in the Land of the Free* by James Kelman. *The Telegraph,* May 30, 2004. http://www/telegraph.co.uk/culture/books/3617979/Tales-of-a-wild-eyed-loon, accessed September 12, 2011.

Welsh, Irvine, "A Scotsman abroad", review of *You Have to be Careful in the Land of the Free* by James Kelman. *The Guardian,* Saturday 22 May 2004. http://www.guardian.co.uk/books/2004/may/22/features reviews, accessed September 12, 2011.

A PERPETUAL CRISIS?
9/11 AND THE AMERICAN PARANOID
HISTORIES

MICHAŁ RÓŻYCKI

Introduction

Americans, as General George Patton emphatically, though somewhat less accurately, claimed, "have never lost nor will ever lose a war; for the very idea of losing is hateful to an American." Yet despite this debatable invincibility, most conflicts and military interventions the United States got involved in were, at the onset, quite unpopular affairs. Before the attack on Pearl Harbor, most Americans rejected the notion of their country entering the Second World War[1]; likewise did the very idea of mounting yet another invasion of Iraq seem ludicrous before the 9/11 attacks. Yet even when such events provided the nation with a *casus belli*, some detractors continued to challenge the legitimacy of a particular intervention, going beyond the realm of the purely ethical. A specific subgroup of them turned in their rhetoric to paranoid and conspiratorial interpretations of the events, claiming that they had been engineered by a narrow cabal for their own benefit. Such claims, while often removed from mainstream discourse – and at times encountering even outright hostility[2] – have consistently reoccurred throughout the American history. Not only was every US conflict, such people would claim, actually fought against the American society, but the society was always on the losing side.

---

[1] Kathryn S. Olmsted, *Real Enemies: Conspiracy Theories and American Democracy, World War I to 9/11*, (New York: Oxford University Press, 2009), 48.

[2] Katherine Olmsted provides a number of examples, one notable dating from the eve of American entry into the First World War, and referring to Senator Charles Lindbergh, an ardent isolationist. The politician had to be escorted during anti-war rallies by his son, the future aviator and celebrity Charles A. Lindbergh, who was always ready in a car with the engine running to rescue his father in case the rally was attacked by a lynch mob (20).

Indeed, such conspiratorial claims regarding the attacks on the World Trade Center (WTC) in 2001, and the subsequent wars in Afghanistan and Iraq, use surprisingly similar arguments as those voiced when the US was entering the Second World War, starting the Spanish-American War of 1898, or intervening in the Vietnam War.

The goal of the following text will be to outline the nature and the origins of such revisions of American interventions. Taking the aftermath of 9/11 as a point of departure, it will look backwards in history and trace the historical and cultural motifs that led some to believe the wars waged by the Americans are, and were, in fact engineered by a conspiracy of un-American, subversive forces.

Defining conspiracies

Discussing the role and purpose of conspiracy theories in any given culture may, at first glance, seem quite straightforward. Yet the more one studies the subject, the more intricacies and problems arise, even more so when discussing war. On the surface, the answer to the question: "what is a conspiracy theory" lies in its very name. First, it is a theory, implying that while it is not yet fully verified, yet it is potentially so. As such, it *may* become truth, but is perpetually held short of becoming it[3]. This fact stems out of the other element of the name: conspiracy. A self evident fact, each conspiracy theory supposes the existence of a secretive, influential group. A believer in conspiracy theories seeks to prove their existence, but to remain credible he also has to reinterpret the new data as it appears. This, combined with a focus on interpreting information rather than analyzing it objectively, makes faith the prime criterion for accepting a conspiracy theory. A further problem lies in the fact that one not only has a choice of believing in a conspiracy theory or not, but also of believing what a conspiracy theory *is*. An interpretation of reality which becomes dubbed so effectively becomes treated as nonsense, and a potentially dangerous one. This fact will be developed more in the later parts of this work regarding the narratives and counter-narratives describing 9/11, with both the official and some popular interpretations bearing the hallmarks of a conspiracy theory.

All of the above issues may have led many of the scholars who analyze conspiracy theories to an attempt to avoid the term itself. A case in point would be the seminal work "The Paranoid Style in American Politics"

---

[3] Mark Fenster, *Conspiracy Theories. Secrecy and Power in American Culture,* (Minneapolis & London: University of Minnesota Press, 2008), 103.

(1964) by Richard Hofstadter. This text sought to describe a recurring
phenomenon within the American culture, one that Hofstadter defined by
the term "paranoid style". He explicitly eschewed the use of the term
"conspiracy theory", claiming that "no other word adequately evokes the
sense of heated exaggeration, suspiciousness, and conspiratorial fantasy
that I have in mind"[4]. This trend has been in some parts continued by other
scholars. For Timothy Melley, such narratives surfaced in moments of
"agency panic"[5]. This term, explored in *Empire of Conspiracy* (1999),
denoted a situation where members of the society feel unable to influence
the reality around them, yet at the same time transfer this ability to some
all-powerful agency: the conspiracy itself. A final example out of many
might be the notion of "conspiracy panics" put forward by Jack Z. Bratich.
In his research he concentrated not on the theories themselves, but rather
on the consequences they cause within a society[6].

Despite the above problems, this text will try to use the term in its
common meaning, one that is often intuitively known, that is, an
explanation of reality, a theory, that hinges on the existence of a
conspiracy. Some reservations have to be made, of course. First, no
attempt will be made to verify or disprove the claims of a conspiracy
theory. The texts will be treated and interpreted at their face value, with no
intention, unless otherwise stated, to provide the official, or more
acceptable, interpretation of some events. One has to remember that at
many points in history the US government did indeed conspire, sometimes
against its own citizens, to mention but the Watergate scandal, the Iran-
Contras affair, some elements of the MK-ULTRA program, or the
unfulfilled Operation Northwoods as some examples of true events and
schemes, whose influence and scope was often later blown out of
proportion.

There is, however, the second aspect in need of clarifying, which is a
peculiar course of logic a conspiracy theory narrative usually makes. As
Hofstadter claimed, many such texts are, at the onset, based on facts, but at
some point make an *a priori* assumption – to which they then fit the facts
– usually an assumption, to use Karl Popper's words, quoted in Knight,
"that whatever happens in society – including things which as a rule
people dislike, such as war, unemployment, poverty, shortages – are the

---

[4] Richard Hofstadter, "The Paranoid Style in American Politics," In *The Paranoid
Style in American Politics,* (New York: Vintage Books, 2008), 3.
[5] Timothy Melley, *Empire of Conspiracy*, (Cornell University Press, 1999), 12-13.
[6] Jack Z. Bratich, *Conspiracy Panics: Political Rationality and Popular Culture*,
State University of New York Press, 2008, 6-9.

results of direct design by some powerful individuals or group"[7]. The final element in need of defining is their purpose. A conspiracy theory is, in its most basic form, a response which for some reasons runs counter to the official one. Of all the possible reasons, the prime one would be a lack of an acceptable answer, one that would put sense and meaning into an event, often a tragic one. As Brian L. Keeley claimed, the official reports, seemingly true to the facts, seem to favour contingency over active agency, leaving the public with the conclusion that things "just happen"[8]. On the other hand, conspiracy theorists become "one of the last believers in an ordered universe"[9], who provide the public with a totalizing answer, usually more interpretative than factual, but for this reason more alluring. While not directly, this explanatory function will be an important part of this work.

Conspiracies of conflict

In the ever-growing family of events that spawned conspiracy theories, wars seem to occupy a unique niche. They are, by their very nature, clandestine affairs. Most of the soldiers fighting them never get to know the "full picture", which is even less the case with the civilians. At the same time, however, the public is presented with a contrived image of the conflict, one that attempts the impossible task of making a war both justifiable and appealing. At the same time, one is able to access the other discourse, the "real side" of a conflict, through the testimonies of soldiers, independent war correspondents, and the so-called independent media. The truth, which would probably fall somewhere in between, is nonetheless rarely acceptable for, or indeed available to, the public.

Many scholars, Jean Baudrillard and Judith Butler to name but two, have attempted to tackle this discrepancy. The former's influential work, entitled *The Gulf War Did Not Take Place* (1991), famously interpreted the First Gulf War as a scripted spectacle, which blurred the border between media reality and media fiction, transmitted live directly to our homes. "Fascination and horror at the reality which seemed to unfold before our very eyes mingled with a pervasive sense of unreality as we recognized

---

[7] Peter Knight, "Making Sense of Conspiracy Theories," In *Conspiracy Theories in American History. An Encyclopedia*, ed. Peter Knight, (ABC-Clio, 2006, PDF), 18.
[8] Brian L. Keeley, "Of Conspiracy Theories," In *The Journal of Philosophy* 96, (1999): 109-126, Accessed July 22, 2009, http://www.jstor.org/stable/2564659, 126.
[9] Keeley, 123.

the elements of Hollywood script which preceded the real (...)"[10]. It is a tragic irony that these words, a comment on the practices of the military spokesmen, can also so accurately describe the 2001 attack on the World Trade Center. Even though it was witnessed first-hand by many New Yorkers, most of the global public knows it through media transmissions. This feeling of detachment is by no means lessened nearly twenty years after the Gulf War, as evidenced by a recent book by Judith Butler. Her *Frames of War* (2010) in a way deals with the consequences of the process Baudrillard described. Victims of conflicts become "framed" by various media equipment, and often cease to be considered "living", or even "dead", in the commonly understood sense of the word[11].

Taking the above into account, it is no wonder that some explanations of the origins of wars fall into the realm of the paranoid style. In a sense, therefore, the decisions behind every conflict could be attributed to a conspiracy: "a small group of powerful people combine together in secret to plan and carry out an illegal or improper action, particularly one that alters the course of events"[12]. Likewise, any justification of a declaration of war will bear the traits of the paranoid style by simplifying the political and economic circumstances, rendering the enemy as a "model of malice", and describing the conflict in apocalyptic terms[13]. The problem is that in many situations both the secrecy and potential illegality could be rendered legal by a context, such as the military one. In both official and conspiracy discourses, war is a product of deliberation – a smoothly working and rational, though cruel, machine. The difference lies in the apprehension of the purpose and of the reason why the machine was put into motion. The official narrative often puts emphasis on contingency and necessity, while the conspiratorial – especially in the American cultural context – on deliberation and a gain of the few at the expense of the majority of society.

Making sense of 9/11

9/11 and its aftermath were, in many ways, a case in point. It is quite telling that the official discourse discredited conspiracy theories even before they gained popularity among the American public. A mere two

---

[10] Paul Patton, Introduction to *The Gulf War Did Not Take Place,* by Jean Baudrillard, (Bloomington, IN: Indiana University Press, 1995), 2.

[11] Judith Butler, *Frames of War. When Is Life Grievable?*, (London, New York: Verso, 2010), 1-3.

[12] Peter Knight, *Conspiracy Culture. From Kennedy to The X-Files,* (New York & London: Routledge, 2000), 15.

[13] Hofstadter, 31.

months after the attacks, president George W. Bush emphatically criticized the very act of creating such theories, claiming they move the blame away from the guilty[14]. When the National Commission on Terrorist Attacks Upon the United States, better known as the "9/11 Commission," was formed, its members outright stated that they would not attempt to address any theories that surface, but will present their version of events, one that would render other theories obsolete and unnecessary.

Yet by 2004, a number of vocal groups surfaced that contested the official interpretations of what transpired on September 11th, 2001. Many of them rejected the policies of President Bush, as well as the ongoing wars in Iraq and Afghanistan. Neither Osama bin Laden, nor Saddam Hussein's "weapons of mass destruction" could be found, while American soldiers died, as many claimed, for no apparent reason or benefit to the country. This wave of dissent also comprised those who simply chose not to believe in the explanation the 9/11 Commission had provided. The Report focused heavily on the contingency theory by claiming that even though there were "fault lines within our government – between foreign and domestic intelligence, and between and within agencies", ultimately no blame could be assigned to any of them, as the attacks were so inconceivable and unprecedented in their scale[15]. The text came under attack by those who claimed that, in the words of Jimmy Walter, "it wasn't nineteen screw-ups from Saudi Arabia who couldn't pass flight school who defeated the United States with a set of box cutters"[16]. Members of this loose group became dubbed, by themselves or the media, the "9/11 Truth Movement".

One could wonder, however, why the conspiratorial explanation ever gains any popularity. After all, war-time propaganda makes it both extremely difficult to exhibit pacifistic beliefs without being stigmatized for them, and extremely easy to find comfort in the official line. While a thorough description of such a phenomenon would be beyond the scope of this text, a partial explanation, in relation to 9/11, was explored by Elisabeth Anker in her work "Heroic Identifications: or, 'You Can Love Me too – I am So Like the State'". In this text she attempted to tackle the question that is the reverse of the topics raised by this chapter, namely,

---

[14] Online at http://georgewbush-whitehouse.archives.gov/news/releases/2001/11/20011110-3.html.

[15] *The 9/11 Commission Report. Final Report of the National Commission on Terrorist Attacks Upon the United States,* (Official Government Edition, 2004, PDF), xvi.

[16] James McConnachie and Robin Tudge, *A Rough Guide to Conspiracy Theories,* (London, New York: Rough Guides Ltd., 2008), 397.

why so many Americans support the actions of their government, including "violence, coercion and surveillance over others as well as themselves, and circumscribed their own already restricted access to political power". An answer that is presented is that they did so to regain their mastery over the events, by identifying with the state power, or rather with what "'should have been'– sovereign, self-making – and what it now desires to be 'like'". In a word, such identification gave the capacity to fight the enemy, al-Qaeda in this instance, who would otherwise be untouchable. This could not be an option for many believers of conspiracy theories due to the either in-bred or acquired distrust of the federal government, and the focus of self-reliance and constitutionalism, the hallmark of nativist and militia movements. This problem could only have been solved by shifting the blame to an enemy that could be eliminated – the government itself. While a regular citizen might not have the capacity to strike at terrorists on another continent, he has the democratic tools in place through which to depose the conspiracy/government, and return to the, often idealized, constitutional values. While the influence of such logic may vary, and it is not necessarily connected to conspiratorial thinking, it seems to be underlining in many forms of conspiracy theory narratives picturing the governmental power as the culprit in a conspiracy.

The "Truthers" are in no way a homogenous organization. They include regular citizens disgruntled with the government, some of those who lost their loved ones in the attacks, academics and engineers who saw inconsistencies in the Commission report, political activists, and, of course, conspiracy theorists. Indeed, as *Time* magazine put it, "this is not a fringe phenomenon, it is a mainstream political reality"[17]. Many texts on the 9/11 conspiracy theories open with a version of the following:

> Opinion polls conducted in 2004 found that half of New York City residents believe that U.S. leaders "knew in advance that attacks were planned on or around September 11, 2001, and that they consciously failed to act," and a Scripps-Howard poll in 2006 revealed that more than a third of Americans believe that it is likely or very likely that the U.S. government either actively assisted in the September 11th attacks, or deliberately allowed them to happen because it wanted to go to war in the Middle East.[18]

---

[17] Lev Grossman, "Why the 9/11 Conspiracy Theories Won't Go Away," *Time.com*. Accessed May 17, 2012,
http://www.time.com/time/magazine/article/0,9171,1531304,00.html.
[18] Peter Knight, "Conspiracy Theories about 9/11," In *Centre for International Politics Working Paper Series* 34, (2007): 2, Accessed July 22, 2009.
http://www.socialsciences.manchester.ac.uk/disciplines/politics/researchgroups/cip

Their beliefs, though almost unanimously stemming from the same conviction, are not alike. Many of them have little to do with conspiracism, apart from the 9/11 issue. One example might be Steven Jones, a physicist and former member of the Brigham Young University faculty, who published academic papers claiming that a plane impact could not have caused a building like the Twin Towers to topple, thus becoming "the most scientifically credentialed member of the truth movement"[19]. Their interpretations of the reasons for the attacks are also diverse. Some follow the claims Michael Moore so strongly implied in his documentary *Fahrenheit 9/11*, that the attacks on the World Trade Center in 2001 were a huge blunder of the newly elected Bush administration, while its aftermath was a mixture of shrewd yet cynical policies and a desire for personal gain. Many others, however, contest the government's stance, repeated in the 9/11 Commission Report, that it had no foreknowledge of the attacks. Here one of the persistent leaps of logic occurs: in a paradoxical empowerment of the Bush administration, the conspiracy theorists imply that had the government known about the attacks, it was bound to successfully prevent them regardless of circumstances. As they evidently did not, they must have either allowed for the attacks to take place, or that the Bush administration manufactured them themselves.

The evidence and interpretations resulting from adopting one of the above beliefs differ depending on the given narrative. There are, however, recurring elements that most of them share. The prime division consists of two general beliefs: first, that the US government knew about the attacks and allowed them to happen, and second, that the US government, often at the behest of some external group, used its influence to perpetrate the attacks itself. The first interpretation, to some extent outlined in the previous paragraphs, presents the Bush administration as taking an opportunity to make use of the tragic events to either fortify America's international position, primarily by securing territories in the Middle East, or, in a more paranoid version, to divert the public's attention from the electoral controversies of 2000, to profit from the resulting war, and to pass legislations that would otherwise be decried by the society, most notably the Patriot Act. A legacy of American isolationism, as well as anxiety over the possible abuses perpetrated by the "big government", is visible in such claims, yet they become even more pronounced in the next category.

The second interpretation – which puts more emphasis on the

/publications/documents/Knight_000.pdf.
[19] Fenster, 248-249.

conspiratorial, illicit element – is present in most texts popularly seen as conspiracy theories. Such interpretations suppose that most, if not all, of the official versions of events are a fabrication designed to screen the true perpetrators and their motives. Here the theories can become both very diverse and increasingly implausible. In some the Bush administration is often reduced to the role of the patsy, with the real masterminds appearing as a global corporate entity, a 21st century version of the "money power". In others, especially those of Alex Jones described below, the goal of the conspiracy behind 9/11 was not only to secure profits, both from the war itself and oil revenues, but also to erode American liberties and in the process change the country into a "police state". This category of explanations makes heavy use of the "controlled demolition" theory, which supposes that the hijacked planes hitting the Twin Towers were not the cause of their collapse. As mentioned, scientific studies were conducted, but much of the argument focuses on amateur observation, as well as the case of the often forgotten 7 WTC building, which collapsed even though it was not hit. To present more specific examples, the following second section of the essay will focus on two contemporary conspiracy theory texts, the documentaries *Loose Change: Final Cut* (2007) by Dylan Avery and *9/11: The Road to Tyranny* (2002) by Alex Jones.

Narratives of conspiracy: Dylan Avery and Alex Jones

The history of the work that became *Loose Change* is full of controversy, generated also by the "Truthers" themselves. The movie, as Dylan Avery himself claims, began as a project to create a fictitious 9/11 story revealing that it was an inside job. However, while doing research he became convinced that the inside job scenario was not fiction. The first version of the film was published in April 2005 and attracted the criticism of both the official and the unofficial sources. In 2007 a *Final Cut* version was published, one that is perhaps most widely known today, "purportedly selling over 100,000 copies on DVD and, as of September 2007, enjoying nearly 7 million views (...) on Google Video"[20]. Indeed, the dynamic editing of official footage, juxtapositions of firsthand accounts and vague official responses, combined with the cool and sarcastic voice of the narrator provide an alluring mix.

In essence, *Loose Change* is a case study 9/11 counter narrative. During the two hours of its running, the movie deconstructs the official version of the events that took place on September 11th, 2001, attempting

---

[20] Fenster, 269.

to point out not only its inconsistencies, but undermining the very integrity of the 9/11 Commission. Avery, evidently, proceeds to present his version of events, which is indeed an "inside job scenario", supposing that the 9/11 attacks were orchestrated by certain elements within the US government. Furthermore, according to *Loose Change*, neither Flight 77 nor 93 were destroyed when hitting the Pentagon or crashing into a field near Shanksville, Pennsylvania, respectively. Instead, the Pentagon was supposedly hit by a much smaller plane, while the crash of Flight 93 never took place, the evidence and voice accounts fabricated to create a heroic myth. Finally, it claims that the destruction of the World Trade Center towers 1, 2 and 7 was the result of a controlled demolition. Many other inconsistencies are emphasized, including the notorious story claiming that news channels reported the collapse of the North WTC before the fact of its actually happening , or claims that Osama bin Laden died before the attacks took place.

Where Avery seems to raise questions and contests the official version, Alex Jones' *9/11: The Road to Tyranny* tries to supply the viewer not only with answers, but also the "big picture". In the very first words of the movie he defines a "New World Order", a "criminal global elite" consisting of "power-mad megalomaniacs" bent on creating a totalitarian world-state. To achieve this, Jones claims, they have perpetrated a string of terrorist attacks, often against their own countrymen, and used the resulting crises to enforce legislations that brought them closer to their goal "by making people exchange liberty for the so-called security"[21]. To demonstrate this, *9/11: The Road to Tyranny* tries to put a then very recent event in a historical context, one which supports Jones' conspiracy theory. As with many a conspiratorial text, *9/11: The Road to Tyranny* provides a convincing argument until one ceases to take the enormous amount of facts it provides at face value; yet what is intriguing in Jones' text is his conspiratorial interpretation of war.

According to Jones, war is a tool used to centralize power as well as a "unifying force to control populations", for "humans instinctively shift into mindless group-think when confronted with an external enemy, real or manufactured". None of the historical events featured in *9/11: The Road to Tyranny* are presented as results of an accident – all are the results of deliberation. Even though he vehemently supports the American's right to bear arms, Jones is inherently pacifistic in his convictions, strongly

---

[21] Among such consequences of conflicts he mentions the near-absolute power given to Adolf Hitler after the burning of the Reichstag, the formation of the "globalist" United Nations after WWII and the Patriot Act passed after the 9/11 attacks.

implying that if the power of a centralized government was limited, armed conflicts would cease to happen. His theories seem to be a result of the growing banality of death combined with the need to oppose wars, to which, due to the media, we have grown accustomed to. In yet another paradox, Jones creates a reason for the people to reject military conflicts: a tangible conspiracy with a clearly defined agenda; he effectively manufactures enemies, the action for which he blames the "tyrannical" governments.

A history of conspiracies and conflicts

One line of similarity between the two discussed texts lies in them referencing past events, most notably the 1941 Japanese attack on Pearl Harbor. For Jones, and less so for Avery, the September 11 attacks were a part of a historical trend, or rather "plan", consisting of events that took place for the same purpose – giving the conspiracy a chance to start a war and profit from it. Here, one seemingly encounters an "egg-or-chicken" question. Did the conspiracy theorists combine unconnected events and *casus* to aid credibility to their theories[22] or were they themselves influenced by a cultural motif present in the American consciousness? It is a curious paradox, after all, that similarities between 9/11 and Pearl Harbor are drawn easily by both the official and the conspiracy theories, though in a very different way. As this final part of the work will attempt to demonstrate, the latter seems to be closer to the truth. It will outline this motif, starting with some of its first historical occurrences, to continue chronologically and leading up logically to 9/11.

(1)The Antebellum

The decades leading up to the American Civil War were full of conflicts both ideological and military, as well as their paranoid interpretations. As the year 1861 drew closer, both sides of the slavery debate levelled ever more accusations against each other. Most notably, many of the abolitionist writers alluded to the existence of a "slave power" that "molded (…) the general policy of the country"[23]. What was

---

[22] Richard Hofstadter identified this as a common characteristic of the paranoid style. He observed that conspiracy theorists frequently make their works appear scholarly to gain credibility (37).
[23] William Goodell, "The Role of the Slave Power in American History." In *The Fear of Conspiracy. Images of un-American Subversion from the Revolution to the Present.* David Brion Davis, ed. Ithaca and London: Cornell University Press, 1979, 112.

essentially a lobby of southern politicians, this group was believed to have dictated the laws for the benefit of their states at the expense of the North. Among their goals was to both strengthen and expand the South, primarily by creating new states south of the Mason-Dixon Line. The ultimate purpose of this political manoeuvring was, as more radical abolitionists claimed, to gain a majority in the Senate and impose slavery on the whole country, ruining the Northern way of life and possibly even introducing white slavery[24]. It was this goal that supposedly dictated the United States' relations with Mexico in the first half of the 19th century, and ultimately led to the annexation of Texas in 1845 and the resulting war with Mexico[25]. The attitude towards this conflict, which ended with a definite US victory and won them huge new territories south of 36°30', was probably best summed up by William Goodell, who, referring to the 1812 war with Britain, claimed that "had Canada been adjacent to the slave States, and adapted to slave culture, there can be no reasonable doubt that it could have been conquered as expeditiously as were California and New Mexico"[26].

Finally, it should be mentioned that the case against these claims was not helped by the circumstances surrounding the actual declaration of war, which is the so-called Thornton Affair. After the Texan victory over the Mexicans, the captured president Antonio Lopez de Santa Anna agreed to set the territory's border on the Rio Grande River. The Mexican congress claimed that Santa Anna had no rights to do so, and argued the border should run along the Nueces River. Soon after the annexation of Texas the president James K. Polk moved four thousand troops commanded by General Zachary Taylor to the Rio Grande, still considered as their territory by the Mexicans. A small cavalry unit led by Captain Thornton was sent to scout the banks of the river, and while doing so encountered and was defeated by a much larger Mexican force. As some at the time claimed, the affair itself was instigated by president Polk, a stern believer in the notion of Manifest Destiny, who saw not only Texas, but most of Mexico's territory, as a target for American expansion, and supposedly planned to convince the Texan president Anson Jones to create an incident to provide the US with the reason to attack its neighbour, whom it

---

[24] David Brion Davis, *The Fear of Conspiracy. Images of un-American Subversion from the Revolution to the Present,* (Ithaca and London: Cornell University Press, 1979), 104.

[25] James C. Foley, "Slave Power," In *Conspiracy Theories in American History. An Encyclopedia,* ed. Peter Knight, (ABC-Clio, 2006, PDF), 660.

[26] Goodell, 116.

overshadowed in military strength[27].

(2) The Spanish-American War

An interestingly similar situation took place over half a century later, when the USS *Maine*, docked in Havana, suddenly exploded, an event leading to the Spanish-American War of 1898. On February 15th that year the USS *Maine*, anchored for three weeks in Havana, was utterly destroyed in a massive explosion that killed two thirds of its crew. The ship's mission was to observe the development of the Cuban uprising against Spain, and evacuate any American citizens should the conflict escalate. The explosion resulted in an uproar from the US public, fuelled to some extent by anti-Spanish sentiments, but primarily by the publications of newspapers owned by William Randolph Hearst and Joseph Pulitzer, which featured titles such as "Maine Explosion Caused by Bomb or Torpedo?"[28]. An official American investigation decided that the explosion was indeed external, but failed to put the blame on any party, while a Spanish inquiry claimed that the explosion originated from a mechanical error within the ship[29]. Regardless of the findings, by April 25th, 1898, President McKinley asked the Congress to declare war on Spain. The aftermath of the conflict left the erstwhile global power ultimately crippled, and won America most of the Spanish colonies, as well as Cuban independence.

Two primary questions arise from the sinking of the USS *Maine* – the first concern the conspiratorial reinterpretations of the event itself, the second, the circumstances surrounding its nature and the precedent the event set. The truth behind the event, the reason for the explosion, was still unclear even as America declared war on Spain, so it comes as no surprise that some would claim that the US either capitalized on the explosion, using the yellow press to whip the society into an anti-Spanish frenzy, or it went as far as to sacrifice its own ship. Even a layman could see, the argument went, that the US could only gain in a war with the deteriorating

---

[27] Rolando Avila, "Mexican-American War," In *Conspiracy Theories in American History. An Encyclopedia,* ed. Peter Knight, (ABC-Clio, 2006, PDF), 465.

[28] Amanda Laugesen, "USS *Maine*," In *Conspiracy Theories in American History. An Encyclopedia,* ed. Peter Knight, (ABC-Clio, 2006, PDF), 710.

[29] A final investigation into the matter was carried out in 1976 by Admiral H. G. Rickover. His conclusion was that the most likely cause must have been a spontaneous ignition of the coal dust inside the *Maine*, which in turn led to explosion of the stored munitions. He was also very skeptical of the 1898 inquiry, though his results were a subject of controversy as well (Laugesen,711).

Spanish Empire. The one thing president McKinley lacked was a motive[30]. The Spaniards did not provide it – they welcomed the presence of the USS *Maine*. Its explosion, regardless of being an accident, attack, or "friendly fire", gave the *casus belli* for a war that, given America's interest in acquiring Cuba, seemed most beneficial for Washington. More importantly, however, the Spanish-American War for the first time fully demonstrated how much public opinion can be swayed in favour of a potentially unpopular decision by a single event, regardless of the doubts surrounding it. In analyzing this particular event, Amanda Laugesen highlights two issues. The first is the role of the media, or any other power, which can effectively create a version of events, a truth, for their own purposes. The second is the importance of "technical or scientific evidence" and investigation, often viewed as conclusive only by the virtue of the scientific nature. Laugesen claims that the story of the *Maine* "also reveals that technical evidence (which is not infallible) can be given too much power"[31]. In the confusion surrounding the fate of the *Maine* the search for objective truth became a secondary issue, swept aside by hysterical jingoism, which painfully demonstrated how a manufactured truth can be used to sway a society's opinion, and which, regardless of the complexity of a conspiracy theory, returned in the aftermath of 9/11.

(3) The First World War

If the Spanish-American war was perceived as a conspiracy of American making, the US involvement in the First World War combined this element with the notion of serving a foreign interest. It was different from the 1898 conflict, however, in the sense that the reason to enter the war was unequivocally provided by the enemy-to-be: Germany renewed its total naval war doctrine in 1917, which resulted in the sinking of a number of American ships. Furthermore, once the US entered the war, president Woodrow Wilson's administration, elected in 1916 on an anti-war platform, was so expert in creating pro-war propaganda, one which presented Germany as an "evil empire" which conspired against freedom and democracy, that any dissenters were not only ridiculed, but often lynched[32]. It comes as no surprise, therefore, that most of the revisionist writing appeared in the 1920s. Many of the historians who penned it were actually employed by the US as propagandists, yet changed their convictions when the full horror of the war became apparent, combined

---

[30] McConnachie, Tudge, 359.
[31] Laugesen, 711.
[32] Olmsted, 21.

with the realization that not only did the Germans bear the sole responsibility for it, but the Entente itself was revealed as "partly guilty of the charge that their war aims were based on selfishness and greed"[33].

Most of those revisionist writings embraced those beliefs deemed taboo during the war, employing the tropes of a conspiracy theory to varying degrees. Some, like the ex-propagandist Harry Elmer Barnes, attempted to combat the official "conspiracy theory" with a contingency theory, eschewing clear divisions between the "good" and the "bad" side. Others, however, took to identifying an agency that purposefully caused the US to enter the war, ushering in a disaster for the common citizen. One of the small groups that benefited from the conflict was to be the "money power" of the Populist rhetoric that had been present in American culture since the early 19th century. In the case of WWI such claims were not fully unfounded: the US allowed both sides to buy their goods, while in the period between 1915 and 1917 American banks loaned close to $3 billion to European powers, primarily to the Entente. This led to a belief that the US is a "financial oligarchy", with the president fully controlled by the "money power", that wanted to profit from selling arms to either side and maundered the country into helping the English and the French to secure their victory and ability to pay back the loans Wall Street gave them[34]. Such claims would continue to have weight and returned in the years following the Wall Street crash of 1929, most notably in Gen. Smedley D. Butler's *War is a Racket* (1935). The second motif is that of outside influence, especially that of Britain. A vivid example are the theories surrounding the sinking of HMS *Lusitania*, a passenger ship that was destroyed by a German U-boat torpedo on May 7th, 1915, killing 1198 passengers, including 128 Americans. The disaster was supposedly allowed to happen by the British, who withdrew its escort and allowed it to sail through dangerous waters despite German warnings, in hopes of provoking America to enter the war[35]. More successful activities were attributed to British propagandists working in America as well as pro-British elements that counselled the president. Of the first group, the most notable was to be Sir Gilbert Parker, who claimed that his activities in forming the American public opinion were both successful and extensive, while Col. Edward House and Walter Hines Page, the ambassador to the United Kingdom, were numbered in the second[36].

---

[33] Olmsted, 21-22.
[34] Olmsted, 23.
[35] McConnachie, Tudge, 323.
[36] Olmsted, 24.

(4) Pearl Harbor and the Second World War

The paranoid revisions of either of the World Wars form a mirror image. Just like its predecessor, the Second World War was interpreted as an example of foreign powers forcing America to enter a conflict against the convictions of its citizens. Before 1941, the US public was vehemently against participating in what was slowly becoming a World War on any front. Politicians on both fronts favoured American non-intervention as well – President Franklin D. Roosevelt famously claimed during the 1940 elections that he would not send American soldiers to fight a foreign war. All of them, however, changed their minds after the sudden Japanese attacks on the military base in Pearl Harbor on December 7th, 1941. This allowed Roosevelt to declare war on Japan, and consequently on Nazi Germany, a contribution which ultimately allowed the Allies to emerge victorious.

As mentioned, one of the most common conspiratorial interpretations of the Pearl Harbor attack supposes – in a vein similar to its counterparts of 9/11 – that Roosevelt's administration either knew about the Japanese plans and yet did nothing to counteract them, or that the president's diplomatic staff did everything in their power to aggravate Tokyo, force it to commit to war and use a humiliating defeat to rally the public opinion[37]. In the words of Charles A. Lindbergh, America got into the European war through the Asian Back door[38]. This thesis originated from the controversies surrounding the investigations into the reasons behind the dramatic loss, which was originally blamed on Pearl Harbor's commanders. However, evidence surfaced even during the war that some censure of FDR was issued only after his death. Over the years the significance of the attack evolved, and in the eyes of some, Pearl Harbor became the prime example of the American government sacrificing both the lives and reputation of its servicemen for what it perceived to be the greater good.

(5) Vietnam War and the Cold War

The Cold War era was a time presented as a Manichean conflict between good and evil, coupled with an unprecedented level of secrecy and deceit; as such, it became the ultimate breeding ground for conspiracy theories. If, as Katherine Olmsted argues, by the end of WWI the

---

[37] McConnachie, Tudge, 360-363.
[38] Olmsted, 45.

Americans had started to believe that their own government has enough influence to plot against them, by the 1980s many became fully convinced that this was indeed the case. The notorious MK-ULTRA program not only introduced the term "brainwashing" into the vernacular, but also shocked many with its blatantly experimental use of unknowing subjects. The Central Intelligence Agency rose to complement the Communist Other, a home-grown "Gestapo" of great power and un-American secrecy[39]. The assassination of President John F. Kennedy, and the unsatisfactory findings of the Warren Commission, made a dent in the public trust. The revelations of the Watergate scandal and the Iran-Contra affair turned this dent into a wide gap and proved that presidential power can be abused for personal gain, regardless of public opinion or democratic values.

Within this context, the notion that one of the most traumatic conflicts in American history – the Vietnam War – was started and conducted only for the benefit of the industrialists and financiers was bound to appear. Most of the revisions of this conflict concentrate on the Gulf of Tonkin incident from August 2nd and 3rd, 1964. During these days the USS *Maddox* was allegedly attacked by ships of the communist Democratic Republic of Vietnam while in its territorial waters, supporting the pro-American Republic of Vietnam with information from its surveillance equipment. On the 3rd of August, however, the *Maddox* and another ship, the *C. Turner Joy*, were supposedly attacked by torpedoes. No evidence of enemy ships was found, however, due to bad weather. In the event's aftermath president Lyndon Jonson was given "a free hand to escalate U.S. military action in Southeast Asia", even though it was entirely possible that no torpedo attack had taken place[40]. The Vietnam War itself was reinterpreted to be waged either to prevent the spread of Communism in the region, to secure the local resources, mostly oil and gas, or even to provide profits for the money power, turning the conflict into a war that could not be won[41].

Conclusion

The tragic events of September 11th, 2001, are the final link in this chain of events, one that has in truth little to do with some conspiracy's centuries-long master plan. The fall of the WTC towers saw a return of a

---

[39] Olmsted, 122.
[40] Nicholas Turse, "Tonkin Gulf Incidents," In *Conspiracy Theories in American History. An Encyclopedia.* ed. Peter Knight, (ABC-Clio, 2006, PDF), 690.
[41] McConnachie, Tudge, 374-375.

cultural motif already embedded within the American psyche. As this paper has tried to demonstrate, wars provide a breeding ground for conspiracy theories for a number of reasons. First, there is no way for the public to see the "truth" behind a conflict, most if not all of the information reaching it will invariably be propaganda, constructed narratives and anti-narratives. Most of the conspiracy theories divide the world into an apocalyptic struggle of "us" versus "them", caused by deplorable, clandestine actions, and in doing so they fit Richard Hofstadter's definition of the paranoid style. Paradoxically, by shifting the blame on a shadowy, all-powerful force, the conspiracy theorists empower both themselves and their country. They suppose that political events *can* be controlled, that wars are not started due to human error or the machinations of history, but due to conscious human agency. Moreover, in many instances they whitewash their nations by claiming that they were not to blame for the state of affairs – after all, they were powerless against a conspiracy. In the end, a conspiratorial interpretation of wars and interventions may be a false one, but remains comforting, for in supposing that there is an absolute evil orchestrating wars, it makes these disastrous events something more than "only the cold hearted killing of innocent people"[42].

Filmography

Avery, Dylan. *Loose Change*. Internet Video. Directed by Dylan Avery. 2007.
Jones, Alex. *9/11: The Road to Tyranny*. Internet Video. Directed by Alex Jones. 2002.

Bibliography

The 9/11 Commission Report. Final Report of the National Commission on Terrorist Attacks Upon the United States. Official Government Edition, 2004. PDF.
Anker, Elisabeth. 2012. "Heroic Identifications: or, 'You Can Love Me too – I am So Like the State'". in Theory & Event. Vol. 15, Issue 1. Jodi Dean, Davide Panagia eds. The Johns Hopkins University Press. Accessed 03.04.2013. https://han.buw.uw.edu.pl/han/MUSE/ muse.jhu. edu/journals/theory_and_event/v015/15.1.anker.html
Avila, Rolando. "Mexican-American War." In *Conspiracy Theories in*

---

[42] Knight, 3.

American History. An Encyclopedia. Peter Knight ed. ABC-Clio, 2006. PDF.

Barkun, Michael. *A Culture of Conspiracy: Apocalyptic Visions in Contemporary America.* Berkeley: University of California Press, 2006.

Bratich, Jack Z. *Conspiracy Panics: Political Rationality and Popular Culture.* State University of New York Press, 2008.

Butler, Judith. *Frames of War. When Is Life Grievable?.* London, New York: Verso, 2010.

Davis, David Brion ed. *The Fear of Conspiracy. Images of un-American Subversion from the Revolution to the Present.* Ithaca and London: Cornell University Press, 1979.

Fenster, Mark. *Conspiracy Theories. Secrecy and Power in American Culture.* Minneapolis & London: University of Minnesota Press, 2008.

Foley, James C. "Slave Power." In *Conspiracy Theories in American History. An Encyclopedia.* Peter Knight ed. ABC-Clio, 2006. PDF.

Goodell, William. "The Role of the Slave Power in American History." In *The Fear of Conspiracy. Images of un-American Subversion from the Revolution to the Present.* David Brion Davis, ed. Ithaca and London: Cornell University Press, 1979.

Grossman, Lev. "Why the 9/11 Conspiracy Theories Won't Go Away." *Time.com.* Accessed May 17, 2012.
http://www.time.com/time/magazine/article/0,9171,1531304,00.html

Hofstadter, Richard. "The Paranoid Style in American Politics." In *The Paranoid Style in American Politics.* New York: Vintage Books, 2008.

Keeley, Brian L. "Of Conspiracy Theories." In *The Journal of Philosophy,* Vol. 96, No. 3 (Mar., 1999), pp. 109-126. Online at http://www.jstor.org/stable/2564659. Accessed: July 22, 2009.

Knight, Peter. *Conspiracy Culture. From Kennedy to The X-Files.* New York & London: Routledge, 2000.

Knight, Peter. "Conspiracy Theories about 9/11." In *Centre for International Politics Working Paper Series,* No. 34, August 2007. Accessed July 22, 2009.
http://www.socialsciences.manchester.ac.uk/disciplines/politics/researc hgroups/cip/publications/documents/Knight_000.pdf

Knight, Peter. "Making Sense of Conspiracy Theories." In *Conspiracy Theories in American History. An Encyclopedia.* ed. Peter Knight. ABC-Clio, 2006. PDF.

Laugesen, Amanda. "USS *Maine.*" In *Conspiracy Theories in American History. An Encyclopedia.* Peter Knight ed. ABC-Clio, 2006. PDF.

McConnachie, James. Robin Tudge. *A Rough Guide to Conspiracy*

Theories. London, New York: Rough Guides Ltd., 2008.

Melley, Timothy. *Empire of Conspiracy*. Cornell University Press, 1999.

Olmsted, Kathryn S. *Real Enemies: Conspiracy Theories and American Democracy, World War I to 9/11*. New York: Oxford University Press, 2009.

Patton, Paul. Introduction to *The Gulf War Did Not Take Place* by Jean Baudrillard. Bloomington, IN: Indiana University Press, 1995.

Turse, Nicholas. "Tonkin Gulf Incidents." In *Conspiracy Theories in American History. An Encyclopedia*. Peter Knight ed. ABC-Clio, 2006. PDF.

FROM "INFREQUENT SHOCK TO [...] MAIN THREAD OF THE PLOT": PROFESSIONAL TECHNIQUES OF TORTURE AND THE DISCURSIVE PARTICIPATION OF FOX'S TV-SERIES *24* SINCE 9/11

DANIEL ŠÍP

"Time to Think about Torture"[1] – this was the headline for an appeal Jonathan Altar made in the US-American *Newsweek Magazine* in November 2001. He argued that September 11, 2001[2] laid the ground for an introduction of torture as a legal and governmental practice of interrogation. The law-scholar and practising lawyer Alan M. Dershowitz led the debate a step further. In the beginning of 2002 the *San Francisco Chronicle* published his proposition to allow regimented and controlled torture as a state practice. In cases of immediate threats by terrorists, he proposed, "torture warrants" should be issued which would grant US-investigators torture as a means to interrogate terrorists.[3] Dershowitz's proposition relied heavily on a threat scenario, which has been repeatedly popularized as the *ticking time-bomb-scenario*. In this scenario, torture would be necessary if a time bomb hidden by terrorists is about to explode at a secret location. In such a case, torture would be, as Dershowitz argued, the only way to effectively extract the information about the bomb's location.

Both articles were met by strong objections and re-started a discussion

---

[1] Jonathan Altar, "Time To Think About Torture," *Newsweek*, November 5, 2001
[2] From here on I will refer to this date with the common abbreviate *9/11* – this is done for pragmatic reasons and in an awareness of the term's problematic connotation and discursive instrumentalisations. I am not using the abbreviation as a self-evident sign.
[3] Alan M. Dershowitz, "Want to Torture? Get a Warrant." *San Francisco Chronicle*, January 22, 2002, A 19.

about the legitimacy of torture and the moral and legal framework of liberal democracies. Up until 2004 the US-American public discourses on torture were grappling with the question if governments should be allowed to use torture. The arguments of the opponents of torture are various. Their reasons range from legal-pragmatic to moral objections, from medical to psychological cautioning. Underlying all arguments, however, is a fear of the effect torture bequeaths upon the victim and the condoning society. Proponents of torture primarily rely on the argument that , in times of national security, it is an abhorrent but necessary instrument to adequately respond to the new threats of terrorism.

A problem for proponents as well as opponents of torture has been the question whether torture is an operable and efficient technique of interrogation. Opponents of torture tend to regard torture as inefficient and unreliable. Torture, from this perspective, overwhelms the victim and makes him say everything and anything to stop the further infliction of pain. Interestingly, a look into interrogation manuals by the American military and CIA reveal that the infliction of pain is understood as a very risky affair, endangering a subjects' will to cooperate.[4]

Despite such widespread uncertainty, there are historical records of successful torture, as Lutz Ellrich has argued after discussing the question with a former Nazi interrogator.[5] The most recent revelations about US-American interrogation techniques in the war against terror reveal that the assumption that pain can be a fast way of extracting information remains seductive. In 2004 a number of memorandums were published under the Freedom of Information Act which proved to an American public, discussing if torture after *9/11* was justified, that the US-American administration had been researching and had resorted to enhanced interrogation techniques since 2002.

Both sides cannot make a conclusive case for or against torture's reliability. But an answer to the question if torture is a legitimate tool in times of national security apparently hinges on the respective opinion about torture's reliability.[6]

---

[4] See for example KUBARK's section on the infliction of pain.

[5] Ellrich, Lutz, "Was spricht für die Folter?," in *Wahrheit und Gewalt. Der Diskurs der Folter in Europa und den USA*, Ed. Weitin, Thomas (Bielefeld: Transcript, 2010), 267-84.

[6] Curiosity moved one US-American reporter so far as to expose himself publically to *waterboarding* to test the method's effect. Cf. "Waterboarding: Historically Controversial." *Harrigan on the Hunt*, November 7, 2006, Fox News.

The legitimacy of torture representations

A number of British and US-American television series have portrayed torture since 9/11 and hence participated in the precarious discourse on torture's legitimacy as outlined above. They have been making offerings to the question if torture works.

This participation or the representation of torture in general has been problematized by scholars and authors alike. Elaine Scarry has come to the conclusion that pain is hardly representable. In her very pertinent study *The Body in Pain* she argues that pain is at best approachable in metaphoric terms, such as a "burning pain".[7] Obviously, this is a general problem of language, but with regard to torture it can turn into a dramatic failure of language with political implications. If the reality of pain is inaccessible to anyone who is not experiencing it, as Scarry claims, then representing the pain of torture victims entails the danger of misrepresentation. The representation of torture is constantly exposed to tests of adequacy and legitimacy. The right choice of words and a careful degree of explicitness are essential. Literary representations are not devoid of this issue as Nobel laureate J.M. Coetzee pointed out:

> [...] The dark, forbidden [torture] chamber is the origin of novelistic fantasy *per se*; in creating an obscenity, in enveloping it in mystery, the state creates the preconditions for the novel to set about its work of representation.

Yet there is something tawdry about following the state in this way, making its vile mysteries the occasion of fantasy. For the writer the deeper problem is not to allow himself to be impaled on the dilemma proposed by the state, namely, either to ignore its obscenities or else to produce representations of them. The true challenge is how not to play the game by the rules of the state, how to establish one's own authority, how to imagine torture and death on one's own terms.[8]

With this in mind, this paper sets out to analyze the fourth season of the US-American TV-Series *24*. This particular season has been widely criticized for its depiction of torture and includes more torture scenes than any of the previous seasons. To refine the analytical focus, the analysis will concentrate on torture scenes that depict a reliance on knowledge

---

[7] Elaine Scarry, *The Body in Pain: The Making and Unmaking of the World* (New York: Oxford UP, 1985), 7.

[8] J.M. Coetzee, "Into the Dark Chamber: The Novelist and South Africa," *New York Times Books*, January 12, 1986. Section 7; Page 13, Column 1.

which, as stated in the show, stems from research or manuals on interrogation.

This paper aims at showing how the TV-series made concrete offerings to a discourse which was struggling with the question if torture should be legalized, and in 2004, the period of the screening of season four entered a phase of concretization. Nearly simultaneously with the publication of the "torture memos" in 2004, the events of Abu Ghraib came to public awareness. Most importantly, however, the scandal surrounding the torture memos revealed that, secretly and unofficially, knowledge about potentially illegal interrogation manuals was circulating within the US-American administration.

Production and Screening and the Constellation of the Torture Discourse

Season four of *24* premiered in the United States on January 5 and ended on May 23, 2005. From the scarce information on the series' production, it is deducible that the production of season four will have begun at the latest around the end of May 2004. As all the previous seasons were filmed into their screening period we can assume that the production of season four ended towards the end of May 2005, just before the season finale was screened.

The year 2004 was particularly reminiscent of 9/11, both for the United States and for Europe. The March 11, 2004 Madrid train bombing too, which killed 191 people, was initially connected to Al Qaeda. On October 29, 2004 Al Jazeera broadcast a video recording showing Osama bin Laden taking responsibility for the attacks on the World Trade Center, but accusing the Bush administration of having brought the attacks on themselves. In September 2004, George W. Bush accepted his nomination as candidate for the Republican Party for the 2004 presidential election. He was re-elected for his second term in November 2004. This was a victory by a slim margin against the democratic candidate John Kerry. The presidential race was dominated and decided by issues of national security in times of terrorism, the war in Iraq and, not least, about torture. Two events that were picked up by the US-American torture discourse will be particularly formative for this analysis: 1. The successive release of *torture memos* on interrogation techniques from the Bush administration; 2. The publication of images showing prisoner abuse at the Abu Ghraib detention facility in Afghanistan. These incidents, which were accompanied by accusations of torture voiced through US-American and international public media outlets, mark a change in the public discourse on torture in the United States. The change is particularly striking when it is compared to the time directly after the attacks of September 11, a time of a rather abstract evaluation of torture's dangers and potentials. I consider the change as a moment of substantiation or concretization. The production and screening period of *24*'s season four encompassed these events and their aftermath.

Constellation and Position of Season Four

Season four enters this discourse configuration with the season's pilot on January 09, 2005. Few indications are given about the season's time frame. While the pilot's narration begins in the morning hours of "Day 4"[9], the year it is set in is not mentioned. One can deduct from the information given in this season that season four is set in the year 2004, possibly at the beginning of 2005, which means it broadly overlaps with the time of its screening.

The plot can be loosely structured into four phases which are organized along the complex and interlaced plan of Habib Marwan. Marwan is identified by the Counter Terrorist Unit (CTU) as the head of a terrorist organization including a number of sleeper cells, who have initiated a large scale attack on the US initiated from American soil.

In the first phase (episodes 1-8) one of Marwan's terrorist cells kidnaps Secretary of Defence James Heller and his daughter/assistant Audrey Raines. Heller is supposed to be subjected to a web-broadcast trial for "crimes against humanity". CTU works tirelessly to prevent the staged trial, Heller's certain execution, and the nation's humiliation. CTU agent and the show's protagonist Jack Bauer is able to rescue them just in time before a cruise missile, sent as a final resort on President Keeler's order, hits the compound in which Heller is held.

In phase two (episodes 9-13) CTU discovers that Heller's kidnapping was only diversionary and that the terrorists were actually acquiring a device to melt down all of the US-American nuclear power plants. CTU and Jack succeed in preventing the majority of plants from melting down.

In the meantime, Marwan has used the chaos of the moment as another diversion to initiate phase three (episodes 14-19). In this phase Marwan orders the attack on Air Force One and President Keeler. Air Force One is successfully struck, President Keeler nearly killed and in a coma. Vice

---

[9] Since one season in *24* is the equivalent of a day, the show's seasons are titled according to the day they portray within the shows overall narrative. Season four is therefore titled "Day 4".

President Logan becomes acting president.

Jack Bauer uncovers that this, too, was only a diversionary attack to achieve the main goal. In this last phase (episodes 15-24) codes and instructions to US-American nuclear missiles are stolen from the wreck of Air Force One. Marwan's men acquire a nuclear warhead which is mounted on a cruise missile and launched from Iowa against Los Angeles. Jack is able to find and kill Marwan and the missile is shot down before it hits its target. This effectively ends Marwan's grand scheme to make the American nation pay for their "imperialism" and "ignorance".[10]

Torture in Season Four

Season two had already introduced terrorists of a Muslim background. Season four uses the concept of Muslim sleeper cells for terrorists operating within the United States. It is particularly reminiscent of the investigations and evidence presented on the attackers in the aftermath of 9/11. But the season additionally appears to make references to the more recent events. In the first episode, Habib Marwan initiates his plan with the derailment and explosion of a train. Marwan's rhetoric during the recording of a confession video has a striking resemblance to the video message of October 29, 2004, in which Osama bin Laden accused the US-American administration and the American people for having brought 9/11 upon themselves. James Heller's online trial is reminiscent of the online decapitation of Nick Berg,[11] kidnapped in Iraq and killed by a group of men allegedly connected to Abu Musab al-Zarqawi. Zarqawi was believed to be a leading Al-Qaeda operative.[12] In their statement – minutes before Berg's execution – the kidnappers refer to Abu Ghraib as a legitimisation of their actions. These visual and rhetoric indications continuously remind a sensitive audience of 9/11 and its subsequent investigations. But it is the depiction and negotiation of torture that stands out in season four. Torture representations in this season make the most explicit offerings to a US-American discourse that has been engaged in tackling the question of torture's legitimacy since 2002.

Season four spends twenty-three minutes in the torture cell and

---

[10] "Day 4 - 01:00 A.M. – 02:00 A.M." *24*, (April 25, 2005), Fox.

[11] The set-up of the trial and Heller's clothing bear a striking resemblance to the decapitation video of Nick Berg, which was released on May 14 on an "Islamist Website" as the *NY Times* called it

[12] Craig Whitlock. "Al-Zarqawi's Biography." *The Washington Post,* June 8, 2006, http://www.washingtonpost.com/wp-dyn/content/article/2006/06/08/AR2006060800299.html.

constitutes – after season two – the second torture peak in the history of *24*. It distributes these representations over ten different scenes, as many as season two. And, just like season two, season four reiterates the majority of its torture scenes in its retrospective summaries or recaps at the beginning of each episode, underlining their essential significance for the plot. The reception of the season was even more critical and, in its aftermath, reviews and academic articles moved torture to their headlines when discussing the show. In his article "Torture and Morality in Fox's *24*", Douglas L. Howard commented on season four:

> Season Four is more violent in terms of the number of tortures that take place. In more than half of the episodes, the plot revolves around some form of torture. The guilty certainly do get tortured. Bauer and his fellow agents torture the innocent and the guilty alike. [...] regardless of how unrealistic and absurd it all may be, if *24* enables us to deal with that darker drama currently playing out in the streets and cities of the world, then, in the end, it is a guilty pleasure that is worth the time.[13]

24's handling of torture – and particularly season four – became an issue to the extent that in 2006 a U.S. Army Brigadier Specialist, accompanied by a group of professional interrogators, visited the show's writers and producers to dissuade them from depicting torture. One of the visitors reported instances of abuse in Iraq which had happened right after interrogators had watched the TV-Show.[14] In May 2005 Adam Green of the *NY Times* asked, if "'24' [had] descended down a slippery slope in portraying acts of torture as normal and therefore justifiable?"[15] Despite the assumed danger of the show's depiction of torture, none of the reviewers take a closer look at how the episode, and *24* in general, participates in the contemporary torture discourse. As remains to be shown, only in dissecting *24*'s complex order of torturers and tortured is it possible to understand its participation in a discourse that is asking the question if torture is a legitimate tool in the war on terror.

The term "torture" is uttered in sixteen instances, three times as often as in season two. Seven actions are retrospectively called torture, while

---

[13] Douglas L. Howard, "Torture and Morality in Fox's 24," in *Reading 24: TV against the Clock*, Ed. Stephen Peacock (London, England: I.B. Tauris, 2007), 137, 144.

[14] Jane Mayer, "Whatever It Takes: The politics of the man behind '24'," *The New Yorker* 12, 2007,
<http://www.newyorker.com/reporting/2007/02/19/070219fa_fact_mayer>.

[15] Adam Green, "Normalizing Torture on '24', *NYTimes*, May 22, 2005,
<http://www.nytimes.com/2005/05/22/arts/television/22gree.html?pagewanted=all>

three scenes that are structurally similar remain unnamed. The scenes called torture by characters in season four can be broadly arranged into two major groups: 1) torture by terrorists and 2) torture by US government officials. The latter group needs to be distinguished by three sub-categories: a) torture by government officials without special training; b) torture by professional torturers whose sole function is to torture and whose methods differ from anyone else in *24*; and c) torture by Jack Bauer. The concern of the torture discourse since 2004 focuses on the government agents and their methods. Accordingly, a similar perspective with regard to *24* promises to be particularly insightful for the series' handling of torture.

Governmental Torture

The first torture by government agents begins in episode three and comes to an end in episode six, screened on January 10 and 24, respectively. Its narrative thread reappears in episode 22, screened on May 16. This torture scene is one of the most debated within the season and, because of its constellation, very revealing. It is the torture of Richard Heller, son of Secretary of Defence James Heller. CTU suspects he has connections to the terrorists who kidnapped his father.

Richard is characterized in a discussion that occurs between him and his father only minutes before the kidnapping. He is an open critic of President Keeler's politics and of the administration his father is involved with. James Heller's intention is to dissuade Richard from speaking against President Keeler's policy at a rally in "Lockheed". Their discussion shows how *24* tries to participate in the contemporary US-American political discourse of the year 2004:

> *Richard Heller*: I'm going, Dad. And there's nothing you can do to stop me. How many cars do you need to get places? [in reference to the autocade outside Richard's house]
> *James Heller*: I didn't come here to argue about the environment, Richard.
> *Richard*: I didn't ask you to come at all.
> *James*: I do not want you to attend or to speak at that rally at Lockheed this afternoon.
> *Richard:* You don't have any leverage over what I do anymore. You haven't since I stopped taking your money.
> *James*: Can't you ever think of anything besides yourself? If you do this, it will humiliate the President, and it will be dangerous to national security.
> *Richard*: What could be more dangerous than 2,500 missile delivery systems?

> *James*: Oh, spare me your sixth-grade Michael Moore logic. The world is a little bit more complicated than that, Richard. We do not live in a utopia. America has enemies.
>
> *Richard:* Enemies who were our friends a year ago. And in another year, it'll change again, unless people stop supporting your psychotic need to control the world.
>
> *James*: Psychotic need?! We serve our country! We serve the cause of freedom! What do you do?!
>
> *Richard*: Why don't you just go back to your little motorcade and drive somewhere where people actually buy the lies you're selling?
>
> *James*: Okay, look, look, we don't have to do this, okay? We do not have to.
>
> *Richard*: Fine, Dad. What do you want to do?
>
> *James*: Do not disrespect me. I am your father.[16]

Richard and James become allegorical characters that can be read as representing the political factions, as they were understood to be in 2004, the year of the US-American presidential race which ended in Bush's narrow re-election in November 2004. James Heller's concern for national security seems to be confirmed as adequate when the terrorists strike in Richard's front yard, and his indicated fate, if read against the gruesome decapitation of Nick Berg, offers to side with his take on questions regarding national security – a provocative proposal if read against representations of the societal climate since Bush's reelection.[17] James Heller tries to marginalize Richard's argument with a patriarchal tone and by referencing George W. Bush's prominent and controversial critic, Michael Moore. However, for a country that was seen as divided and still grappling with the aftermath of 9/11, Richard widens the perspective on terrorism. His criticisms of opportunistic American foreign relations that backfired, was a criticism raised also after 9/11, and also by Michael Moore.[18] The argument is not decided in this season. Marwan's final nuclear attack originating from the heart of America's "corn belt", Iowa, allows a critical stance on the proliferations of nuclear weapons, but also on the argument in support of strengthening national security. The fight

---

[16] "Day 4 - 07:00 A.M. – 08:00 A.M." *24*. (January 09, 2005), Fox.

[17] An exit poll done in 2004 indicates that 54% of the voters who cast a vote felt they were "safer from terrorism" since 2001. 79% of these were Bush voters. 41 % of the voters of 2004 election felt less safe from terrorism since 2001 and of those 85% gave their voice to John Kerry.

[18] Michael Moore's *Fahrenheit 9/11* (2004) repeatedly criticizes George Bush senior's support of the Taliban in the 1970s and 1980s. In *Bowling for Columbine* (2002) Moore addresses Lockheed Martin's role as a weapons manufacturer in the context of the Columbine shooting.

between the two sets the tone for the ensuing torture of Richard.

After James Heller has been kidnapped, Richard is immediately apprehended by CTU. Upon arrival at the CTU headquarters, he is brought in for interrogation. All the while, the audience has no knowledge of any relation that Richard might have had with terrorists. CTU is also working on circumstantial evidence. Two reasons make Richard a suspect: 1) He is the only person who survived the attack but was not kidnapped; and 2) James' visit was unscheduled and not officially announced, and Richard was the only person who could have leaked the information to the terrorists. In an attempt to substantiate the evidence, Chief of Staff Curtis Manning and the head of CTU Erin Driscoll, who is in charge, connect a polygraph to Richard. Though not fully conclusive, the polygraph reveals that Richard holds back information.

Richard unwaveringly maintains that he is unaware of any terrorist plot to kidnap his father. His stance convinces Erin Driscoll to bring in agent Richards, one of the few trained interrogation experts in *24*. Curtis seems uncertain about the decision to include Richards, as becomes clear in the short conversation between him and Driscoll:

> *Driscoll*: You think he's lying?
> *Curtis*: It's possible. Richard was the only one who knew where his father
> would be this morning. And he may have told someone about it.
> *Driscoll*: Why would Richard protect somebody who's betrayed him?
> *Curtis*: Because he's too arrogant to believe that's what's happened.
> > *Driscoll*: It'll take days to go through his phone records. I want you to
> > see if you can get the name out of him another way.
> *Curtis*: What do you mean?
> *Driscoll*: You know what I mean.
> *Curtis*: Erin, we're not even sure if he's guilty of anything.
> *Driscoll*: This is how we'll find out. Get started.[19]

This is a typical conversation for *24*: by creating a "ticking-time-bomb-scenario" torture methods are legitimized by the characters. Driscoll's final comment also highlights that *24* is concerned with the efficiency problem of torture. But Driscoll seems pressured into ordering Richard's torture, despite the risk of torturing an innocent person. This might explain why Driscoll does not use the word "torture" here. It is obvious that she demands harsher techniques than the usual questioning, and is ordering something that both feel reluctant to pronounce.

The fact that Driscoll and Curtis bring in Richards underlines that the

---

[19] "Day 4 - 09:00 A.M. – 10:00 A.M." *24*. (January 10, 2005), Fox.

universe of *24* incorporates a professional hierarchy of torture. While Curtis has received a rudimentary training of improvisational methods for in-field interrogation and inflicting pain, Driscoll herself never tortures and does not appear to be trained. Richards, in contrast, is a mono-functional professional of torture.

Upon entering the interrogation room, Richards displays a suitcase filled with syringes and a serum that, as Curtis explains to Richard, "makes every nerve ending in your body feel like it's on fire."[20] This is the first time that the effect and function of a torture technique is explained in *24*.[21] Yet, Curtis interrupts Richards before he can inject his serum. He feels reluctant to use "inappropriate use of force" on somebody who might not have been involved "knowingly". Driscoll is upset and tries to order Curtis back into the interrogation room but he refuses unless she is prepared to give this order "in writing", which Driscoll is not. Torture seems to constitute a practice that has negative legal consequences if it can be traced. The fact that Curtis is not so much concerned about torturing a person but with torturing an innocent further stresses what was already indicated in season two: torture is a practice used in governmental circles of *24*, even though a legal or moral framework appears at work that fosters the condemnation of the practice – a technique applied outside the view of the public.

Curtis then proposes a different technique, which he calls "sensory disorientation", adding "I have seen good results with [it]". He goes on explaining it: "Cut off his sight, saturate his auditory. It's noninvasive". Driscoll agrees and orders him to "[t]ry it".[22]

The camera does not return to the interrogation room for another fifteen minutes and when the audience is led back to Richard, he is already prepped to a sophisticated machine, wears light-blocking goggles and is forced to listen to a sinus-like sound transmitted via headphones. The sound permeates the headphones slightly, and the audience gets an impression of what Richard is exposed to. Curtis explains the technique to Richard, highlighting its effectiveness.

> *Curtis*: How long do you think you've been sitting here like this?
> *Richard*: Three, four hours.
> *Curtis*: It's been less than 30 minutes. Time is the first thing you lose track

---

[20] Ibid.

[21] In particular, historical research is well acquainted with the fact that the mere display of torture tools, of what will happen to the victim, is often a much faster way of breaking the subject.

[22] "Day 4 - 09:00 A.M. – 10:00 A.M." *24*. (January 10, 2005), Fox.

off with sensory disorientation. And it only gets worse.[23]

Even though visibly stressed by the sensory deprivation, Richard maintains his innocence and Curtis puts the headphones back on, leaving Richard for an unspecified amount of time. For the audience, Richard's guilt is still uncertain and he is not seen again until season six. In the narrated time of *24* this would mean that Richard had spent at least four days at CTU, but it remains unclear how long he is exposed to the SDT.

Before coming to the conclusion of the sensory disorientation episode it is important to clarify the degree of discourse participation made possible by this scene. As with other torture scenes in the episode, it shares a "subterranean aspect"[24] with the Abu Ghraib images and the torture memos, as Lindsay Coleman already observed. Against this background three moments stand out in the scene just analyzed: 1. Driscoll's reluctance to give Curtis her order in writing. Secrecy, the characteristic of our modern day discourse on "torture", is epitomized in Driscoll's reluctance as well as in the scandal surrounding the publication of the *torture memos*; 2. The fact that torture techniques and their effects are explained for the first time by practitioners in *24* overlaps with a phase in which the audience is able to read about and see evidences of torture in US-American newspapers and released memorandums; and 3. Curtis' remark that he has seen "good results" with sensory disorientation and the following application of SDT is provocative and screened at a sensitive time.

Just a few days prior to the screening began the trial of Army Reserve Spec. Charles A. Graner Jr., the highest ranking participant seen in the pictures from Abu Ghraib. He was sentenced on January 15, to 10 years in prison, longer than any of the other tried in the case. The trial revived the debate of US-American torture in Iraq – a debate that was trying to untangle the web of responsibility.

The debate on Alan Dershowitz's proposition had lacked the substantial material which the *torture memos* and images from Abu Ghraib provided in 2004. During this time the term *sensory disorientation* or *sensory deprivation* had received considerable attention in the context of this

---

[23] Curtis' imprecision with the duration of Richard's sensory disorientation is possibly intentional, furthering Richard's loss of a sense of time; an effect supported by the interrogation manual KUBARK.

[24] Coleman, Lindsay, "'Damn You for Making Me Do This': Abu Ghraib, 24, Torture, and Television Masochism," in *The War Body on Screen*, Eds. Karen Randell, Sean Redmond and Joanna Bourke (New York, NY: Continuum, 2008), 199-214; 212.

substantiation. The technique's status as torture is, as I have shown, debated.

However, *sensory deprivation* goes back to the C.I.A.'s 1963 KUBARK interrogation manual which addresses the technique in its chapter on "Deprivation of Sensory Stimuli".[25] Several copies of the manual were seen by *The New Yorker* staff writer Jane Mayer lying in the offices of the writers of *24*, when she visited the production team.[26]

The *LA Times* was the first, on May 11, 2004, to connect the methods described in manuals such as *KUBARK* to Abu Ghraib.[27] Many understood the images from Abu Ghraib as a photographic expression of the results of what was discussed in the torture memos. The memo by Diane E. Beaver to Donald Rumsfeld, which the *Washington Post* obtained in June 2004, proposed "the deprivation of light and auditory stimuli"[28] as an approved method of interrogation. In Abu Ghraib "the marvel of digital technology allowed Americans to see what their soldiers were doing to prisoners in their name", Marc Danner claimed in January 2005.[29] However, none of the images from Abu Ghraib depicted a technique similar to what Richard was exposed to. The images from Abu Ghraib also represent more violent and less sophisticated procedures than the memos describe. A reading of *24*'s torture by governmental agents might refine the view for these subtleties.

After James Heller is saved by Jack Bauer, he is brought to CTU and informed about his son's detention and interrogation. Heller immediately understands what has happened to his son and criticizes Driscoll in front of Jack:

> *Heller*: You subjected my son to SDT?
> *Driscoll*: Yes, sir, we did. But it was stopped the moment you were

---

[25] Central Intelligence Agency. "IX.E." *KUBARK Counterintelligence Interrogation.* 1963.
http://www.gwu.edu/~nsarchiv/NSAEBB/NSAEBB122/index.htm#kubark.

[26] Jane Mayer, "Whatever It Takes: The politics of the man behind '24.'".

[27] Mark Matthews, "U.S. practices at Abu Ghraib barred in '80s," *Los Angeles Times*, May 11, 2004, http://www.latimes.com/news/nationworld/nation/wire/bal-te.interrogate11may11,0,932867.story?page=1.

[28] Diane E. Beaver, "Memorandum for Commander, Joint Task Force 170: Legal Brief on Proposed Counter-Resistance Strategies," in *The Torture Papers: The Road to Abu Ghraib*, Eds. Karen J. Greenberg, Joshua L. Dratel. (Cambridge et al.: Cambridge UP, 2005), 234.

[29] Mark Danner, "We Are All Torturers Now," *NYTimes*, January 6, 2005, http://www.nytimes.com/2005/01/06/opinion/06danner.html?scp=13&sq=sensory+deprivation&st=nyt.

> rescued.
> *Heller*: Jack, did you know about this?
> *Jack*: No, sir.
> *Heller*: I want to see my son now.
> [...]
> *Heller*: Erin, I realize you've been under a lot of pressure these past few
> hours, but you better have cause for this.[30]

Heller's final remarks set the tone of the ensuing debate he has with his son. Heller does not voice a fundamental criticism of Driscoll's action and torture order. Instead, he indicates that he supports her, if there was a legitimate reason for torturing his son. His encounter with Richard in the interrogation room is similarly determined by James' sober tone.

> *Heller*: They said they were using some interrogation techniques.
> *Richard*: They were totally out of line. I am going to sue them blind.
> *Heller*: I think it'll be a little more effective, if you let me deal with it. I
> promise you, if they were out of line, heads will roll.
> *Richard*: What do you mean, "if"?
> *Heller*: Why did they think you were holding something back from them?
> *Richard*: I don't know.
> *Heller*: Richard, if you know something that would shed some light on
> what happened to me...
> *Richard*: What, you don't think I would tell them, if I thought it was
> relevant?
> *Heller*: So there is something?
> *Richard*: Now you're giving me the third degree?
> *Heller*: Son, do you have any idea what your sister just went through? If
> you know anything that would help us find the people behind this, tell
> me now.
> *Richard*: Dad...I'm glad you're alive. I... I really am. But I am not going to
> tell these people things about my private life that they don't need to
> know.
> *Heller*: That you don't think they need to know. Richard, these people were
> trying to save our lives![31]

James Heller suspects that his son is withholding crucial information and he authorizes Curtis "to do whatever you feel is necessary to get this information out of [his] son". It is telling that Heller never uses the term "torture" in Richard's presence. Richard's threat against CTU, the legal claim of a torture victim, if publicly raised, is a powerful one in *24*. But

---

[30] "Day 4 - 12:00 P.M. – 01:00 P.M." *24*. (January 24, 2005), Fox.
[31] Ibid.

for James Heller the situation of an imminent terrorist threat demands measures that include sacrifices like torturing your own son. This is summarized in his concluding remark to his son in which he explains: "I love you, son, but I have a duty to my country." After the second session of interrogation, which *24* does not depict, Richard still does not reveal any information. Heller is enraged and uses the torture word for the first time accusing Curtis: "You tortured my son for almost three hours and ended up yielding nothing?"

It dawns on James Heller and CTU that Richard is innocent. Heller releases Richard and tries to apologize.

> *James Heller*: I'm sorry this had to happen, Richard, but we had to make sure that you weren't withholding anything from us.
> *Richard*: I hate you. I never want to see you again.
> *Heller*: Please understand that I am responsible for the lives of millions of people.
> *Richard*: You torture me and now you want me to forgive you? This just confirms everything I always knew about you. Am I free to leave?
> *Heller*: Yes.[32]

James subtly confirms Richard's claim that he was tortured by not denying it. But, similar to Driscoll's omission to substantiate torture in a written order, he also does not use the term "torture" in Richard's presence. This reluctance on Heller's part is reminiscent of Secretary of Defence Donald Rumsfeld, who, in a less subtle way, responded to the Abu Ghraib scandal:

> My impression is that what has been charged thus far is abuse, which I believe technically is different from torture […] therefore I'm not going to address the 'torture' word.[33]

In *24* – as in the universe of Donald Rumsfeld – torture is an accusation of considerable impact. But *24*'s take on the torture by governmental agents is a much more sophisticated one than Rumsfeld's rejection of the "torture" term. It is closely linked to the professional order of torturers and the effectiveness of their tortures.

The torture of Richard is eventually rendered unsuccessful when Richard is summoned again, and brought back in after CTU discover new evidence connecting him to Habib Marwan. At this point Jack is present

---

[32] Ibid.
[33] Susan Sontag, "Regarding The Torture Of Others," *NYTimes*, May 23, 2004, http://www.nytimes.com/2004/05/23/magazine/regarding-the-torture-of-others.html?pagewanted=all&src=pm.

and about to torture Richard. Richard caves in after his sister speaks to him and warns him of his imminent torture. When James enters the room as well, the pressure increases and Richard eventually reveals that he had sex with a man weeks before the attacks and, as CTU discovers, an accomplice of Richard's liaison tapped James Heller's son's phone. This clarifies how the terrorist could have known about James Heller's unscheduled visit to Richard, freeing the latter of any responsibility. It remains an open question if Richard was not willing to reveal his homosexuality to CTU and his father, or if his affair was an occurrence he did not know had "anything to do with these attacks" as he claims.[34]

Conclusion

CTU and James Heller may have evaluated the danger of Habib Marwan correctly, but the torture of Richard, even with methods that seem to have a successful history in professional interrogation, was not the 'right' choice. Only Jack's reputation brought CTU closer to finding Marwan. This scene cannot be read as a proposition or normalization of torture but, to the contrary, as a careful warning.[35] This is an essential and recurring statement which *24* makes.

Many scholars have remarked on Jack Bauer's outstanding role as torturer and his symbolic but ambivalent function as tragic hero.[36] However, his character and function in the TV-series is much more complex than scholars have outlined as of yet. Despite trained torturers and ongoing research about enhanced interrogation techniques, it is only Jack Bauer, the hero of the show, who can, and does, efficiently and successfully torture. His success, however, does not stem from training in sophisticated interrogation techniques but intuition. He himself relies on instinct, intuition and what he "feels is the right thing to do", as he advises

---

[34] "Day 4 - 04:00 A.M. – 05:00 P.M." *24*. (May 16, 2005), Fox.

[35] This reading is not invalidated even if Richard's homosexuality is understood as a reference to the open homosexuality of Dick Cheney's daughter. James Heller's patriarchal tone with Richard could indicate that he considers his son's sexual preferences a choice; a choice and part of his son's utopian world view and unruly behavior.

[36] Jörg Häntzschel, "Folter als Teil einer nationalen Mythologie," (25 Mar 2007), *süddeutsche.de*. (November 11, .2011), http://www.sueddeutsche.de/politik/us-fernsehserie-folter-als-teil-einer-nationalen-mythologie-1.842820; Jane Mayer, "Whatever It Takes: The Politics of the Man behind '24'"; Coleman, Lindsay, "'Damn You for Making Me Do This': Abu Ghraib, 24, Torture, and Television Masochism".

his apprentice Renee Walker in a later season.

However, the observation from the above analysis – that professional torture and torture based on scientific research is portrayed as unsuccessful and the torturing characters as incompetent – does not reveal, if contrasted with Jack's *ability* for interrogation and torture, that *24* portrays the opinion that torture is justified. Instead, it proposes that torture is necessary, but only successful if the right "man" does it, a man of dubious talents.

Lutz Ellrich is right in arguing that the responsibility which a state might delegate to a Jack Bauer would hollow out its legal system and moral basis.[37] Talent is not an entity which participants in a discourse on the efficiency of torture can rely on. It is a question of a belief in the right man. The medium of the TV-series can make this sort of trust appear plausible. However, a lawyer deciding if or not he should hand out *torture warrants* will tread on precarious ground if he bases his decision on the belief in the talent of the interrogators.

Bibliography

Waterboarding: Historically Controversial. Harrigan on the Hunt. Fox News, 2006.

Alter, Jonathan. "Time to Think About Torture". *Newsweek*, November 5, 2001.

Beaver, Diane E. "Memorandum for Commander, Joint Task Force 170: Legal Brief on Proposed Counter-Resistance Strategies". In *The Torture Papers: The Road to Abu Ghraib*, edited by Karen J. Greenberg and Joshua L. Dratel, 229-236. Cambridge et.al.: Cambridge UP, 2005.

Central Intelligence Agency. "Kubark Counterintelligence Interrogation". 1963. http://www.gwu.edu/~nsarchiv/NSAEBB/NSAEBB122/index.htm#kubark.

Coetzee, J.M. "Into the Dark Chamber: The Novelist and South Africa". *New York Times Books*, January 12, 1986, Section 7; Page 13, Column 1.

Coleman, Lindsay. "'Damn You for Making Me Do This': Abu Ghraib, 24, Torture, and Television Masochism". In *The War Body on Screen*, edited by Karen Randell, Sean Redmond and Joanna Bourke, 199-214. New York, NY: Continuum, 2008.

Danner, Mark. "We Are All Torturers Now" *New York Times*, January 6, 2005.

---

[37] Lutz Ellrich, "Was spricht für die Folter?", 58.

http://www.nytimes.com/2005/01/06/opinion/06danner.html?scp=13&s
q=sensory+deprivation&st=nyt

Dershowitz, Alan M. "Want to Torture? Get a Warrant" *San Francisco Chronicle*, January 22, 2002, A 19.

Ellrich, Lutz. "Was spricht für die Folter?". In *Wahrheit und Gewalt. Der Diskurs der Folter in Europa und den USA.*, edited by Thomas Weitin, 267-84. Bielefeld: Transcript, 2010.

Green, Adam. "Normalizing Torture on '24'". *The New York Times*, May 22, 2005.
http://www.nytimes.com/2005/05/22/arts/television/22gree.html?page wanted=all

Häntzschel, Jörg. "Folter als Teil einer nationalen Mythologie". *süddeutsche.de*, Mar 25, 2007. http://www.sueddeutsche.de/politik/us-fernsehserie-folter-als-teil-einer-nationalen-mythologie-1.842820

Howard, Douglas L. "Torture and Morality in Fox's 24". In *Reading 24: TV against the Clock*, edited by Stephen Peacock, 133-145. London, England: I.B. Tauris, 2007.

Matthews, Mark. "U.S. Practices at Abu Ghraib Barred in '80s". *Los Angeles Times*, 2004.
http://www.latimes.com/news/nationworld/nation/wire/bal-te.interrogate11may11,0,932867.story?page=1

Mayer, Jane. "Whatever It Takes: The Politics of the Man Behind '24'". *The New Yorker*, February 19, 2007.

Scarry, Elaine. "The Structure of Torture: The Conversion of Real Pain into the Fiction of Power". In *The Body in Pain: The Making and Unmaking of the World*, edited by Elaine Scarry, 27-59. New York: Oxford UP, 1985.

Sontag, Susan. "Regarding the Torture of Others". *The New York Times*, May 23, 2004.
http://www.nytimes.com/2004/05/23/magazine/regarding-the-torture-of-others.html

Surnow, Joel, and Robert Cochran. "24 - Day 4". Television Broadcast created by Joel Surnow and Robert Cochran. Los Angeles: Fox Television, 2005.

Whitlock, Craig. "Al-Zarqawi's Biography". The Washington Post, June 8, 2006. http://www.washingtonpost.com/wp-dyn/content/article/2006/06/08/AR2006060800299.html?nav=rss_world/africa

FILM REPRESENTATIONS OF THE MUSLIM IN AMERICAN 9/11 MOVIES: AN ATTEMPT TO UNDERSTAND THE OTHER

ELŻBIETA WILCZYŃSKA

Since 2006, each year has seen the release of almost two or three so-called 9/11 movies. Some of them are entirely devoted to the attack itself and its immediate consequences. Others, on the other hand, focus on the broadly termed war on terror, depicting the involvement of the United States of America as a country or its individuals in the fight against terrorists or in building democratic systems in many Islamic countries in the first two decades of the 21st century.

The Atlantic Monthly from May 2011 reports that many of those movies "have had a notoriously hard time finding audiences."[1] This article lists over twenty of them and compares the budget spent on the movies and the income each of them has brought, making a point that almost none of them has earned any money despite good plots, fantastic actors, and all the technological know-how invested in many of them. Obviously, one conclusion may be that they have cost too much, but the conclusion presented in the article is that "Most Americans don't want to hear, see or feel anything about Iraq, whether they support the war or oppose it. They want to look away, period, and have been doing so for some time."[2] Martin Halliwell claims that here movies were "perhaps too close to the bone" for the American audience.[3] While producers felt the time had come to take up the issue of the 9/11 attack, the response to their message or artwork has

---

[1] "Will Bin Laden's death make 9/11 movies easier to watch?", *Atlantic Monthly,* May 2^{nd,} *2011,* http://www.theatlantic.com/entertainment/archive 2011/05/will-bin-ladens-death-make-9-11-movies-easier-to-watch/238192. (accessed: July 20, 2011).

[2] "Will Bin Laden's death make 9/11 movies easier to watch?", *Atlantic Monthly.*

[3] Martin Halliwell, "Contemporary American Culture", in: *American Thought and Culture in the 21st century,* eds. Martin Halliwell and Catherine Marley (Edinburgh: Edinburgh University Press, 2008), 223.

not appeared to be enthusiastic. Nevertheless, as today's society is greatly affected by various media, which operate through a system of verbal and non-verbal representation, they must have had a substantial influence on how the post 9/11 reality is perceived as still quite a few people did see the films.

It is worthwhile to analyze a number of American movies produced between 2006 and 2010 and look at the projected image of the Other, of the Muslim, who was an agent of the terrorist attack of 9/11, and thus deduce what society at large might tend to think of the Muslim as a result of their exposition to the movies.[4]

Central to the analysis is the concept of representation as developed by Stuart Hall. "Representation is [...] defined as [the] production of meaning through language, signs or images".[5] In the process of producing representation, the meaning of some concepts is generated in the minds of the recipients through the language, images or signs used. Obviously, such meaning depends on the relationship between things existing in the world and the concepts which we have as their mental representations. These mental representations – in this case of suicide bombers, Islamic extremists or terrorists, the Islamic others – are either reflections of the reality (the literal presentation of people who perpetrated these acts) or the construction of those concepts as conceived by various producers. What counts here is that the so called truthful accounts, based on real life incidents, are mixed with "relativized" and subjective representations, but they all have an equal effect on our perception of the world. Hall puts it in the following way:

> It is the social actors [here directors] who use the conceptual system of their culture and the linguistic and other representational systems to construct meanings, to make the world meaningful and communicate about that world meaningfully to others.[6]

We can always agree or disagree with the image or message because of its reliability, but it nonetheless becomes a factor in a discourse as understood by Michael Foucault. Foucault does not stress the semantic aspect of meaning, but rather focuses on the context, which forces the meaning to become entangled in knowledge/power relations. The context

---

[4] The list of all the movies watched for this project is included at the end at filmography.

[5] Stuart Hall, ed., *Representation. Cultural Representations and Signifying Practices* (London: Sage Publications, 1997), 15.

[6] Hall, *Representation, 25.*

for Foucault is linked to the concept of discourse. By 'discourse', Foucault means a group of statements which provide a language for talking about [things] – a way of representing the knowledge about a particular topic at a particular historical moment. Discourse is about the production of knowledge through language.[7]

In this way the 9/11 movies constitute and contribute to the discourse which produces some knowledge about Muslims and Islam. What generates this knowledge we use to infer about Muslims? If paraphrasing Foucault, in a discourse, knowledge is related to power, but what power generates this knowledge and information and why?

Before making an attempt to answer these questions, one has to be reminded that here the focus is on the image of the Muslim constructed in the movies. Movies as such form part of a culture, are embedded as a popular type of entertainment and are supposed to generate "the pleasure or response to drama, comedy, or melodrama,"[8] depending on the genre. This is crucial to bear in mind throughout the analysis because few go to the movies to learn about a war in Iraq or Afghanistan. Instead, most go to watch a story, which – as the audience knows – will be related to the topic of war and will entertain the viewers in a way dependent on the genre. The knowledge of the audience about the genre is important, because, as Gledhill claims, each genre builds a different set of expectations, which are already known to the viewers cognizant with the conventions of the genre.[9] All this – the type of genre, the element of entertainment, and the intended representation – forms a filter through which the audience watches the movies. They are part of an imaginary world, of fiction, however close to reality they are.

The movies that are the subject of the analysis are classified either as dramas or war movies (action movies or thrillers), in which we expect to find two warring sides of villains and heroes. What is also important is that the movies tell stories of particular real incidents or about real or fictionalized people. For example, in the movie *World Trade Center*[10] we have a narrative of survival of two policemen wounded during the 9/11

---

[7] Peter Hamilton, "Representing the social France and Frenchness in post-war humanist photography", in *Representation,* ed., Stuart Hall (London: Sage, 1997), 44.

[8] Christine Gledhill, "Genre and Gender: The Case of Soap Opera", in *Representation,* ed. , Stuart Hall (London: Sage, 2009), 351.

[9] Ibid.

[10] *World Trade Center,* directed by Oliver Stone (2006; Paramount Pictures, CA, 2009), DVD.

rescue operations; in *A Mighty Heart*[11] we have a story of abduction and then murder of an American reporter in Pakistan, Daniel Pearl, whose death epitomizes the plight of many journalists active in the Middle East. Other movies refer to disclosed practices; e.g. *Rendition*[12], while yet others illustrate the vicissitudes of the lives of individual real soldiers, whose characters or life stories are, however, fictionalized. This attribute is essential because as Ien Ang argues "Only through the imagination – which is always subjective, is 'objective reality' assimilated."[13] Indeed, the same content may be found in many documentaries, but documentaries are watched by relatively small audiences. In movies, the focus is on fiction, which triggers the imagination of the public, which, in an indirect way, wants to get an insight into the experience of modern war or different cultures. Few watch the beheading of a soldier in a documentary or a Y-tube, but they will willy-nilly watch it in the movie, where it is fictionalized; yet it stays in the imagination and memory for a long period of time, exerting a long term and short term influence.

From the very first movies we learn that the enemy that caused the havoc of 9/11 comes from Islamic countries, that all the enemies are evil on account of the scale of the "utter hell"[14] on earth they have caused, and that they should be attacked because the life of the victims of the attack should – as one marine who rescued the policemen buried under the debris of the World Trade Center said – be avenged. Also, in this movie from the beginning we all know who is the villain and who is the hero, thus the ideological message is very clear and straightforward, though with the passage of time and the benefit of hindsight fewer and fewer Americans tend to subscribe to the clear thesis that the revenge should have had the form of war, which definitely is the tendency to be observed in the last Hollywood productions.

In the next movie, also released in 2006, *United 93*,[15] from the very first scene the hijackers are presented as devout, pious men, who read or cite Koranic verse. They seem very tranquil, yet apprehensive. Though they speak Arabic, we can sense the support they show to each other, and

---

[11] *A Mighty Heart,* directed by Michael Winterbottom (2007; Paramount Vantage, 2010), DVD.

[12] *Rendition,* directed by Gavin Hood (2007; Level One Entertainment, USA, 2011), DVD. Here this term implies apprehension and extrajudicial transfer of a person from one state to another.

[13] Ien Ang, *Watching Dallas* (London: The Chaucer Press, 1985), 83 (books.google.pl/books?isbn=0416416306...) (accessed August 10, 2011).

[14] *World Trade Center*, 2006.

[15] *United 93*, directed by Paul Greengrass (2006: Studio Canal: USA, 2008), DVD.

we sense their brotherhood when they hug or just look at each other. The tranquillity stays with them till they board the plane. When the hour of the strike comes, they transform into attackers, displaying the well recognized attributes of kamikaze hijackers with bomb vests. They terrorize the passengers into submission by threats and shouts, and if anybody stages resistance, they kill them, always repeating "in the name of God". The actors playing the hijackers are young, clean shaven, and look intelligent and educated, an accurate representation when comparing them to the pictures of the real hijackers. This is where the reality stops because though the audience knows the end of the movie all the scenes are either fictionalized or imagined behavioural patterns deduced from the phone calls of the passengers to their close relatives short of their tragic death. The images of the terrorists, though not homogenous, are uniformly defined as evil and the psychological underpinnings of their deeds are rather shallow, rendered as an unreflective obedience to Allah and Muslim leaders.

The image of bomb-strapped men recurs in many movies: we see them in *The Kingdom*,[16] when they detonate themselves in the American part of a city when the Americans are playing baseball, or in many scenes in *Body of Lies*,[17] when jihadists stage attacks in a few Muslim or European cities. The most poignant depiction of a jihadist is portrayed in *Rendition*, when a presumably North-African protagonist, a suicide bomber, a student of art and a gifted artist himself, is pushed to commit this act to avenge his brother, killed by anti-terrorist forces. Apparently, this is one of the motives that drives young Muslims to such actions: the death of a Muslim killed by an infidel should be atoned by the death of his compatriot or a relative. Even when having deep doubts, foreboding, or being deeply in love, thus likely to give up the task, they cannot resign from their suicide mission because they have been told to believe they cannot turn back. Custom sends them on this path of action. If they hesitate or are thwarted, there is always a sniper who kills them, thus causing an explosion anyway. Even in *Rendition*, where the terrorist gets the romantic attention of one of the main protagonists, the picture of a jihadist-suicide is never really deepened. Here the audience gets the impression that, in some way, all terrorists are intrinsically abhorrent. In fact, however, as most experts claim for the most part they are not. Recruits are not drawn from the impoverished or uneducated masses; most are professionals, young,

---

[16]*The Kingdom,* directed by Peter Berg (2007; USA: Relativity Media, 2010). DVD.
[17] *Body of Lies,* directed by Sir Ridley Scott (2008; Scott Free Productions: De Levine Pictures. WBP, 2011), DVD.

married (often with children) college educated and middle or upper class men with no pattern of mental illness. They are not deranged in seeking personal gain and glory. Most are convinced that they are fighting a righteous defensive battle...[Moreover] most recruits are not violent personality types. They are sucked into a subculture that provides a sense of community that is missing from their lives. Once recruits connect with the group, they adopt a new social and psychological identity within a context of physical and financial security.[18]

Representations of the terrorist groups that provide such a welcoming feeling and thus have been successful in recruiting new suicide volunteers can be found in *A Mighty Heart, The Kingdom, Rendition, Body of Lies and Green Zone*[19]. The representation is produced through two main pictures: of secret meetings held in Mosques, where the Muslims are united in praying, reading verses from the Koran, or by listening to their leaders; or squatting in the middle of a Mosque on a floor, throwing their fists up and echoing verses after their leaders. These terrorist recruits represent an intimidating picture, as possessed maniacs, though – as was stated above – they may be very different from such a depiction.

The state of possession and obsession is linked to what the terrorist recruits are exposed to, that is their leaders, who – as the main child character in *The Brothers* says – are the bad guys. "The ones with the beards."[20] Very often such leaders claim to be direct descendants of a prophet, who preach that "We will avenge the American war in the Muslim world. We will come at them everywhere. We will strike continuously at random. We have bled, now they will bleed."[21] They promise to avenge Muslims via bombings detonated in public places or on hijacked planes, to destroy the infidels. They hate America, the embodiment of civilization, progress, power, and economic subjugation through the colonization period. America, as they assert, threatens their religion and the identity of countries where the religion is practiced. The chief of the CIA in *Body of Lies* asserts that "[such leaders] want to establish universal caliphate across the face of the earth and they want every infidel converted or dead."[22] This is indeed the idea that some Sunnis and Shiites preach, but what the American heroes of the movies do

---

[18] Carl Ciocacco, Howard Gambrill Clark and James Van de Velde, "Ending al-Quaeda,". *American Interest* vol. VI, No. 6, *2011* July/August, 44..

[19] *Green Zone*, directed by Paul Greengrass (2010; Universal Pictures, 2011), DVD.

[20] *Brothers,* directed by Jim Sheridan, 2008.

[21] *Body of Lies,* directed by Paul Greengrass, 2010.

[22] Ibid.

not say, is that those saying it are only a tiny minority. Such a minority has thus drawn the greatest attention of the non-Muslim world. It has also become a symbol of all the Islamic people, who are often opposed to the minority, but are unable to conquer it.[23]

Naturally, in scenes showing the jihadists, the focus is on the authority of the fundamental leaders who are knowledgeable about Islam and the teaching of Koran. These leaders need Islam warriors ready to defend their religion, world and custom, and they shape the young impressionable minds saying that Allah is the greatest value and worth receiving the greatest gift of their lives. This is the most precious gift they can give. As the movies suggest, many of the leaders were educated in American universities, where they mastered their talent of public speaking and skills to indoctrinate, as well as developed their dislike of American life, with all its vices – as they claim – including freedom of speech, religion, democracy and social and moral decay. This they all drop on the young minds during individual meetings in Mosques or by recording their speeches and then either broadcasting them on the Internet or circulating their message via DVDs.

All the above images constitute one type of representation of the Muslim – a terrorist, the one who uses violence, or threats to use violence, in order to achieve some political or ideological aim. Among the aims we can list revenge on the injustice done to Muslim countries (the invasion of Afghanistan in *Lions for Lambs*[24] or of Iraq in *Green Zone* and *Fair Game*[25]), or the imposition of the western political system, which is alien to their culture. Stuart Hall claims that "representation when dealing with difference, engages feelings, attitudes and emotions, and it mobilizes fears and anxieties in the viewer at deeper levels than we can explain in a simple, common sense [journalistic] way."[26] This may be the reason that though the terrorist figures are not the central protagonists, any suspense in the movie is built in reference to them. Hence they arouse the most intense emotions in the viewer, contributing to the construction of the prevailing type of a Muslim as the terrorist. They are the most extreme

---

[23] Cf. "Nowoczesność bez granic" [Modernity without borders], Europa No. 7. One section of this edition of the journal is devoted to the issue of the Arab Spring of 2011, and it is made of interviews and articles by academics and journalists specializing in the Islam World, e.g. John Gray, Ian Burma and Olivier Roy.

[24] *Lions for Lambs,* directed by Robert Redford (2007; Clermont, USA, Hong Kong, MGM, 2009), DVD.

[25] *Fair Game*, directed by Doug Liman (2010; River Road Entertainment, USA, 2011), DVD.

[26] Stuart Hall, "The Spectacle of the Other", Stuart Hall, ed., *Representation, 226.*

type of the Other, with reference to which the American identity is strengthened.

Apart from the terrorist figure, there is usually the good "Muslim" figure as well – the one that sides with Americans and represents anti-terrorist views. In *A Mighty Heart, The Kingdom, Rendition*, and *Body of Lies,* this figure is a man, usually a policeman, who knows that Muslim terrorist groups misrepresent them, whether they are Jordanians, Syrians or Iraqis, and thus does whatever is necessary to capture and punish the terrorists. Such characters have a sense of great duty towards their country, feeling it is their responsibility to keep law and order and introduce elements of democracy, preferably following the American model. In a very powerful scene in *A Mighty Heart,* a good policeman interrogates one of the men responsible for capturing the journalist Daniel Pearl and asks his captor who is a good Muslim, and who carries out his responsibility of a Saudi better: one who cooperates with a foreign regime which is an intruder in the country or one who safeguards Saudi values and wishes to expel the foreign element and thus cause violence? The answer to that question of course belongs to the viewer.

In two cases, in *The Kingdom* and in *Rendition,* the policemen are married men, with children and loving wives. In the latter movie the policeman is an interrogator who uses cruel methods to extract information from his prisoners. At home, however, he is a good, sincere man, the patriarchal-type of a husband. In his private life he abides by Muslim principles. He is thus not very happy that his daughter is dating a young man and looks up to his sister who lives according to western ways. He forces his daughter into an arranged marriage against her will, which makes her leave her home and find a refuge in her aunt's abode. This once again shows that a traditional Muslim family is sometimes internally torn by conflicts along western and traditional Islamic lines. This message is secondary to the plot, thus its power in constructing the image of the Muslim is smaller, yet it contributes to the wider picture of the context, proposing other images of the Other.

Another type of a Muslim is the wealthy royal family member, whom we see only in *The Kingdom*. Wealthy, enjoying the benefits of the oil business, living a leisurely life quite distant from the ordinary folks they rule, such royals are not represented as ones who evoke authority. In fact, they barely sustain the respect worthy of a sovereign. Though traditionally dressed in the white igal, they are presented not as very religious, rather as corrupt and vain, whom the American government nonetheless supports. This actually has some reference grounded in reality, if we take into account the events of 2011 in Egypt or Libya. The full reality is obviously more complex; for example, it is never mentioned in the movies that such royals are in power because they are tied to tribal loyalties, whom they favour and whose help they can count on under any circumstances. Thus they can always find refuge and assistance among their kin.[27]

Yet movies are often not meant to be a fully realist account or an educational tool; nevertheless, by stirring the emotional side, such images tend to stick in the mind of the audience, who, in the majority, do not delve into the subject to broaden their knowledge about the situation in the Middle East. Thus such images tend to convey information which builds knowledge about the countries. If this knowledge translates into power, then it serves the American government, who needs control over the countries that drill oil, so indispensable to the American economy and way of life. Or, if interpreted the other way around, such knowledge of such facts undermines the authority of the American state, which is represented as giving support for economic interests to a side which is so rife with vice. The latter message seems to prevail in the movies made more recently, where the credibility of the American government was undermined by exposing the fallacy of the main reason that prompted Americans into war, namely, that Iraq had weapons of mass destruction [WMD]. Halliwell posits that such a close connection between politics and cultural productions has recently arisen due to "the cultural vanguard that has formed due to the Bush presidency".[28]

A separate category of protagonists featured in the movies and one that should be distinguished from the rest is that of women. Only a few of them stand out as major subordinate characters. In *Rendition* there are two female protagonists: the already mentioned younger generation daughter of the interrogator, who – despite wearing the hijab – tries to free herself from the traditional arranged marriage scenario planned by her father. A similar split from traditional behaviour is exemplified by her aunt, who not only wears western style clothes but also adopts the western style of living. Yet she is shunned by the rest of the family, a sign that the modern type of a woman who discards the head-dress and the traditional role of a woman as a mother has a hard time being accepted. Another female Muslim character is also Aisha, a nurse in *Body of Lies,* who decides to begin a romantic affair with an American, but she tries to achieve it in a Muslim way: by receiving the acceptance of her older sister and inviting the American to dinner to make her sister approve of her choice. This once

---

[27] Bernard Lewis, *Co sie właściwie stało? O kontaktach Zachodu ze światem islamu* [*What went wrong? Western Impact and Middle Eastern Response*], trans. Jolanta Kozłowska (*Warszawa: Dialog, 2002*).

[28] Halliwell, "Contemporary American Culture", 223.

again stresses the fact that a liberated type of a Muslim woman in the Middle-East needs to negotiate her Muslim identity between the demands of tradition and the modern lifestyle, and that the number of such women is low. A slightly different view was reported by Bobby Ghosh who has found out that many women in contemporary Egypt would:

> wear [...] a sleeveless top and [their] hair is uncovered. In [his] experience, Salafis, adherents of a very strict school of Islam, take a dim view of such displays of femininity. I recall [he continues] a time in Baghdad when a Salafi preacher cursed me for bringing a female photographer to our interview, and an occasion in the Jordanian city of Salt when another Salafi leaped from his chair and thwacked his teenage daughter on the arm when she accidentally entered the room without covering her face from my infidel eyes.[29]

So it seems that what is exception in the movies, in some Arab places, definitely great cites, has become more widespread. So again reality drags behind the typified image of women transmitted by the media. With reference to young people as a whole, Ghosh makes a remark that:

> this generation – which is intimately interconnected by new communication technologies like satellite television, social media and the Internet – has formed a new kind of transnational identity, one that cannot be contained by any ethnic, national or sectarian borders. It is an identity founded on young people's shared ambition to free themselves from the grip of their corrupt and inept political, religious and economic institutions and thus to return their culture and society to the days of glory it achieved in Ibn Battuta's time.[30]

This type of view of young people is nowhere to be found in the movies yet, and they clearly counter the dominant type of a Muslim that the 9/10 movies are saturated with. As a result, what we remember is rather the above mentioned Muslims avowing hatred towards westernization and the United States.

Similarly as with the women types, the mix of child protagonists is very limited, and they are usually background figures. Yet in a way they foreshadow the possibilities life presents to adults in this part of the world. So among the jihadists there are always armed boys, who – as in

---

[29] Bobby Ghosh, "The Rise of Moderate Islam," *Time Magazine Travels Through Islam,* June 21, 2011.
[30] Ibid.

Brothers[31] – serving as errand boys still witness the torture and execution of both American soldiers and their own family members. At a young age they are already indoctrinated and involved in the Al-Qaeda network. One fictional Saudi boy witnesses the death of his grandfather involved in the Aamas terrorist group. When shot by an anti-terrorist group, the grandfather whispers in his grandson's ear: "We will kill them all, son". Such a message is powerful, serving as guidance for the grandson to continue the fight. The movie consequently suggests that the show will go on; especially that one American anti-terrorist fighter also whispers the same words to his fellow American, whose friend has been killed in a terrorist suicide attack. The opposing sides are clenched in a battle which the contemporary audience of the second decade of the 21st century really does not know who has started and why. The deep-rooted cause for the hatred linked to post-colonialism can be learnt from books that have a limited readership,[32] but not from Hollywood movies.

Also offering a glimpse into children's lives is the depiction of a Jordanian family in *Body of Lies*, with two boys who watch American movies, relish hamburgers and hotdogs and detest home cuisine. Undoubtedly, they signify the westernization trend that the Islamic world fears and tries to prevent and escape from[33], as such ways are believed to subvert Islamic culture. Indeed, from the special issue of TIME magazine *Travels through Islam* a picture of a new type of a Muslim emerges. Reza Aslan, a renowned Iranian-American activist and a writer in his article "World Wanderer" published in the above mentioned edition of *TIME* asserts:

> I find that Islamists of all stripes – from extremist Salafis to members of more orthodox groups like the Muslim Brotherhood – say they are breaking with the past and reinventing themselves as the moderate mainstream. "We can no longer be the party that says 'Down with this' and 'Down with that,'" says Essam el-Erian, a top Brotherhood leader. "The thing we stood against is gone, so now we have to re-examine what we stand for."[34]

Jihadists try to thwart this trend, but what is important for the present

---

[31]*Brothers*, directed by Jim Sheridan (2009; Studio Michael DeLuca Productions, 2011), DVD.
[32] Jean Ziegler, *Nienawiść do zachodu* [La haine de l'Occident], trans. Ewa Cylwik (Warszawa: Wydawnictwo Książka i Prasa, 2009).
[33] Bernard Lewis, *Nienawiść do Zachodu*.
[34] Aslan, Reza, "World Wanderer," *Time Magazine Travels Through Islam,* June 21 (2011).

analysis, depiction of this trend is almost missing in the analyzed movies. Except for a few individuals who cooperate with the Americans (*The Kingdom*) and a liberal journalist who escaped from Pakistan (*A Mighty Heart*) or a so-called decent Muslim (*Green Zone*) these Hollywood productions do not give any hint of any liberating social and political widespread changes taking place among the Muslims.

Beside the above mentioned Muslim characters that feature as subordinate protagonists in such movies, we have a plethora of background protagonists, who are imbued into the setting, from which we may read quite different and contrary messages. On the one hand, we are mesmerized by the images of colour-filled bustling and crowded cities like Baghdad, Tikrit, Kabul, or Amman, where people are engaged in trading, talking, drinking, or gossiping. One Iraqi family of a physicist father enjoys their family time, Aisha works in a hospital, a family has their dinner. These thriving colourful scenes seem to suggest that life in these countries is not all as 'evil' and filled with constant danger as it is often painted, at least for a majority of people living there. Most people lead normal lives and live in peace and quiet, while being good and devout "Muslims."

That this task of leading a normal life is not easy for them to realize and for the viewers is hard to accept as normal is illustrated through many protagonists of the movies in question. American combatants or CIA agents in such movies as *Stop Loss*[35], *The Lucky Ones*[36], or *Brothers*, even *Body of Lies* repeat, like a mantra, that those apparently innocent people, elements of the setting, may actually pose dangers and threats. There is always the possibility that such people are in service to the terrorists. Nobody knows who the enemy is: it might be a child, a woman wearing a burqa, or a man dressed in an igal; anybody can be carrying a gun, a bomb, a grenade, or a knife. Children may serve as shields to thwart the attack of American soldiers, who then may die from a grenade thrown out by a surviving child. Therefore, as the CIA head, played by Russell Crow, says in *Body of Lies*: "Nobody likes the Middle East."[37] At least nobody that looks from the perspective of Washington. Meryl Streep as the head of the Defense Department in *Rendition* reminds us that all Muslims are potential terrorists who may pose a danger to the Americans.[38] This is why officials have to be both unscrupulous and harsh. Such officials are often

---

[35] *Stop Loss,* directed by Kimberley Peirce (2008; MTV Films: Paramount Pictures, 2011), DVD.

[36] *The Lucky Ones,* directed by Neil Burger (2008; Koppelman and Levien Productions, 2009), DVD.

[37] *Body of Lies*, directed by Paul Greengrass, 2008.

[38] *Rendition*, directed by Gavin Hood, 2007.

immune to the harm they inflict upon mostly peaceful, individual Muslims. This element tends to occur more and more often in the latest movies: the callous American government is contrasted with innocent Muslims who fell prey to the scheme of the American government aimed at capturing terrorists, whatever the cost. Often the American protagonists of the movies are caught in the inner struggle of loyalty to their own country and its policy, which, on the one hand, is supposed to liberate the Muslims, but, on the other hand, brings misery both to the American soldiers (*Stop Loss, Brothers*, and *In the Valley of and Elah*[39]) and the common people of the Islamic world. In these movies the focal point is on the hurt American individuals, and thus the Muslims are hardly represented.

It should follow from the analysis that Hollywood has masterfully stereotyped the Muslim. Out of the few types of Muslims that have been presented as featuring in the movies, some definitely stand out and overshadow others. One that usually catches our attention and riles our emotions is the jihadist, terrorist, or an orthodox leader. According to Stuart Hall, stereotypes differ from plain types in that they "take hold of the memorable characteristics, reduce them, exaggerate them, and simplify them, fix them without change or development to eternity. So stereotyping reduces, essentializes, naturalizes and fixes differences."[40] Though there is quite a panorama of Muslims of Hollywood movies, the focus is on hatred towards the West, suicide bombers, bearded preachers, and women wearing a burqa or a hijab. These elements are shown as natural because they stem from the very theology of Islam, which – as Lewis claims – cannot be reconciled with Christianity. Moreover, the stereotype fixes itself into a binary opposition: us as Christians, and them as Muslims; us civilized, them barbaric; us liberal, them fundamentalists; us oriented forward, them oriented backward, yet both vengeful. Such classification conveys affective meanings, deeply rooted in the grand American narrative of progress, which are expressed in the emotionally-marked representations of the Muslims.

In this way stereotyping is a signifying practice: it sends some messages and meaning, which influences or constructs the way of thinking of the audience. In this representation practice inherent also is the Foucauldian power to "mark, assign and classify."[41] Hollywood definitely has exercised the power to represent Muslims in a certain way, within the

---

[39] *In the Valley of Ellah,* directed by Paul Haggis (2007; Summit Entertainment: USA, 2010), DVD.
[40] Stuart Hall, *"Spectacle of the Other",* Stuart Hall (ed.). *Representation* (1997, 258.
[41] Ibid., 259.

above "regime of representation". So within the regime of representation all Muslims are potentially involved in life-and-death theology, martyrdom, or turning their faith into a killer, not a healer. Such a representation undoubtedly leads to Islamophobia, where the hated Muslims also hate Americans universally and want them out of their holy land.

In these movies, as is in many books,[42] it is hinted that the world is divided into two international opponents – the Muslim world and the West, represented by Americans, and only one may win. When seen through the regime of representation, Americans' presence, against all odds, is needed, and Americans should continue backing new revolutions and nascent governments in many Arab countries, because only thanks to this support will the democratic forces win. On the other hand, with the passage of time it becomes more evident that each post 9/11 movie paradoxically becomes an anti-American government movie because it conveys the message that Americans are dying on foreign soil for reasons they do not necessarily support (*Stop Loss, The Lucky Ones, Lions for Lambs*). In *The Green Zone* and *Fair Game* definitely, and more implicitly in *Lions for Lambs*, the government is presented as lying to Americans and conniving with corrupt regimes, for different reasons. The movies, made by liberal American directors, prove that freedom of speech rules, but often at the cost of undermining the credibility of their country.

Subsequently, by no means can we say that the movies represent the power of the government; although the first ones gave support to the American policy, they rather represent the power of Hollywood liberal directors, who express the doubts of the "public" concerning the war on terror and throw these doubts into the public discourse. Many experts on the war on terror remind us that some movies, by stereotyping American heroes and the enemy they fight a war with, do a disservice to the country. Halliwell expresses this very forcefully when he writes that "the right accuse the left of treason and siding with the nation's enemies" in the culture war that takes place between the west and the Middle East countries. He continues, that in the culture war "[t]he left (here the American Hollywood liberal directors) accuse the right of ... cosying up to big business, even abusing political power in the name of aggrandizement."[43] Political scientists warn that the impact of the media seems to resemble the one on the Vietnam war, foreboding a failure in this

---

[42] Cf. Olivier Roy, *Secularism confronts Islam* (New York: Columbia University Press, 2007); John Gray, "Nieliberalna demokracja [Non-liberal Democracy], trans. Łukasz Pawłowski, *Europe* 7. Bernard Lewis, *Co się właściwie stało*".
[43] Halliwell, 214.

mission as well.[44]

Such movies have introduced into the discourse the image of Muslims as the Other, which has perhaps replaced a previous other, namely, the black Other, or the Native American one. Since, according to Hall, each culture needs an Other as a reference point to identify itself, the Muslim as the Other may have appeared just in time to fill in any void. Thus simplified and stereotyped, the image of the Muslim as a jihadist and terrorist, the villain, prevails. In such movies secondary Islamic characters are peripheral. Though they feature as people of a broader perspective, they are deprived of celebrity status or heroic charisma (though this seems to be changing in the last 2010 movies). As a result, the glamour and pleasure of identification are accorded to the white heroes of the movies, and rarely to the "good Muslim type." This is also implied by the producer and the genre that these themes are represented through. Yet such stereotyping misrepresents Muslims, who, in the majority, are moderate and wish for freedom and prosperity. The 'Muslim spring' in North Africa is clear evidence that young, disillusioned Muslims may just as well prefer resorting to democratic methods of changing their country than joining Al-Qaeda, as the events in Libya of 2011 prove. Yet it seems that this stereotyped Muslim figure will overshadow them unless the media image is saturated with equally powerful examples of Muslim liberals.

Bibliography

Primary Sources

"Will Bin Laden's death make 9/11 movies easier to watch?" *Atlantic Monthly,* May 2011,
http://www.theatlantic.com/entertainment/archive/2011/05/will-bin-ladens-death-make-9-11-movies-easier-to-watch/238192
(accessed July 20, 2011).

Ang, Ien. *Watching Dallas.* London: The Chaucer Press, 1985.
http://*books.google.pl/books?isbn=0416416306...)* (accessed August 10, 2011).

Aslan, Reza, "World Wanderer," *Time Magazine Travels Through Islam,* June 21, 2011.

Ciovacco, Carl, Howard Gambrill Clark and James Van de Velde. 2011.

---

[44] Robert Baer, *Oblicze Zła. Prawda o wojnie z terroryzmem we wspomnieniach oficera CIA* [Faces of Evil], trans. Grażyna Górska (Warszawa: Wydawnictwo Magnum, 2002), 25.

"Ending al-Quaeda". *American Interest* vol. VI, No. 6 July/August (2011), 40-49.

Gledhill, Christine. "Genre and Gender: The Case of Soap Opera." In *Representation: Cultural Representations and Signifying Practices,* edited by Stuart Hall, 337-386. London: Sage Publications, 1997.

Ghosh, Bobby. "The Rise of Moderate Islam." *Time Magazine Travels Through Islam,* June 21, 2011.

Hall, Stuart, ed. *Representation. Cultural Representation and Signifying Practices. London:* Sage, 1997.

Halliwell, Martin. "Contemporary American Culture". In: *American Though and Culture in the 21st Century,* edited by Martin Halliwell and Catherine Morley. Edinburgh: Edinburgh University Press, 2008.

Hamilton, Peter. "Representing the Social: France and Frenchness in Post-War Humanist Photography." In *Representation: Cultural Representations and Signifying Practices,* edited by Stuart Hall, 75-150. London: Sage Publications, 1997.

Lewis, Bernard, *Co sie właściwie stało? O kontaktach Zachodu ze światem islamu* [What went wrong? Western Impact and Middle Eastern Response], translated by Jolanta Kozłowska. *Warszawa: Dialog,* 2003.

Pawłowski, Łukasz. "Nieliberalna demokracja arabska" [Non-liberal Arab Demoracy]. Interview with John Gray." *Europa,* no 7 (May 25, 2011), 5-9.

Roy, Olivier. "Czy możliwe jest Oświecenie bez przemocy. Rozmowa ze znawca Islamu Olivierem Rayem." *Europa,* no. 7 (May 25, 2011), 29-32.

Stuart, Hall. "Introduction." In *Representation: Cultural Representations and Signifying Practices,* edited by Stuart Hall, 1-12. London: Sage Publications, 1997.

—. "The Work of Representation." In *Representation: Cultural Representations and Signifying Practices,* edited by Stuart Hall, 13-75. London: Sage Publications, 1997.

Ziegler, Jean. *Nienawiść do zachodu* [La haine de l'Occident]. Translated by Ewa Cylwik. Warszawa: Wydawnictwo Książka i Prasa, 2010.

Secondary Sources

Baer, Robert. *Oblicze Zła. Prawda o wojnie z terroryzmem we wspomnienie oficera CIA* [Faces of Evil]. Translated by Grazyna Górska. Warszawa: Wydawnictwo Magnum, 2002.

Jałoszyński, Kuba and Janusz Skosolas, *Media wobec współczesnego*

terroryzmu. Warszawa: Collegium Civitas Press, 2008.
Laqueur, Walter, Ostatnie dni Europy [The Last Days of Europe]. Wrocław: Wydawnictwo Dolnośląskie, 2007.
Marranci, Gabriele. 2009. *Understanding Muslim Identity. Rethinking Fundamentalism.* Pal grave: McMilliam.
Weigel, George. *Wiara, Rozum, i wojna z dżihadyzmem* [Faith, Reason and the War with Jihadism: A Call to Action].Translated by Krzysztof Jasiński. Warszawa: Fronda, 2007.

Filmography

A Mighty Heart. Directed by Michael Winterbottom. 2007. Paramount Vantage, 2010. DVD.
Body of Lies. Directed by Sir Reedley Scott. 2008. Scott Free Productions. De Levine Pictures. WBP, 2011. DVD.
Brothers. Directed by Jim Sheridan. 2009. StudioMichael DeLuca Productions, 2011. DVD.
Fair Game. Directed by Doug Liman. 2010. River Road Entertainment, USA, 2011. DVD.
Green Zone. Directed by Paul Greengrass. 2010. Universal Pictures. 2011. DVD.
In the Valley of Ellah. Directed by Paul Haggis. 2007. Summit Entertainment. USA. 2010. DVD.
Lions for Lambs. Directed by Robert Redford. 2007. Clermont, USA, Hong Kong, MGM, 2009. DVD.
Rendition. Directed by Gavin Hood. 2007. Level One Entertainment, USA, 2011. DVD.
Stop Loss. Directed by Kimberley Peirce. 2008. MTV Films. Paramount Pictures, 2011. DVD.
The Kingdom. Directed by Peter Berg. 2007. Relativity Media, USA, 2010. DVD.
The Lucky Ones. Directed by Neil Burger. 2008. Koppelman and Levien Productions. Overnight Production, 2009. DVD.
United 93. Directed by Paul Greengrass. 2006. Studio Canal: USA, 2008. DVD.
World Trade Center. Directed by Oliver Stone. Paramount Pictures, 2009. DVD.

"On the Transmigration of Meaning": Essay on the Remembrance of 9/11 in Symphonic Music

Ákos Windhager

> *"When people experience traumatic events,*
> *sharing through creative mediums*
> *can begin the process of healing."*
> *(Pierre Jalbert)*

Introduction

The articulation of identify takes place in the social sphere, where the notion of I/we gains its distinct meaning from that of the Other labelled as you/they. This socialisation usually is a cultural (and of course, psychological) interaction between the self and society. How can a culture deal with the lack of any self-identification items? The institutionalised culture can borrow some from other cultures. For example, the lack of national American funeral music was replaced by European classical masterpieces by Beethoven, Brahms and Mahler.

The present paper analyses compositions written in remembrance of 9/11. The focus is on merging and separating art and politics in music in order to grasp the concept of "we" and "they". I am presenting an interpretational model of the first and third persons plural, "we" and "they", "us" and "them" through the case study of Tchaikovsky's *1812 overture* and Bartók's *Concerto for Orchestra*. Finally *On the Transmigration of Souls* by John Adams and *American Symphony* by Leonardo Balada are analysed from the perspective of community including both we and they.

The hermeneutics of the symbols employed in music

In a piece of literature we can identify ourselves with the protagonist or the narrator through the text by the overall narrative; a phenomenon analysed in several studies. Moreover, Italo Calvino's (1923-1985) *Se una notte d'inverno un viaggiatore* (*If on a winter's night a traveller,* 1979) describes the process of identification, which is manifested in everyday-life activities.[1] The same identifying mechanism works in songs, operas or cantatas as well, because the text also has a primary importance in these works. Program-music can also be characterised by these features, for its title or plot describes the situation.

In non-program orchestral pieces (like symphonies or concertos) identification is less accessible, since music employs abstract symbols. However, there are some external tools that guide the receivers' emotion, like the citation of well-known melodies, sounds or sonic symbols. Thus, we can consider musical symbols exclusively by their receptions; for music has no universal meaning, being rather based upon a consensus rooted in common interpretation. Turning to concrete examples, in Ludwig van Beethoven's (1770-1827) *Symphony No. 3* (*Eroica,* 1804) the audience is carried away by the great sorrow of the music, which means that we can include ourselves into the first person plural.

In Beethoven's *Symphony No. 5* (1807) the dynamic opening motif of the fourth movement alludes to Napoleon's political fanfare, that is why all the French guardians – listening to the première – were jumping up and shouting *"Long live the Emperor!"* (See Table 1.) Later this part lost its political connotation and the audience itself transformed into the first person plural.

However, Beethoven composed an explicitly political piece of music, the *Siegessymphonie* (Wellington's Victory, 1813); the orchestra is divided into two groups: the French and English "armies". The bands of both "political sides" play the national marches: *"The Rule Britannia"* for the British and the *"Marlborough has left for the War"* for the French. Beethoven intended a similar effect with *La Marseilles*, but it was considered subversive. Thus, the first and third plurals have clear positions, and the identification process can be done with absolute efficiency. This battle music met with success, political support and fortune for Beethoven, although it has little merit. Fortunately, it vanished from the concerts.

---

[1] *If on a winter's night a traveller* (Italian: *Se una notte d'inverno un viaggiatore*) is a 1979 novel by the Italian writer Italo Calvino (1923-1985). The narrative is about a reader trying to read a book called *If on a winter's night a traveller.* In every odd-numbered chapter the "author" addresses the readers in the second person singular, and provides a detailed description of what is going on in the readers' mind. The even-numbered chapters are separate stories that the fictitious reader is trying to read. The book was published in English in 1981.

Furthermore, Peter Ilyich Tchaikovsky (1840-1893) – in his *The Year 1812 festive overture* (1880) – symbolised the attacking French by fragments from the hymn of liberty, *La Marseillaise*, and the defending Russians by the anthem *God Save the Tsar!* (See the motifs on Table 2.) The composer employed two more citations, from a Russian orthodox prayer (*God Preserve Thy People!*) and a folk dance (*At the Gate, at Grandfather's Gate*). If we interpret the music with an awareness of the historical facts, it is clear that finally the Russians won. However, if we interpret the music through the musical symbols, we can conclude that the Russians were fighting against the warriors of freedom. That's why Tchaikovsky employed a totally different triumph-motif (which is a military fanfare) in the finale, and the monumentality of this finale even by the music of the Russian imperial anthem – with a large symphony orchestra, brass band and real cannons – gives a brotherly hug to every nation in the universe.

Although this interpretation could appear as if it was exaggerating, the facts can verify it. *The Year 1812* has become an important part of the American national music canon, especially for concerts on Independence Day.[2] The well-composed, simple work of art, which tells the fairy-tale like story of Good and Bad, has gained a wide popularity due to its mild and epic melodies, the heroic finale and the involved cannon solos. In the USA this overture lost its original national connotation (like the above mentioned *Symphony No.5* by Beethoven) and even during the Cold War it became part of the pan-American tradition. The audience receiving the usual Hollywood-like narrative reinterpreted it, as if it had been about the American triumph over the British! Since 1976, the bicentenary festival, Tchaikovsky's overture has been saturated with American patriotism.

On the contrary, in Europe, this piece is rarely played to convey its original political meanings as European culture has been Francophone rather than pan-Slavic, although its bombastic finale has a good reception. Thus, the first person plural is presented through the victorious community with fanfares and cannons, and the third person plural is accidental, even with its well-identifiable fanfares. The first person plural identifies itself with its idealistic historical point of view, but not with any historical facts...

Another level of the musical characterisation can be found in Béla Bartók's (1881-1945) symphonic poem about Lajos Kossuth (1802-1894), the leader of the Hungarian War of Independence in 1848-49. The *Kossuth* symphonic poem (1904) consists of a heroic Hungarian main theme and a

---

[2] Andrew Druckenbrod, *"How a rousing Russian tune took over our July 4th?"*

contrasting episodic theme, which is a demonised variation of the Austrian imperial anthem, the *Gotterhalte*.[3] (See Table 3.) Every listener could differentiate the first and third person plural, that is, every listener was able to learn from the symbols who were the Good and who were the evil. The mock was so obvious that the Austrian musicians of the première at Budapest refused to attend the concert. Bartók had to pay them two glasses of beer each to convince them to play…

In his *Concerto for Orchestra* (1943), which is the last finished piece of Bartók, the composer employed a similar stylistic technique. Bartók's *Concerto* is considered to be his swan-song of his passionate nostalgia for his homeland. In the fourth movement, which is called: *Intermezzo interrotto* Bartók alludes to a popular Hungarian patriotic operetta-melody: "*Hungary, You Are So Marvellous*" in hymnal form (See Table 4.). However, this sublime tune is harshly destroyed by a trump march, a scathing parody of the "invasion theme" from Dmitry Shostakovich's (1906-1975) *Symphony No. 7* (1941).[4] Shostakovich's piece is called "*Leningrad-symphony*", inspired by the devastating combat between the German and the Soviet Armies around Leningrad (See Table 5.). Thus, Bartók's fourth movement could be interpreted as the tragedy of Hungary, since the precious homeland is demolished by German boots. (See table 6.) The identification of "us" with Good and "them" with the Devil is obvious from the tunes.

Bartók recognised that the above mentioned Shostakovich-motif is a melody from the *Merry Widow* (1905) by Ferenc Lehár (1870-1948). Lehár was a worldwide popular Hungarian operetta-composer. This melody portrays an old cavalier flirting with show-girls singing: "*Love has more value than any patriotism*". Bartók, who knew both pieces, merged the two melodies into an ironical parody of false nostalgia. Turning back to Shostakovich – one of whose favourite melodies was this Lehár-arietta – we should add that his truly patriotic symphony is built on the melody of flirtation. How can we interpret this choice? If we are consistent, we should destruct the political undertone of the *Leningrad-symphony* – which means that the visible border between the first and third person plural becomes absolutely elusive.

Summing up, we see that there are some external features in the non-program musical works of art that serve to separate "us" from "them"; however, these allusions have more than one meaning.

---

[3] David Schneider, *Bartók, Hungary and the Renewal of Tradition*, 66.
[4] David Cooper, *Bartók: Concerto for Orchestra*, 57.

9/11 in classical music

> *"America ... did not have a single orchestral work
> that could satisfy the need for collective emotional experience
> that a seriously traumatized public maintained
> in those jarring days after the attack."[5]*
> *(John Adams)*

The trauma of 9/11 has been expressed in several musical pieces. The best known is John Adams's (1947*) *On the Transmigration of Souls,* commissioned by the New York Philharmonic in 2002. This piece received the Pulitzer Award for its painful beauty. In the same year Eric Ewazen (1954*) performed his wind ensemble lamentation, the *A Hymn for the Lost and the Living.* It is followed by Leonardo Balada's (1933*) *American Symphony* in 2003, written for the Pittsburgh Symphony Orchestra. Jay Greenberg (1991*, sic!) composed his *Skyline Dances* in 2008 on the commission from a consortium of youth orchestras. William Basinski (1958*) released his *Disintegration Loop 1.1* in 2002, which was reconstructed in 2011 for the Wordless Music Orchestra. Finally three new pieces have been composed for the tenth anniversary, the cantata *And None Shall Be Afraid* by Paul Aitken (1970*), the orchestral song *Shades of Memory* by Pierre Jalbert (1967*) and the orchestral remembrance *One Sweet Morning* by John Corigliano (1938*) which premiered on 30th September 2011.

Among the eight composers only three, Adams, Aitken, and Corigliano employ a wide variety of text, by which we can identify ourselves as the first person plural. John Adams chose some sentences from survivors' letters, notes, and messages. Paul Aitken employed peace prayers from five different religions, like the Jewish *"Come Let Us Go"*, the Native American *"Spirit of Our Ancestors"*, the Muslim *"Praise Be to the God of the Universe"*, the Christian *"Lord in Heaven"*, and finally *"If There is to be Peace in the World"*, a philosophical statement by Lau Tse. The third composition, John Corigliano's prayer for the future is based on the anti-war poem *"One Sweet Morning"* by Yip Harburg. This poem looks forward to *"One sweet morning"* when, *"out of the flags and the bones buried under the clover,"* *"spring will bloom"*...*"peace will come."*

The next five pieces are compositions without lyrics and any external program, even though they employ some symbolic gestures that suggest possible interpretations. For example Eric Ewazen's *A Hymn for the Lost and the Living* is composed for trombone solo and wind ensemble. The

---

[5] John Adams, *Halleluja Junction*, 262.

trumpets or trombones symbolise transcendence in the symphonic culture; since the *Book* of *Revelation* seven trumpets have been recognized as announcing the Apocalypse. Another example, Jay Greenberg's *Skyline Dances*, is non-program music, in spite of the composer's reflection on a tightrope walker's 45 minutes performance between the World Trade Center towers in August 1974. As Greenberg explained:

> While it has no extra musical or programmatic associations, it is linked in my mind to the city of New York itself and its position as a centre for creative works of all kinds.[6]

William Basinski's remembrance piece, the *Disintegration Loop 1.1* is in reality only the soundtrack of his "cinema verite elegy" (sic!) about the smoke of the collapsing towers. Pierre Jalbert uses the Gregorian chant, the *Dies Irae* (The day of wrath) motif to picture the doomsday atmosphere that invaded the city in those days. Jalbert employs also the *Agnus Dei* (The lamb of God) motif, in which the *Dona Nobis Pacem* (Give us peace) is emphasised. The three Gregorian sounds evoked here convey a suggestive message of hope even without the use of lyrics. These two thousand-year old chants can symbolize the journey from terror to healing.

The American institutional intention for musical identity

The tragedy of 9/11 shed light on the lack of any authentic funeral music pieces. On the first memory concert of the New York Philharmonic, Kurt Masur conducted the *German Requiem* by Johannes Brahms.[7] Since 2002 the memorial concerts of 9/11 have contained the same program – even by the New York Philharmonic – as it was rendered at the Kennedy memorial events; the *Symphony No.3* (*Eroica*) by Beethoven and the *Symphony No.2* (*Resurrection*) by Gustav Mahler (1860-1911).[8] There are only three American pieces for tragic occasions: *The Unanswered Question* by Charles Ives (1874-1954), the *Adagio for Strings* by Samuel Barber (1910-1981) and the *Quiet City* by Aaron Copland (1900-1990).[9] However, these three works are short and cannot bear the *gravitas* of the national pain of 9/11.

---

[6] Jay Greenberg, Skyline Dances, op. 15 – Programme Note.
[7] Greg Cahil, *New York Phil 9/11 Tribute Concert to be Viewed Worldwide*, post.
[8] See the concert program on November 24, 1963! on: Digital Archives of the New York Philharmonic.
[9] John Adams, ibid., 262.

The musicologist Nicholas Tawa presents the story of a heroic aspiration for the American national music canon; which could be interpreted as a national funeral music or celebration. This process had been under way in Europe a century earlier. For instance, the Italian identity continues to be rooted in Verdi's operas. In 1935, during the years of the Great Depression and the Second World War the American government funded the Work Progress Administration, which supported – among other cultural projects – the new-born, American contemporary classical music.[10] The WPA did not command or order any piece, but organised the concerts.

In this period, 1935-1950, a huge part of American society attended the American contemporary (symphonic) concerts.[11] Aaron Copland, Samuel Barber, and Leonard Bernstein (1918-1990) have become famous outside of America, but after the Roosevelt era their identical American orchestral pieces could hardly survive even in the American concert halls. Even now, the national burial prayer is still absent, as we can see by the memorial concerts of 9/11. Furthermore, in the Golden Age of the United States, symphonic music belonged to the established cultural canon which expressed civilised existence; currently classical music has become an alternative subculture. Thus, the contemporary funeral music is completely different from the symphonies of the Golden Age, even if they even resemble each other.

*

Which musical elements (symbols, signs, and significant sounds) can be attached to an "American" symphony? How can a composer become "the bard" of the States? To these questions, every composer has to respond in his own way. The earlier mentioned scholar, N. Tawa, analysed 18 American composers' symphonies in his study, but during their reading we cannot find the secret code of essential Americanism. However, Jeff Dun, a San Francisco music critic, presents a list of some features of American music. Dun strictly judged the completely new *American symphony* by Christopher Theofanidis (1967*).

Those who envision a typical America as big and brash, can-do, no-nonsense, powerful, mostly optimistic, energetic – and not too thoughtful or profound – should acclaim the latest release, on ASO Media, as an

---

[10] Nicholas Tawa, *The Great American Symphony,* 14.
[11] Tawa, ibid, 27.

exemplary candidate for the Great American Symphony of the new century.[12]

Adam Schoenberg, contemporary author, composed his *American symphony* in 2011. The Schoenberg-symphony is built on the symphony model of Copland, although besides him Schoenberg refers to two other American composers: movement IV pays homage to Barber and Gershwin as a prayer with a chorale. However, Schoenberg does not proclaim that his finale is based on an allusion to the most famous American march: *Stars and Stripes For Ever* by John Philip Sousa.[13] His symphony begins with a fanfare, contains a choral-prayer and ends up with *Stars and Stripes*. Could this be short selections of the secret "ingredients" of a "real" American symphony?

The institutional remembrance after 9/11

There is a common expectation towards the composers composing memorial music in the name of American society, that is, to identify themselves with the suffering caused by the traumatic event. Chris Becker, a journalist, looks back to the bygone times when the community had communal rituals for tragedies and collective singing had been one of the most important acts during a burial. People needed music to express their sorrow, both collectively and as individuals:

> In times of collective trauma, human beings need music, whether in the form of a great song or a piece for chorus and orchestra. Music in any and all of its forms will speak to us individually and as a community. And again, our always hard-to-define and very personal responses to music (or any kind of art) somehow... bring us closer to the people around us.[14]

Many of the critics and essayists have looked for healing in the field of the arts. John Adams, the aforementioned composer laureate admits the magic power of music that can touch the hidden layers of the human soul. This touch can be the real aim of composing:

---

[12] Jeff Dun, "A New 'American' Symphony."
[13] He mentions only the following: "Movement V is the longest movement, and is essentially conceived in three larger sections: *Stars, Stripes*, and *Celebration*." Schoenberg, ibid.
[14] Chris Becker, "Speaking to tragedy: 9/11 in music and memory."

Modern people have learned all too well how to keep our emotions in check, and we know how to mask them with humour or irony. Music has a singular capacity to unlock those controls and bring us face to face with our raw, uncensored and unattenuated feelings. That is why during times when we are grieving or in need of being in touch with the core of our beings we seek out those pieces which speak to us with that sense of *gravitas* and serenity.[15]

However, even he warns of the overestimated role of music. In his view human beings can only heal themselves through music by using it as a tool. His aim has been to write music that creates a tender link between the collective memory and personal wounds:

I am always nervous with the term 'healing' as it applies to a work of art. ... So it's not my intention to attempt 'healing' in this piece. The event will always be there in [the] memory, and the lives of those who suffered will forever remain burdened by the violence and the pain. Time might make the emotions and the grief gradually less acute, but nothing, least of all a work of art, is going to heal a wound of this sort. Instead, the best I can hope for is to create something that has both serenity and the kind of '*gravitas*' that those old cathedrals possess.[16]

The audience's demand goes as far as that the composers' absence from New York deprives their pieces of their authenticity. However, it is worth noting that the personal tone of these compositions is not built on firsthand experience of 9/11, but rather on various experiences of human disasters.

The following two musical *ars poetica* represent variations of the artistic truth – reconstruction, and the replacement of personal presence. Adam Schoenberg (1980*) reflects on 9/11 from the point of view of his joy over Barack Obama's electoral victory, and links together all the tragedies that happened in the last decade:

While not a patriotic work, the symphony reflects a respect and responsibility for the great potential of our nation and a hunger to affect positive change. It is about our collective ability to restore hope within ourselves and our neighbours, both here and around the world. ... The movement IV, Adagio is dedicated to those lost in 9/11, hurricane Katrina, and all victims of violence and war.[17]

---

[15] Elena Park, "A Commemorative Commission (Interview with John Adams about "On the Transmigration of Souls")."

[16] Park, ibid.

[17] Adam Schoenberg, "American Symphony (2011)."

Pierre Jalbert was far away from New York at the moment of 9/11; however, his brother was taking an aeroplane at that time. Jalbert merges this personal experience, as he saw a woman shouting in terror and refusing to leave the train at the former station of the WTC. His music is built upon the universal language of sorrow.

> It was quite difficult at first; I didn't know how to wrap my head around it. I felt like an outsider looking in. Yes, it was a national tragedy that changed things personally, nationally and internationally, but my exposure to it was limited. I came up with the idea to write an elegy, a type of musical memorial. Music happens in time, it's temporary. The memorial will exist for 13 minutes and the experience of listening to it serves to honour those who lost their lives. I knew early on I didn't want to craft a tone poem, or something that would pictorially represent 9/11 like Penderecki's *Threnody to the Victims of Hiroshima.*[18]

Institutionalised culture needs institutions, for example philharmonic orchestras, cultural foundations and the government. They can support the national healing process by inviting compositions for national mourning. In contrast to the Golden Age, when the WPA did not stipulate what to compose, these contemporary institutes have to define their goals, e.g. what is a requiem-symphony, etc. However, the musical harvest would be completely open to question. Joshua Kosman, critic at the *San Francisco Chronicle*, articulated the arguable topic well.

> But the purveyors of orchestral music like the Philharmonic still need someone to call when they want to make a contribution to the national mourning process, just as monarchs employ court composers and poets to mark momentous national events. And it has to be someone whose artistic voice, like Copland's, is distinctively and recognizably American.[19]

As we saw in the quotations, Adams, Jalbert and Balada composed music, commissioned by philharmonic orchestras, in the name of the American people. How can a contemporary classical composer write a piece of art claiming to speak for all the inhabitants of the United States? Memory-building needs time, invention and an audience. The ingenuity that is essential for invention cannot be enforced, or provoked, even by the most tragic events.

---

[18] Joel Luks, *"Shades of Memory," Culture map Houston* (09.16.2011).
[19] Joshua Kosman, *"Voice of America: Composer Adams Speaks for the Nation"*, 6.

Adams answered the Philharmonic's call, and rose to the challenge of creating a public utterance of enormous dignity and tenderness. But it was only with 'My Father knew Charles Ives' [Adams's composition from the same year 2003 – ÁW], as I hear that score, that he accepted the full responsibility of being the nation's musical representative in the way that Copland was before him.[20]

More precisely, Pierre Jalbert expressed the ambiguity of the commissioned remembrance music. As we can assume from the citation below, he considered his piece as an entity on its own and left it open for interpretation and criticism.

Musically, it can stand on its own outside of its commemorative spirit, not unlike Shostakovich's *String Quartet No. 8* which is dedicated to victims of Fascism, for example. I'd love to see it performed more. But whether it will be is not up to me. That's up to others to decide.[21]

From abstract to ethnic

The *Symphony No. 5* by Leonardo Balada was commissioned by the Pittsburgh Symphony, directed by Maris Jansons. Balada's *American symphony* is also non-program music; however, the titles of the movements suggest some possible interpretations. The first movement is called *9/11: In Memoriam*, the second is named *Reflection*, and the finale is entitled *Square Dance*. In the symphony the dramatic and abstract first movement evolves through a slow second part inspired by a lamenting African-American spiritual into an uplifting square-dance.

Leonardo Balada was born in Barcelona, Catalonia, Spain, in 1933. He graduated from *Conservatorio Superior de Música del Liceu* in Barcelona and immigrated to the United States, where he graduated from the *Juilliard School* in New York. Balada studied composition with Aaron Copland as well as conducting with Igor Markevitch. His role in the American classical music is really unique, as Philip Guerrard adds:

...Music such as Leonardo Balada's – which is not minimal, serial, aleatoric or stochastic, but is, rather, intensely allusive – does not require a label so much as some identification of its salient features. The influence of Stravinsky is apparent in Balada's snarling brass parts, the frequent use

---

[20] Joshue Kosman, "Voice of America: Composer John Adams Speaks for the Nation," *San Francisco Chronicle*, May 18, 2003.
[21] Luks, ibid.

of ostinati, the sometimes diatonic choral writing, and asymmetrical rhythms.[22]

Since 1970 Balada has been teaching at Carnegie Mellon University in Pittsburgh. His extensive catalogue of compositions includes operas, and orchestral, chamber, instrumental, vocal and choral works. He has had a long-standing relationship with the Pittsburgh Symphony since 1969, when his *Guernica* was premiered. Balada usually composes his symphonies in dedication, for example his *Symphony No. 1* is "*Sinfonia en Negro - Homage to Martin Luther King*", the *Symphony No. 3* is the "*Steel Symphony*", dedicated to Pittsburgh's steel factory, and his *Symphony No. 6* is the "*Symphony of Sorrows*," dedicated to "the innocent victims of the Spanish Civil War".

In the same way the *Symphony No. 5*, the *American Symphony*, is dedicated to the victims of 9/11. The symphony's first movement is organised chaos with *ad libitum* playing. Dry, loud and desperate sonorities are presented in the most abstract, tense and driven manner. The composer told in an interview that "the first movement is foreboding and tragic, with the interval of a minor third heard throughout." The monsters of this music are reminiscent of the sonic experience which could have been a reality during the attacks. By this sonic image we can identify ourselves with survivors in the first person plural. Balada similarly to Adams and Basinski, tried to use the real sounds of the event in order to verify their abstract music – however, Balada opted for the musical chaos and abstained from using the original recordings.

In the second movement, *Reflections*, the music becomes optimistic. The above mentioned melancholic "minor third" is transformed into a delicate fabric of melodic lines based on an African-American spiritual. Here all is quiet, peaceful, and hopeful and to a degree melodious. The identification is strengthened by the use of the spiritual, which belongs to a celestial, transcendent culture and a common sonic environment in the States. The third, *Square Dance* movement, is a toxic, vivid part, merged with some Native American folk-tunes in the style of *Rodeo* by Copland. The significant accord of the first movement, the minor third, is applied to this dance melody. Thus, the musical symbol of sadness can transform into remembrance, reflection and a furious life-dance. The identification is easier than before; we are all one in the waving tumult. In Balada's vision '*All Mankind become brothers / Where the gentle wings of this dance hold sway*'.

The critic, Jonathan Woolf evaluates the new *American symphony* in the following words:

---

[22] Philip Guerrard, "On the music of Leonardo Balada."

My impressions of Balada so far have not been unmixed, but he's a composer difficult to ignore. The three movement (sic!) Symphony No.5 *American* features the vestigial use of some extreme avant-garde effects with more 'ethnic' material, to use Balada's own word. It was written *In Memoriam 9/11* and moves from the darkness of the first movement to the communing light of the second.[23]

The CD-reviewer, S.G.S., finds the piece flat; however, his aesthetics is based on the classical European forms, but not fixed on the American symphonic techniques. However, Roy Harris, former American composer laureate, who never developed his themes, but rather employed fugue and counterpoint techniques, was immensely appraised for his *Symphony N. 3*, which is considered to be the most popular American symphony. S.G.S., nevertheless, lauds other features of Balada's composition.

It seems to me that a Big Subject requires more inspiration, rather than less, but Balada seems to be working on automatic pilot throughout much of the movement – chaotic opening, programmatic rendering of the twin-tower crash, nothing you couldn't predict and, worse, nothing more either. The entire symphony emphasizes the interval of a third, without ever once harvesting a truly musical idea from it. There's no argument and no progression, consequently, no transformation. It's music that squats. (…) Everything comes at you on the same level of importance. I strongly suspect that audiences react to the 'spiritual program', rather than to the music itself.[24]

Balada was most probably aware of the complexity of his task when he decided to compose an American symphony. There are many U. S. related symphonies; among them the most popular is Antonin Dvorak's *Symphony No. 9* ("From the New World"); however, the most "American" American symphony was written by Aaron Copland (it is his *Symphony No. 3*, 1946).

If we compare the remembrance music under consideration, we should recognise the specialities of Balada's composition. For example, it is the only remembrance music which concludes in a happy, optimistic way, and with a notion of healing. Further, we should be aware of the fact that Balada composed his fifth symphony for his seventieth birthday, since we can recognise his auto-citations.[25] In the first movement he recalls fragments and techniques from his *Steel Symphony*. Simultaneously, he

---

[23] Jonathan Woolf, "Leonardo Balada."

[24] S.G.S., "BALADA: Symphony No. 5 'American' (2003)."

[25] Michelle Pilecki, "High Five, A Long-Time Local Composer's Creation of His Dream Symphony.", *Pittsburgh Magazine* (November 2003): 19.

remembers his childhood experience of the barbaric bombing of Guernica – another auto-citation, because his first Pittsburgh composition was *Guernica*.

As mentioned earlier, concerning the '*Quest of Essential Americanism*', each composer has to deal with the matter of national identification, or put more simply: every author is obliged to reveal the first person plural in her/his music. Balada's auto-citations could support the listeners' identification with the "us" of the music – if the author had a worldwide reputation. Beyond his auto-reflection Balada responds to the necessity of the identical quest in three other ways. The first movement represents the victims and survivors of the attack, generally the New Yorker (metropolitans) in our time. The strongly rhythmic, tireless, black spiritual of the second movement gives a symbolic tribute to the African-Americans living for centuries in the States. The Copland-like country dance of the third movement reveals the cowboys, the farmers, and the villagers. Thus, Balada designates the Americans by special elements linked to their three origins. The first person plural of Balada's *American symphony* is constituted by these three relevant social groups in a manner of the aesthetic horizon of the Golden Age.

The Apolitical National Requiem

"I'm sure there will be some who would have preferred something more Copland-esque, more messianic, more patriotically uplifting to commemorate the memory of that fateful day..." [26]
(Ed Uyeshima)

The composer laureate of the States, John Adams also emphasises the importance of common memory that can help the personal memory in dealing with trauma. For Adams the remembrance music might have been a challenge, because he is well-known for his leftist (green) commitments, and his non-conventional political attitude, exemplified by his opera *The Death of Klinghoffer*. This piece deals with the Achille Lauro hijacking for which some critics accused him of anti-Semitism. [27] Adams summed up his

---

[26] Ed Uyeshima, "Masterful Memoriam of Our Defining Moment", October 7, 2004, *Amazon.com*

[27] The opera's Palestinians appear to be noble victims; its Jews seem to have stepped out of an episode of Seinfeld. Soon after 9/11 the Boston Symphony cancelled previously scheduled performances of choruses from *Klinghoffer*. – David Schiff, "Memory Spaces," *The Atlantic Monthly* (April 2003): Volume 291, No. 3; 127-130.

intentions with the following words:

> At first I didn't think it was an appropriate thing for me to do, but it was a very serious request from the philharmonic, so I had to find a way to be meaningful and not exploitative of the emotions... *On the Transmigration of Souls*, a work that is neither an official public memorial, nor a personalised response, but rather ... a memory space – you can be alone with your thoughts but hear a continuum of sound, with other people's footsteps, outside noises, and above all, you feel in the presence of eons of souls all around.[28]

Adams's intention was to avoid the above mentioned heroic gestures, and instead he wrote a symphonic melodrama, which he called, a "memory space". He emphasised many times that he could not tolerate the "orgy of narcissism" of the Bush-governments.[29] He judged the state communication as a "kitschification" of 9/11, in accordance with Philip Roth's arguments.[30] In his biography Adams also mentions the politically unpleasant topic of warfare bombings by the US Air Force during the last few wars. In summary, the composer has indeed been moved by the national pain; however, he has insisted on staying out of governmental reactions. This personal point of view can explain the very strange genre of his memorial work of art. Furthermore, his personal feelings account for his strong criticism of the Pulitzer Award during his own award ceremony.

On the Transmigration of Souls is one slow orchestral movement with constant vocal sounds and recorded street noises. The choirs recite the victims' name and the survivors' messages posted on the walls of Ground Zero. Adams employs his minimalist style, which means strong repetitive effects, modal atonality and a huge variety of rhythms. The orchestral music resembles movie soundtracks, although there is a hidden classical structure. While Adams rejects the Romantic orchestral explosions, he uses a big ensemble consisting of many deep instruments, for instance bass clarinets, contrabassoons or tubas.

The *Transmigration* has been rendered in several places all over the world. We can consider it a huge success, like the mentioned Pulitzer Award in 2003, or the Grammy Award in 2005. Its fans have described it as "*A Requiem for the 21st Century*", "*A Memoriam and Refuge*", or "*A*

---

[28] Pierre Ruhe, "An American classic: John Adams brings a common touch to the highbrow symphonic world."
[29] Adams, ibid, 264.
[30] Adams, ibid, 263.

Temple of Music".[31] However, there are negative criticisms, too. The dissenting opinions are divided into two groups: the first rejects the minimalist music style, and the second finds it too mundane.

A BBC commentator, Germaine Geer, felt it to be dry, plain and premature.

> First of all, the experience hasn't gelled. We haven't got the distance. We don't understand its significance really. We haven't got any kind of objective correlative for it and the very worst way of approaching it in my view was to make it a kind of souvenir of 9/11. Here are the names; here are this and that. The musical structure isn't dense enough. There isn't a tone or a pulse that comes out of it that becomes the sound of that moment.[32]

Another commenter, Mark Kermode, leans toward the second group:

> I think the problem is that he was so worried about doing anything in the words that would offend people; somehow using the words which people wrote on walls themselves, the names of people, seems justified, it seems honest, it seems like it has integrity and it does have all of those things. What it doesn't actually have is any kind of artistic validity and that's the problem.

In Adams' music we can clearly find the first person plural as the choirs whisper the names of the victims. Adams reformed the model of the concerts by this piece, because the audience can listen to not only orchestral music, but also murmurs. In addition to the "memory space" concept, the audience can take part in the concert by repeating their deceased friends' names. The concert-goers are involved in the memorial process, as they were in the real events, especially if they resided in the US at the time of the attack.

Another fingerprint of the identification can be recognised in the artistic tribute to Charles Ives' *The Unanswered Question* (see Table 6.). Adams confessed in his biography that he was inspired by the structure of Ives' piece. The slow, motionless strings of both works expand time into infinity. This eon-like existence is disturbed in both pieces by a trumpet solo. Adams´ response to the quest of the essential American can be easily interpreted: everything is essential, which comes from Ives, the stubborn

---

[31] See on the micro site of On the Transmigration of Souls on the Amazon.com website, ibid.
[32] Tim Marlow, *Newsnight Review discussed John Adams' On The Transmigration of Souls*, BBC News, 4 August, 2003.

non-European composer. Beyond this national identification Adams' "us" is everybody, all who can feel sympathy for the victims and the mourners.

Summary

In conclusion we can assume that the long '*quest for the American musical identity*' has not been completed – insofar as we consider the establishment of a national canon as a primary criterion. On the one hand, the heroic endeavour of Copland, Barber and Bernstein in the Golden Age was doomed to fail in the overburdened political milieu of McCarthyism. On the other hand, contemporary composers – in spite of their conscious reference to the aesthetic horizon of the Golden Age – did not use direct political references – as expected – in their musical articulation of the 9/11 experience.

Beethoven, Tchaikovsky and Bartók composed political music, but these became soon forgotten. Beethoven and Tchaikovsky commented on their above mentioned battle music as the worst they had ever composed, and Bartók went as far as to hide the score from the public two years after the successful première. Even in those compositions that were meant to be apolitical, they used political symbols; however, they loaded them with new implicit meanings. As we can notice, 'the transmigration of meaning' is a vivid process in the music culture, in which even the notion of "we" and "they" are elusive and therefore open to various interpretations.

The American concert canon is filled with European compositions, with no or hardly any tribute to the masterpieces of American composers, whose commitment was to serve their audience rather than political agendas. The 'transmigration of meaning' is an ongoing phenomenon in the American musical life; however, it is in the reverse direction: the burial prayers by the apolitical Balada and the openly leftist Adams were highly acclaimed for their supposed political references, and received laudation from the public. However, in the absence of any efforts to establish a national canon, their future remains somewhat obscure. Will they be soon forgotten as it happened to Beethoven's *Siegessymphonie* or Bartók's *Kossuth-symphony*? Or will they be divested of their historical reference and used as a sentimental soundtrack of a Hollywood movie? Finally, will any of them be nominated as the creator of American funeral music *par excellence*?

Bibliography

Books

Adams, John. *Halleluja Junction*. New York: Farrar, Straus, Giroux, 2008.
Cooper, David. *Bartók. Concerto for Orchestra*. Cambridge: University Press, 1996.
Schneider, David. *Bartók, Hungary, and the Renewal of Tradition* Los Angeles: University of California Press, 2006. .
Tawa, Nicolas. *The Great American Symphonies*. Bloomington and Indianapolis: Indiana University Press, 2009.

Scores

Adams, John. *On the Transmigration of Souls*. Boosey & Hawkes, New York, 2002.
Bartók, Béla. *Kossuth*. Budapest: Editio Musica, 1963.
—. *Concerto for orchestra*. Piano version by the composer. Boosey & Hawkes, New York, 2001.
Beethoven, Ludwig von. *Symphony No.5*. Piano version by Liszt, Franz. Leipzig: Breitkopf & Härtel, n.d. (1865).
Tchaikovsky, Peter Ilyich. *The Year 1812*. Military band version by L.P. Laurendau. United States Military Band Journal, New York: Carl Fischer, 1904.

Articles in journals

Pilecki, Michelle. "High Five, A Long-Time Local Composer's Creation of His Dream Symphony." *Pittsburgh Magazine* (November 2003): G 3-4.
Ruhe, Pierre. "An American classic: John Adams brings a common touch to the highbrow symphonic world." *Atlanta Journal Constitution*, May 25, 2003, http://www.earbox.com/inter-ruhe2.html)
Schiff, David. "Memory Spaces." *The Atlantic Monthly* 291,3 (April 2003):127-130.

Articles online

Alicino, Christine. "John Adams 9/11 transmigration: premiere in New York",
http://www.boosey.com/pages/cr/news/further_info.asp?newsid=10394

&LangID=1.

Becker, Chris. "Speaking to tragedy: 9/11 in music and memory." *Culturemap Houston* (09.09. 2011), http://houston.culturemap.com/newsdetail/09-05-11-20-16-rare-birds-911-music-and-memory/.

Cahil, Greg. *New York Phil 9/11 Tribute Concert to be Viewed Worldwide,* post on webpage Strings, http://www.allthingsstrings.com/News/News/New-York-Phil-9-11-Tribute-Concert-to-be-Viewed-Worldwide

Digital Archives of New York Philharmonic (Session 1963/64) http://archives.nyphil.org/index.php/artifact/6c0ec546-3916-4217-85f9-a3539ab8191b?search-type=singleFilter&search-text=*&doctype=program&x=31&y=11&search-dates-from=11%2F22%2F1963&search-dates-to=12%2F30%2F1964

Dun, Jeff. "A New 'American' Symphony." *San Francisco Classical Voice* (05. 07. 2011), http://www.sfcv.org/reviews/a-new-american-symphony.

Druckenbrod, Andrew. "How a rousing Russian tune took over our July 4th". *post-gazette.com A&E* (04.07.2003), http://old.post-gazette.com/ae/20030704overtureae3.asp

Greenberg, Jay. "Skyline Dances" – *Programme Note,* http://www.chesternovello.com/default.aspx?TabId=2432&State_3041=2&workId_3041=37237.

Guerrard, Philip. "On the music of Leonardo Balada." http://www.newworldrecords.org/linernotes/80442.pdf..

Kosman, Joshua. *"Voice of America: Composer Adams Speaks for the Nation".* San Francisco Chronicle* (May 18, 2003), http://www.earbox.com/inter006.html.

Luks, Joel. "Shades of Memory." *Culturemap Houston* (09.16.2011), http://houston.culturemap.com/newsdetail/09-16-11-shades-of-memory-pierre-jalbert-former-teaching-assistant-quizzes-him-on-his-houston-symphony-premiere/.

Marlow, Tim. *"Newsnight Review discussed John Adams's On The Transmigration of Souls".* BBC News (4.08. 2003), http://news.bbc.co.uk/2/hi/programmes/newsnight/review/3123759.stm.

Park, Elena. "A Commemorative Commission" (Interview with John Adams about "On the Transmigration of Souls") New York Philharmonic web site (September 2002), http://nyphil.org/attend/guests/index.cfm?page=interview&interviewNum=27&selectedNav.

Schoenberg, Adam. "American Symphony (2011)",
    http://www.adamschoenberg.com/asymphony.html.
S.G.S., "BALADA: Symphony No. 5 'American' (2003)." *Classicalcdreview*
    (May 2007),
    http://www.classicalcdreview.com/8557749.html.
Uyeshima, Ed. "Masterful Memoriam of Our Defining Moment" (October
    7, 2004),
    http://www.amazon.com/On-the-Transmigration-of-Souls/product-
    reviews/B0018AX1UC.
Woolf, Jonathan. "Leonardo Balada." *Naxos Review* (2005),
    http://www.musicweb-international.com/classrev/2006/Apr06/balada
    _8557749.htm.

Appendix

1. table
L. v. Beethoven: Symphony No. 5, IV. mvt (Allegro),
Piano version by F. Liszt,
"Long live the Emperor!"- Motif

2. table
P. Tchaikovsky: The Year 1812, Overture
(Military band version by L.P.Laurendau)
The tunes of *La Marseillaise* in the central staves

3. table
Bartók: *Kossuth*. The tunes of *Gotterhalte* in the parts of comic
instruments (bassoons) in the upper staves

4. table
Bartók: *Concerto for Orchestra*, 4th mvt.
Operetta melody (42-47. bars in the upper staves) in hymnal style

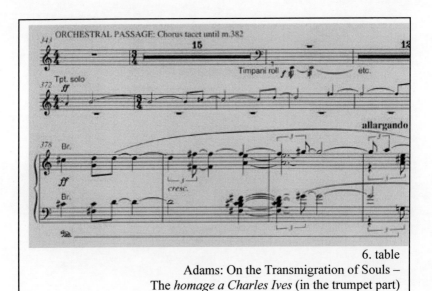

5. table
Bartók: Concerto for Orchestra, 4th mvt.
The *Invasion theme* of Shostakovich (originally a Lehar-melody)
in parody style (in the third stave)

6. table
Adams: On the Transmigration of Souls –
The *homage a Charles Ives* (in the trumpet part)

GEORGE ORWELL'S COLONIAL OTHER: THE PERVERSITY OF IMPERIALISTIC STEREOTYPING

UWE ZAGRATZKI

Based on his personal experience in Burma, where he served with the Imperial Police between 1922 and 1927, George Orwell produced a few lesser known texts on the East, of which the novel *Burmese Days* (1934) stands out as the most acclaimed one of the species. However, it is his shorter texts "A Hanging" (1931) and "Shooting an Elephant" (1936) which are keys to the author's notion of the Eastern (Colonial) Other.

Michael Sheldon in his committed biography meticulously traces Orwell's post-Eton public-school career.[1] Wavering between pursuing the path to an academic title and his "taste for adventure" he finally opted for a 'return' to the East, where he had been born on 25 June 1903 in Motihari, Bengal, near the border with Nepal and four hundred miles northwest of Calcutta and which he had left for England with his mother and sister in 1904.[2] His father stayed behind – in Orwell's words – as "an official in the English administration" of India, covering up the fact that he worked to secure the British government opium monopoly in Bengal.[3] Now at the age of 19 without his father's financial support of his university education, young Orwell set his eyes on the East again. He aimed at a career in the Indian Imperial Police, and when he had passed the admission exams held by the India Office – doing well in Greek and Latin, bad in riding – he left England for Burma on 27 October 1922. Burma, in those days a province of India and a politically unstable backwater, had been Orwell's first choice, as police service in the country offered him promising opportunities to secure his life financially. Besides,

---

[1] Michael Sheldon, *Orwell – the authorised biography* (London: Secker and Warburg, 1996).
[2] Sheldon, 86.
[3] Sheldon, 14.

he may have been misled by false images about the country, since his maternal grandmother still lived there detached from the life of the Burmese.

Orwell joined the service as a probationary Assistant District Superintendent of Police. During his five years in Burma he was posted to five different districts, where he did extremely well. Responsibility was constantly growing, and at one post – the Syriam refineries – he oversaw the security of British India's most important oil supply, whilst he was also in charge of 200 local policemen. So, by and large, there was a bright future in the Imperial Services ahead of him. Why, then, did he quit the post, while he was on sick leave in England in 1927? His texts about Burma, written in retrospect, tell a sub-plot he would not be able and willing to tell while in service.

In his programmatic essay of 1946 "Why I Write", Orwell laid down the criteria of what writing meant to him. Among the "four great motives for writing... prose" there are (items 3 and 4):

> 3. Historical impulse. Desire to see things as they are, to find out true facts and store them up for the use of posterity.
> 4. Political purpose – using the word 'political' in the widest possible sense. Desire to push the world in a certain direction, to alter other people's idea of the kind of society that they should strive after. Once again, no book is genuinely free from political bias. The opinion that art should have nothing to do with politics is itself a political attitude.[4]

In the course of the essay he reiterates the importance of political writing as he feels pushed by the age to "becoming a sort of pamphleteer." He continues: "First I spent five years in an unsuitable profession (the Indian Imperial Police, in Burma), and then I underwent poverty and the sense of failure." He concludes: "And yet it is also true that one can write nothing readable unless one constantly struggles to efface one's own personality. Good prose is like a window pane."[5]

The issues raised above apply in the essay "A Hanging", which was published for the first time in the *Adelphi* in August 1931. The piece revolves around the execution of a Hindu convict presumably at Moulmein jail, where Orwell was posted as the sub-divisional police officer and

---

[4] "Why I Write," in *The Collected Essays, Journalism and Letters of George Orwell*, ed. Sonia Orwell, Ian Angus. Vol. 1 *An Age Like This* (Harmondsworth: Penguin, 1975), 23-30; 26.
[5] All quotes from *The Collected Essays*...Vol. 1, 26; 29-30.

which he may have witnessed voluntarily.[6] Though the tone is detached, it yet shows concern by means of describing in minute details the convict's way to the gallows, thus creating a growing tension through a slowly developing narrative. Relief finally comes for all attendants and the reader only after the man's death. Central passages reveal the epiphanic character of an intimate moment at which the I-narrator realises the senseless extinction of human life:

> It is curious, but till that moment I had never realized what it means to destroy a healthy, conscious man. When I saw the prisoner step aside to avoid the puddle, I saw the mystery, the unspeakable wrongness, of cutting a life short when it is in full tide. The man was not dying, he was alive just as we were alive. All the organs of his body were working.... and his brain still remembered, foresaw, reasoned – reasoned even about puddles. He and we were a party of men walking together, seeing, hearing, feeling, understanding the same world; and in two minutes, with a sudden snap, one of us would be gone – one mind less, one world less.[7]

The vigorous humanism of the paragraph refrains from any accusation of a political regime guilty of this "wrongness", though "the job in Burma had given [him] some understanding of the nature of imperialism."[8] Orwell's anger here is fuelled by the Christian spirit of the Fifth Commandment ("Though shalt not murder!") rather than by a political doctrine like Socialism that he would be in favour of after 1936 according to his reflections above. Against this background it is less of a surprise that the 'double Other' – Hindu and criminal – is neither vilified nor discriminated against on the ground of his race or religion, as would have been expected from a white Imperial policeman, but, on the contrary, considered a valuable human being with undeniably equal rights of existence. The humanism in "A Hanging" points to the essence of Orwell's political philosophy which would be refined in the years to come. Looking back in 1937 to his years in Burma he explains:

> Every Anglo-Indian is haunted by a sense of guilt which he usually conceals as best he can, because there is no freedom of speech, and merely to be overheard making a seditious remark may damage his career. All

---

[6] Sheldon, 113.
[7] "A Hanging," in *The Collected Essays*, Vol.1, 66-71; 68-69. Originally published in *Adelphi* (August 1931).
[8] "Why I write," 26.

over India there are Englishmen who secretly loathe the system of which they are part.[9]

Literature was also the means of articulating emotions as much as political ideas for Orwell. With hindsight he stresses the emotional impulse behind *Burmese Days*:

> I wanted to write enormous naturalistic novels with unhappy endings, full of detailed descriptions and arresting similes, and also full of purple passages in which words were used partly for the sake of their sound. And in fact my first complete novel, *Burmese Days*, which I wrote when I was thirty but projected much earlier, is rather that kind of book.[10]

The first edition of the novel, which was banned in India by the British Government, was published in the USA by Harper & Brothers in 1934, but, as Orwell admits, had been on his mind for some time.[11] After slight changes by the author to avoid libel action, Victor Gollancz published the English version in June 1935.

His 1946 reflections on the book – the same year "Why I write" saw the light of day – tell only half of the truth. Certainly, on the one hand, existential loneliness and sexual frustration are hard to bear for Flory, the English timber trader in fictional Kyauktada, and his emotions run wild so that he kills himself when he finally is rejected by Elisabeth, the young single Englishwoman, who is forced by fate to settle in Burma and live with her aunt and uncle until a protective marriage saves her from utter distress and wretchedness. Yet, on the other hand, the author's comment for unknown reasons covers up an explicit condemnation in the novel of the pervasive Imperial order imposed on English, Burmese and Indian. Daily life, this is made clear from the beginning, is regulated by powerful and unquestioned hierarchies which are anchored in racism: "When a man has a black face, suspicion is proof" (*Burmese Days*, 8).

At the top of the Kyauktada community, English administrators and merchants live the lives of imperial masters, their exclusive "European Club" symbolises the fortress of white power. As the narrative is told from a homodiegetic point of view – Flory's, who belongs to the ruling section, though he is an outsider – the reader obtains an intimate view of white

---

[9] George Orwell, *The Road to Wigan Pier* (London: Gollancz, 1937; Penguin, 1979), 127.

[10] "Why I Write," 25.

[11] *Orwell: The War Broadcasts*, ed. with an introduction by W.J. West (London: Duckworth, 1985), 23. Sketches of the future novel had existed before Orwell left the country in 1927.

racism and moral rottenness.[12] A strong bond among the tiny group of Whites is alcohol. Their attitudes towards the local villagers vary from outright (Ellis) to moderate racism (Macgregor) and include Flory's risky friendship with the Indian surgeon Dr. Veraswami.

Since racism is at the core of Imperialism, it is no wonder that the native population is generally considered by the English figures stupid, ugly, seditious, dangerous, in short inferior to the white race. Only Flory stands as an exception – his facial birthmark makes him stick out from the rest of the Whites, even visibly, emphasising his in-between position. Though he employs local staff in his household and pays a native prostitute for her services, he feels he is part of Burma (*Burmese Days*, 72). It is through Flory's serious talks with Dr. Veraswami that personal grumbles and frustrations, interpersonal or interracial relations and communal affairs, are synthesized by a common denominator.

This is Flory speaking:

> I don't want the Burmans to drive us out of this country. God forbid! I'm here to make money, like everyone else. All I object to is the slimy white man's burden humbug… the lie that we're here to uplift our poor black brothers instead of to rob them. I suppose it's a natural enough lie. But it corrupts us, it corrupts us in ways you can't imagine… We Anglo-Indians could be almost bearable, if we'd only admit that we're thieves and go on thieving without any humbug… The official holds the Burman down while the businessman goes through his pockets… The British Empire is simply a device for giving trade monopolies to the English… (*Burmese Days*, 37/38).

Anger about the injustice caused by imperialism would not leave Orwell until the end of his life. In his essay "Not Counting Niggers" his sarcasm is barely bridled:

> One gets some idea of the real relationship of England and India when one reflects that the per capita annual income in England is something over £80, and in India about £7. It is quite common for an Indian coolie's leg to be thinner than the average Englishman's arm. And there is nothing racial in this, for well-fed members of the same races are of normal physique; it is due to simple starvation.[13]

---

[12] See Lackersteen's lechery in relation to his niece.
[13] "Not Counting Niggers," *Adelphi* (July 1939) in: *Collected Essays*, Vol.1, 434-438; 437.

Flory's counterpart is the "fanatically loyal" Indian Dr Veraswami, who "had a passionate admiration for the English" and thought the Indians "belonged to an inferior and degenerate race" (all in *Burmese* Days, 38). He would counter Flory's arguments on the idea of British progress being brought to Burma:

> Could the Burmese trade for themselves?.... And while your businessmen develop the resources of our country, your officials are civilising us... I see the British, even the least inspired of them... ass [sic!] torchbearers upon the path of progress (*Burmese Days*, 39/41).

Frantz Fanon, the Algerian philosopher and theoretician of colonialism, emphasised the concept of inferiorisation, which makes the colonised doubt their traditions and cultures. Owing to continuous self-degradation the colonised finally adapt the coloniser's values on the grounds of the native culture's backwardness and primitiveness: "Every effort is made to bring the colonised person to admit the inferiority of his culture."[14] Dr Veraswami's elitist position inside the Imperial order privileges him for this concept as he stands fairly detached from his own people. In the eyes of Imperialism, however, he is as much the Other as Flory is, who is anxious to second his friend's admission to the European Club. Consequently, both fail in the end. Another person from the local ranks is U Po Kyin, a Burmese Sub-divisional Magistrate of Kyauktada, a wicked schemer and Dr Veraswami's fiercest rival for admission to the Club. Again an individual figure is linked with the Imperial order, since U Po Kyin utilises successfully British stereotypes and ranking systems in his smear campaign against his competitor, by which he proves that the personal relation to an Englishman determines the social standing of a local native and shields him against libels from his own people.

Imperialism is the overarching discourse and when Flory commits suicide in the end, the immediate trigger is failed love, but the implicit cause appears to be an all-pervasive order he could no longer stand as it turns against both sides – the colonised and the coloniser (*Burmese Days*, 46; 63). Opportunism and bitter "hatred of the atmosphere of imperialism" (*Burmese Days*, 68) consistently grew after Flory's eight years in the East

---

[14] Frantz Fanon, *The Wretched of the Earth* (1967), 190, quoted in: Craig Beveridge & Ronald Turnbull, *The Eclipse of Scottish Culture* (Edinburgh: Polygon, 1989), 5. In a similar vein Antonio Gramsci, the Italian Marxist philosopher, who pointed to the consent of the oppressed to their oppression (*Prison Books* (New York: Columbia University 1999; 2007)).

and results in the realisation that "even friendship can hardly exist when every white man is a cog in the wheels of despotism" (*Burmese Days*, 69).

Marxist readings found Orwell's viewpoint strongly flawed. Terry Eagleton's analysis, to name one, strictly focuses on what he sees lacking in Orwell's lower-middle class description of imperialism. For Eagleton therefore "Flory's raging at imperialism is thus privately motivated, not a normal, reliably 'objective' critic of the system." Consequently, he terms Orwell's novel "less a considered critique of imperialism than an exploration of private guilt, incommunicable loneliness and loss of identity."[15] However, Eagleton's reading of Orwell's ideological immaturity – "Flory is a direct projection of the younger Orwell"[16] – is informed by Marxist views and hence insensitive of any emotional rejection of imperialism which rebels against the pervasive poisoning of all human spheres by imperialistic ideology and policy. Orwell's prose recurrently denounced the bloodlessness of a left intellectualism.

The anti-imperial discourse in *Burmese Days* is incorporated into a melodramatic love sub-plot. In his autobiographical essay "Shooting an Elephant", published in 1936, the author is more to the point. Raymond Williams points to Orwell's "direct experience" replacing the intermediary Flory in *Burmese Days*.[17] The scene is Moulmein, Burma's third largest town, where Orwell served as a sub-divisional police officer from April to December 1926. The young I-as-protagonist narrator in the story, Orwell himself, is called by the villagers to regain control over a tame working elephant gone wild. The scene is set in a climate of mixed timidity and hostility against the imperialist intruders, which the narrator is quick to identify:

> For at that time I had already made up my mind that imperialism was an evil thing and the sooner I chucked up my job and got out of it the better. Theoretically – and secretly, of course – I was all for the Burmese and all against their oppressors, the British... In a job like that you see the dirty work of Empire at close quarters... All I knew was that I was stuck between my hatred of the empire I served and my rage against the evil-spirited little beasts who tried to make my job impossible... Feelings like

---

[15] Terry Eagleton, "Orwell and the Lower-Middle Class Novel," in *George Orwell – A Collection of Critical Essays*, ed. Raymond Williams (Englewood Cliffs: Prentice-Hall, 1974), 10-33; 17.

[16] Eagleton, 14.

[17] Raymond Williams, "Observation and Imagination in Orwell," in Williams, *George Orwell*, 52-61; 59.

these are the normal by-products of imperialism; ask any Anglo-Indian official, if you can catch him off duty.[18]

Called to the scene of the agitated animal, which has calmed down by the time the policeman arrives there, the protagonist is caught between the expectations of the local crowd, the expectations of the Imperial system to restore law and order by sticking to the primary principle of raw power, and his personal moral conflict.

> I did not in the least want to shoot him. I decided that I would watch him for a little while to make sure that he did not turn savage again, and then go home.
>   But at that moment I glanced round at the crowd that had followed me. It was an immense crowd... They were watching me... They did not like me, but with the magical rifle in my hands I was momentarily worth watching. And suddenly I realized that I should have to shoot the elephant after all. The people expected it of me... And it was at this moment,... that I first grasped the hollowness, the futility of the white man's dominion in the East... I perceived in this moment that when the white man turns tyrant it is his own freedom that he destroys... For it is the condition of his rule that he shall spend his life in trying to impress the 'natives' and so in every crisis he has got to do what the 'natives' expect of him... And my whole life, every white man's life in the East, was one long struggle not to be laughed at. But I did not want to shoot the elephant.[19]

In the end he botches up the entire operation, as he is a "poor shot"[20] and leaves the elephant dying in great agony.

Written in retrospect, the epiphany of the moment may be doubtful, yet what stands no doubts and what may have been coloured by Orwell's political development between his years in Burma and the time of publication, is the awareness "of the real nature of imperialism – the real motives for which despotic governments act" (*Burmese Days*, 266). Orwell's parable of Imperialism – solidly enriched by a realistic style – reveals the two faces of Imperialism, which victimises coloniser and colonised alike. Under imperialistic rule, structures are reversed and corrupted – what used to be a policeman, idealistically the neutral guardian of order, is made over into a conquering agent of a foreign power, while what used to be traditions and living cultures is denounced as backward and primitive. Both sides are brutalised and deprived of their

---

[18] "Shooting an Elephant," in *The Collected Essays,* Vol. 1, 265-272; 266.
[19] "Shooting an Elephant," 269/270.
[20] "Shooting an Elephant," 270.

previous functions and in the process lose – and this applies particularly to the white servants of imperialism – the last remnants of humanity. Hence there is not even a place to romanticise the natives.[21]

With bitterness Orwell escaped the corrosive influence of the Imperial order.[22] His decision was driven by a political purpose which added a new dimension to the entrenched constructions of the colonial Other as it initiated an alternative paradigm in British perceptions of the East. Kipling's metaphoric "white man's burden" which was bound to ethical principles regarding the civilising of indigenous cultures to be the outstanding accomplishment of British Imperialism, lost its imagined innocence.[23] Under the rule of imperialism which Orwell's political fiction unhesitatingly puts forward, both white and non-white subjects disgracefully suffer:

> Orwell came less to identify with the Burmese and other oppressed races of the Empire than to see the whole process as debasing the ruler even more than the ruled. The imperialist deceives himself...when he believes he is doing civilising work. The imperialist, he says, 'wears a mask and his face grows to fit it'.[24]

Orwell had a substantial knowledge of Kipling's work, though he considered him "a jingo imperialist... morally insensitive and aesthetically disgusting".[25] In the same essay he puts Kipling's work into a historical perspective[26] and defines his political limits by the optimism of his times –

---

[21] Cf. John Rodden, John Rossi, *The Cambridge Introduction to George Orwell* (Cambridge: Cambridge University Press, 2012), 34.

[22] Rodden, Rossi, *The Cambridge Introduction*, 34.

[23] Take up the White Man's burden –
Send forth the best ye breed –
Go bind your sons to exile
To serve your captives' need;
To wait in heavy harness,
On fluttered folk and wild –
Your new-caught, sullen peoples,
Half-devil and half-child. (First stanza, 1897) .
Orwell´s pithy comment on this: "`White man´s burden' instantly conjures up a real problem, even if one feels that it ought to be altered to `black man´s burden'. "Rudyard Kipling," in *The Collected Essays*, Vol.2 *My Country Right or Left*, 215-229; 225.

[24] John Rossi, John Rodden, "A Political Writer," in *The Cambridge Companion to George Orwell*, ed. John Rodden (Cambridge: Cambridge University Press, 2007), 1-11; 2. See also Rodden, Rossi, *The Cambridge Introduction*, 34.

[25] "Rudyard Kipling," in *The Collected Essays*, Vol.2, 215.

[26] He calls him the "prophet of British imperialism in its expansionist phase"

"he had never had any grasp of the economic forces underlying imperial expansion… Imperialism as he sees it is a sort of forcible evangelizing".[27] Orwell's final verdict of the writer Kipling is fairly balanced. He calls him "a good bad poet" whose "rhyming proverbs" can be shared by highbrow and lowbrow for their emotions. From a political point of view, Orwell – implicitly levelling his critical comments at the conservative middle class of his own times – tones down his rigid criticism of Kipling by pointing to his "sense of responsibility" enabling "…him to have a world-view, even though it happened to be a false one".[28] With this in mind, we can say that Orwell's texts about the East also claim their value as oppositional responses to a dominant class discourse of which Kipling had been the major protagonist.

The long passage of time between the end of his service in Burma (1927) and his propaganda work for the Indian Section of the BBC Eastern Service (August 1941–November 1943) had no effect on his attitude towards Burma in particular, neither on his fierce criticism of British imperial policy in general. When the country fell into Japanese hands, Orwell was ready to vent his rage in an internally circulating memo, in which he did not pull any punches about the culprits, who he identified to be the Burmese and British governments.[29] His overall picture of the Easterner had not altered, but was now aligned with his political sympathies for the Indian independence struggle that he saw more threatened by the prospects of a Nazi victory than by the ruling British imperialism.[30] Hence his involvement with the BBC – and thus indirectly with the British Ministry of Information which as part of the British government had been responsible for the banning of *Burmese Days* in India – aimed at the Nazi German propaganda towards India, which attempted to undermine Indian loyalty to Britain. Apart from the political

---

("Rudyard Kipling," in *The Collected Essays,* Vol. 2, 217).

[27] "Rudyard Kipling," in *The Collected Essays*, Vol. 2, 217.

[28] "Rudyard Kipling," in *The Collected Essays,* Vol.2, all 228. Orwell distinguishes between the man and the man's ideology when he says about Kipling: "What is much more distasteful in Kipling than sentimental plots or vulgar tricks or style, is the imperialism to which he chose to lend his genius….The imperialism of the eighties and nineties was sentimental, ignorant and dangerous, but it was not entirely despicable….It was still possible to be an imperialist and a gentleman, and of Kipling's *personal* decency there can be no doubt," (*New English Weekly*, 23 January 1936, repr. in *The Collected Essays*, vol. 1, 183-184).

[29] *Orwell: The War Broadcasts*, 34/35. See also his uncensored talk about Burma on BBC (*Orwell: The War Broadcasts*, 52).

[30] *Orwell: The War Broadcasts*, 36.

aims Orwell's literary talks on BBC were geared to students of Indian universities reading English literature.

In his political reflections dating from the early 1940s ("The English Revolution") Orwell strongly argued in defence of an immediate granting of Dominion Status to India and the possibility of a subsequent secession after the war.[31] Orwell's governing idea here was "some kind of partnership on equal terms", he claimed was feasible on the grounds of a Socialist government in England.[32]

On a concluding note: In addition to his awareness that ethnic stereotyping serves as the basis of imperialist rule, Orwell's literary politics attempt at subverting the dichotomy of Self and Other.[33] His texts reveal the mechanisms of the imperialistic discourse which eliminates the racial Other to be substituted by an ideological Other deprived of race but related to class as a criterion of othering:

> It is a commonplace that the average Indian suffers far more from his own countrymen than from the British. The petty Indian capitalist exploits the town worker with the utmost ruthlessness…, But all this is the indirect result of the British rule…the classes most loyal to Britain are the princes, the landowners and the business community – in general, the reactionary classes who are doing fairly well out of the status quo. The moment that England ceased to stand towards India in the relation of an exploiter, the balance of forces would be altered.[34]

Or they point to the corruption of the imperialist by imperialist ideology. By defining the constructedness of stereotypes on the basis of a political ideology (itself a chain of stereotypes), Orwell confronts the "effectivity" of a stereotype and in consequence interrupts the forceful naturalisation strategies of normality and difference which Homi Bhabha sees at the heart of stereotyping in general: the norm is the given and defines the Other ruthlessly without revealing the constructedness of both.[35]

---

[31] "The Lion and the Unicorn: Socialism and the English Genius," reprinted in *The Collected Essays*, Vol. 2, 74-134; 119; The passage is part of *England Your England* with the title "The Ruling Class" in *Horizon* (December 1940); see also *Orwell: The War Broadcasts*, 18.

[32] "The Lion and the Unicorn," in *The Collected Essays*, Vol. 2, 122-124; see also "Such, such were the joys," *Partisan Review* (September-October 1952); "Toward European Unity," *Partisan Review* (July-August 1947) both reprinted in *Collected Essays*, Vol.4 *In Front of Your* Nose, 379-422, 405; 423-429, 427.

[33] 73. *As I Please* in *Collected Essays*, Vol.3 *As I Please*, 299-302; 301.

[34] "The Lion…" in *Collected Essays,* 123.

[35] Cf. *Us and them – Them and Us. Constructions of the Other in Cultural*

Discourses about the "Other" climaxed on 11 September 2001 and after. It has been intended here to argue that the processes of othering, though as a rule attributed to the categories of religion, ethics, race or gender, are at their core political but successfully conceal their relation to imperial power. Only assisted by ideological criticism which focuses on the effects that imperial stereotyping has on the very agents of practising othering processes, can its Janus face be revealed. Imperialism and all its concomitant stereotyping turn against coloniser and colonised alike and thus finally corrode the moral givens at the heart of any ideology of superiority: the Guantanamo and Taliban camps are twins of the same imperial stereotyping. It is the credit of Orwell's colonial prose to have shown this inherent link.

Bibliography

Beveridge, Craig & Turnbull, Ronald. *The Eclipse of Scottish Culture*. Edinburgh: Polygon, 1989.

Eagleton, Terry. "Orwell and the Lower-Middle Class Novel." In *George Orwell – A Collection of Critical Essays*, edited by Raymond Williams, 10-33. Englewood Cliffs: Prentice-Hall, 1974.

Gonerko-Frej, Anna, et.al. (eds.), *Us and Them-Them and Us: Constructions of the Other in Cultural Stereotypes*. Aachen: Shaker Verlag, 2011.

Gramsci, Antonio. *Prison Books*. New York: Columbia University Press, 1999; 2007.

Orwell, George. "A Hanging." In *The Collected Essays, Journalism and Letters of George Orwell,* edited by Sonia Orwell and Ian Angus, Vol. 1 *An Age Like This*, 66-71. Harmondsworth: Penguin, 1975.

—. "Why I Write." In *The Collected Essays,* Vol.1, 23-30.

—. "Not Counting Niggers." In *The Collected Essays*, Vol.1, 434-438.

—. "Shooting an Elephant." In *The Collected Essays*, Vol.1, 265-272.

—. Rudyard Kipling." In *The Collected Essays,* Vol.2 *My Country Right or Left*, 215-229.

—. "The Lion and the Unicorn: Socialism and the English Genius." In *The Collected Essays,* Vol.2, 74-134.

—. "As I Please." In *The Collected Essays*, Vol.3 *As I Please*, 299-302.

—. "Such, such were the joys." In *The Collected Essays*, Vol.4 *In Front of Your Nose*, 379-422.

—. "Toward European Unity." In *The Collected Essays*, Vol.4, 423-429.

—. *The Road to Wigan Pier*. London: Gollancz, 1937; Penguin, 1979.

Rodden, John (ed.), *The Cambridge Companion*. Cambridge: Cambridge University Press, 2007.

Rodden, John, Rossi, John, *The Cambridge Introduction to George Orwell*. Cambridge: Cambridge University Press, 2012.

Sheldon, Michael. *Orwell – The authorized biography*. London: Secker and Warburg, 1996.

West, W.J. (ed.). *Orwell: The War Broadcasts*. London: Duckworth, 1985.

Williams, Raymond. "Observation and Imagination in Orwell." In *George Orwell...*, 52-61.

CONTRIBUTORS

Thomas Bauer, Dr.phil., Dr.phil.habil. (Erlangen 1989 and 1997) has been Professor of Arabic and Islamic Studies at the University of Münster since 2000. His main research areas are Arabic literature, rhetoric and cultural history from the early times (*Altarabische Dichtkunst*, 1992), and the Abbasid period (*Liebe und Liebesdichtung in der arabischen Welt des 9. und 10. Jahrhunderts*, 1998) up to the Ottoman period. Recent studies focus on Arabic literature of the Mamluk period, especially Ibn Nubāta al-Miṣrī and the popular poet al-Mi´mār. In the field of cultural anthropology of the pre-modern Arabic world, Bauer treats subjects like love and sexuality, death, strangeness, and the tolerance of ambiguity (*Die Kultur der Ambiguität*, 2011). Bauer has been appointed member of the North Rhine-Westphalian Academy of Sciences, Humanities and the Arts in 2012, and has been awarded the Gottfried Wilhelm Leibniz Prize in 2013.

Ryan Dorr currently teaches practical language in the English and American Studies Department at the University of Wuppertal in Germany. His interests include film studies, notions of authenticity and the cinema, and hip-hop studies. His work has previously been published in the volume *Us and Them – Them and Us: Constructions of the Other in Cultural Stereotypes*.

Jarema Drozdowicz, PhD, graduated in ethnology at the Institue of Ethnology and Cultural Anthropology of the Adam Mickiewicz University in Poznań, Poland. Currently working at the Faculty of Educational Studies of the same university. Major fields of research interest lies in the areas of the anthropology of education, the history of anthropological thought, the sociology of education, academic identities, the processes of cultural assimilation, forms of marginalization and discrimination, racism, migration studies, the construction of contemporary identities through popular culture and the cultural ideologies of education. Major publications tackle the problems of the symbolic dimension of culture and the concept of cultural difference constructed through the educational sphere.

Sabine Ernst, M. A., studied Dutch language and literature at the Universität Münster, Germany and Rijksuniversiteit Groningen, Netherlands. Her academic interests include contemporary Dutch literature. Her fields of research are cultural studies, multicultural writers, stereotypes, constructions of cultural identity, constructions of 'self' and 'other' and the contribution of literature to current political debates.

Brygida Gasztold, PhD, holds an MA degree and a doctorate degree from Gdańsk University, and a diploma of postgraduate studies from Ruskin College, Oxford and Warsaw University (British Studies). She is assistant professor at the Technical University of Koszalin, Poland. Her academic interests include American Jewish literature, Canadian Jewish literature, as well as the problems of immigration, gender and ethnic identities. She has published *To the Limits of Experience. Jerzy Kosiński's Literary Quest for Self-Identity* (2008), *Negotiating Home and Identity in Early 20th Century Jewish-American Narratives* (2011) and essays on immigrant literature and ethnicity.

Karolina Golimowska studied English and American Studies, German Literature and Media Studies in Berlin and London. She is a PhD candidate at the Institute for English and American Studies at Humboldt University in Berlin, Germany. Her thesis focuses on the role of cities in post-9/11 novels. She was a Visiting Professor at the University of Richmond, VA in spring 2013.

Dorota Guttfeld, PhD, is an Assistant Professor in the Department of English at Nicolaus Copernicus University in Torun, Poland. Her research focuses on the reception of science fiction and fantasy literature from the perspective of translation studies and the (re)interpretation of history in science fiction and fantasy costume.

Krzysztof Inglot is an English Philology graduate of the University of Szczecin. Currently, he is a PhD student at the same university. His Ph. D. dissertation delves into the methods of translation and interpretation of proper names within electronic games for the English, German, and Polish markets. Krzysztof Inglot's fields of study include English-Polish and English-German translation, onomastics, video game studies, semiotics and linguistics in general. He is also interested in the new media as such, including digitalization, the Internet, its impact on human-to-human and human-computer interaction, and its various channels of communication.

Barbara Poważa-Kurko graduated from Jagiellonian University with an MA and a PhD which dealt with translations and receptions of Harold Pinter's plays in Poland. She worked as a teacher of English and English culture and literature at the Teacher Training College in Cieszyn, and the University of Bielsko-Biała (Akademia Techniczno-Humanistyczna). Since 2006 she has been a lecturer in the State School of Higher Education in Oświęcim, where she has been teaching BA students in English literature and language. Her academic focus is on contemporary English literature and she has presented and published papers on Christopher Reid, Sarah Waters, Iris Murdoch and A.S. Byatt.

Michał Różycki is a graduate of the Institute of English Studies, University of Warsaw, where he also completed his PhD on the role of conspiracy theories in American culture. His academic interests include conspiracy theory narratives, urban legends, cyberculture, and Victorian reinterpretations of folklore. He has contributed on these subjects to both academic publications and popular history journals.

Daniel Šíp is a lecturer at the Institute of English and American Studies at Carl von Ossietzky-University in Oldenburg, Germany. Born in Hamburg in 1981. Studied English (Anglophone Literatures) and Political Sciences at the Carl von Ossietzky-University. Magister-Thesis is on "Literary Representations of Torture from the Gothic Novel to Contemporary Anglophone Fiction." Currently pursuing a PhD on the topic of torture representations in post-9/11 US American TV series. Has interned and worked for political institutions, most recently for the Academic office of the Salzburg Global seminars and for the Salzburg Academy on Media and Global Change. Has published academically and non-academically, most recently a review in *Die Zeit* on the theatrical release of Kathryn Bigelow's *Zero Dark Thirty*.

Elżbieta Wilczyńska works at the Department of Polish-British Cultural Relations, Faculty of English In Adam Mickiewicz University in Poznań. She conducts lectures and classes in British and American studies. She also runs M. A. and B. A. seminars devoted to different aspects of American culture. Her academic interest includes cultural studies, especially the problem of representation and discourse, as well as ethnic America, particularly Native American culture and history. She is also interested in politics and the role of US hegemony. She is a member of the American Indian Workshop and the Polish Association of American Studies.

Ákos Windhager graduated with an MA in History and an MA in Comparative Literature from Eötvös Lorand University, Budapest. His PhD thesis (Eötvös Lorand University, Budapest, 2011) thematises Edmund Mihalovich, a Hungarian Romantic composer, and the cultural workshops of the Austro-Hungarian Empire. It clearly demonstrates a research focus in cultural studies and comparative literature. Windhager has lectured on various topics at international conferences (e.g. in Barcelona, Szczecin, Athens) and published in international reviews (e.g. *News About Mahler Research*, 2013). His university posts include universities in Hungary (e.g. University of Fine Arts) and abroad (e.g. Firenze University, Sapientia Summer PR University Miercurea Ciuc, Romania). Outside his academic career he has been engaged in PR activities for the Arts Harmony Society. His recent projects include politics in music (e.g. 1956 and 1989 in the arts), identity research in mob-culture and the future audience of classics.

Uwe Zagratzki has held various posts at the Universities of Osnabrück, Greifswald, Halle-Wittenberg, Rostock and Oldenburg and has worked as a Visiting Professor at the Universities of Brno, the Czech Republic, and West Georgia, USA. A growing interest in Canadian Studies has been furthered by various scholarships from the International Council of Canadian Studies. He is Professor of British and Canadian Studies and Literature at Szczecin University, Poland. He has widely published in his main fields of interest: Scottish, English and Canadian Literature and Culture, Cultural Studies and War and Literature.

INDEX